GLOBAL SCENES OF BIBLICAL INJUSTICE

Glimpsing the Poor and Oppressed in Today's World

W. R. Brookman

University Press of America,® Inc.
Lanham · Boulder · New York · Toronto · Plymouth, UK

For young Jasper who will, I pray, embrace the
lofty notions of biblical justice throughout his life.

CONTENTS

PREFACE

Throughout Scripture there is a profound and elemental call to practice justice. From the Torah to the Prophets, from the Writings to the New Testament, there is a dominant and reoccurring theme of justice. In the broadest possible sense, there are a number of potential avenues by which one might approach the rather lofty and formidable notion of justice. To be sure, justice is a labyrinth to explore which has a rich and storied history of investigation. Justice is a multifaceted concept that reaches into an array of disciplines. Throughout the ages perspectives on justice have been drawn from arenas as assorted as economic theory, judicial theory, philosophy, and moral theology. At the outset, it should be noted, this book is somewhat modest in its scope. The intent here is to bring some focus on justice from a biblical perspective. Yet, beyond that, the approach is from a different angle—it is via what might be thought of as coming through the back door to get at justice. For the aim here is to consider biblical justice from the frame of reference of injustice as it exists in the world today. That is to say, the intent is to consider justice by viewing examples of injustice. This will be done through presenting a variety of brief vignettes or case studies that will serve as a small sampling of the reality of biblical injustices occurring throughout the world today. Unfortunately, the ones who bear the injustices, almost inevitably, are the poor and the oppressed. This was the case in antiquity, and this is the case today. Thus, the very nature of looking at injustices around the globe will bring a focus upon those who biblical text refers to as the weak, the downtrodden, the poor, and the oppressed.

To be sure, there have been a number of excellent studies on the topic of biblical justice. Yet, the tack taken here is different in that recent and current events will present a glimpsing of contemporary dilemmas and biblical injustices faced by the poor and the oppressed on a daily basis across the entire globe. While the Bible has a lot to say about justice, the contemporary lives of the poor have volumes to speak about injustice. Naturally, if the quest is to truly put biblical justice into practice through the way in which we live our lives, then there needs to be a keen and vivid awareness and an informed understanding of the injustices which are perpetrated in many sectors of life against the poor and oppressed.

The Bible and justice

> Again I saw all the oppressions that are practiced under the sun. Look, the tears
> of the oppressed—with no one to comfort them! On the side of their oppressors
> there was power—with no one to comfort them.
>
> *Ecclesiastes 4:1*

Scholars of the Bible oftentimes seem to agree on very little. Yet, for centuries they have agreed on one particular thing. Namely, they have agreed that the Book of Ecclesiastes can be a difficult work to understand. Even before the time of Jesus, Jewish Rabbis found the book of Ecclesiastes somewhat of an enigma and even discouraged the reading of it.

I have often told students that the Bible has a mysterious, dual reality behind it. There is the complexity of the text, but then there is also the simplicity of the gospel. I know there are intricate textual issues when one examines the ancient manuscripts, and I have actually spent a fair amount of time talking about such things in a variety of classes through the years. That is because I am very interested in textual criticism and the history of the transmission of the ancient manuscripts, and I think it is important. Yet, there is that simplicity of the gospel. When I read the Sermon on the Mount, questions of textual variants fade wonderfully into the background. I'm really not sure how, but these two elements, complexity and simplicity, blend delightfully together in the text of Scripture. Of course, there are those times when the text is not complex, and it is amazingly simple and straightforward. I think one can persuasively argue the point that the verse cited above, Ecclesiastes 4:1, is one of those texts that is simple and straightforward. It speaks of oppressors and the oppressed. It speaks of injustice. It reveals a timeless state of affairs. Just as there was oppression under the sun in antiquity, so it also exists at this very moment in the 21st century. Oppression and justice—these are timeless themes with which every generation needs to wrestle.

Biblical justice in the 8th century B.C. was a huge issue. The prophet, Amos, ranted and raved against injustice, trying with all his might to make it clear to the people that Yahweh doesn't like injustice. However, their ears were closed, and the inhabitants of Israel did not take any kind of action, no concerted effort, to change things. A fair question might be, do the words of Yahweh, spoken through the prophet Amos, have any relevance to us today? Most Christians would say, "Absolutely they do!" Does that mean that we are to be more discerning and even attempt to correct injustices that we observe? If that were the case, might it not be in our best interest to perk up our ears and take note of the situation around us? I'm not convinced that the Church is always the best at taking astute note of the conditions around us, and I write this book, in part, because of this perception that I have. I don't think we are exempt from the wrath of Yahweh if we, like the ancient Israelites of Amos' time, fail to address and correct the injustices around us.

To be sure, the notion of justice is so woven through the entirety of the Scriptures that one would have to be fairly blind not to perceive it. Yet, I would suggest it may, indeed, be the case that many Christians in the 21st century have not apprehended the scope and gravity of biblical justice. This may be particularly true of Christians within the American culture sphere. It may also be the case that we Christians of the modern age are not as fully aware of the reach of injustice throughout the world as we ought to be.

W. R. Brookman
Antigua
February 20, 2010

ACKNOWLEDGMENTS

I would like to thank the students from my course, *Topics in Biblical Justice*, who, over a period of several years, helped provide some of the fodder for the concept of this project through a variety of classroom discussions and questions. Those students, perhaps quite unwittingly, have made a significant contribution to this work, and I deeply appreciate their role in helping me to frame some of the ideas presented this book.

Much gratitude is also due to President Gordon Anderson, Dean Thomas Burkman, and the Board of Regents of North Central University for granting me a generous sabbatical leave during the 2009-10 academic year. It was during that time when much reworking and finalizing of this manuscript took place. Without such support from North Central University, this project would yet be undone.

Working with great colleagues, as we all know, makes life much more fun, and I would like to especially thank Dr. Bob Brenneman and Dr. Nan Muhovich for their long-standing friendship, support and encouragement.

INTRODUCTION

Glimpsing the Poor & Oppressed

For many American Christians, it may oftentimes seem that one must go out of one's way in order to see poverty. For many, seeing poverty is usually a brief experience such as passing through a certain neighborhood in a car or catching a short clip on the evening news—certainly we don't normally get the chance to behold, face-to-face, the teaming masses of poor people around the world. In America it is pretty easy for one to be, almost effortlessly, insulated from those who are poor and oppressed. The Church is also pretty good at insulating itself. Of course, there are exceptions, but the generalization, I think, could be substantiated. Thus, one may speak of our merely *glimpsing the poor and the oppressed*. Indeed, we do catch glimpses of them; we see them in a thirty-second news piece on CNN, or we see them on page A12 and quickly pass by as we thumb hurriedly through the morning newspaper. The fact is, for most of us, it is a set of glimpses that comprise our view of the poor. We usually don't get a good, long look at the poor and the oppressed; we usually get only a glimpse here or there.

A View from the Rich Side of the World

Without a doubt, the glimpses we do get are from a particular perspective. We see the poor and the oppressed from the rich side of the world. We, in the West, who are Christians, generally view the world from this rich side. Hopefully, this book will skew your perspective. All your life, you, most likely, have had a warped view of the world in that you have seen it from only the rich side. The goal is that the little vignettes within this book will prove to present you with a newfound perspective. Yet, merely being presented with a new perspective does not guarantee that you will embrace it to the point of actually changing the way you live your life in any substantive way.

While the Church is pretty good at some things, I have found that many individuals within it are oftentimes quite out of touch with the scope of the human development problem we have. On top of that, I'm not sure churches have been all the effective in bridging us closer to those around the world who are in desperate need. Of course, from the perspective of many people, we don't have the problem; it's others who have the problem. The people of Darfur have the problem. The people of Somalia have the problem. The people in the slums of Mexico City have the problem. Our perspective is, "Thank the Lord, we don't have those problems," and somehow we have learned to be comfortable with that. Yet, as Jesus clearly demonstrates to us, the need of those, even those in a different cultural sphere, or even a different religious sphere, is also our need. For that reason, it may be a good exercise to consider how those of us within the rich, American Church could better deal with issues of injustice, oppression, and poverty. It may be a good exercise for you, personally, to consider how you should specifically deal with issues of injustice, oppression, and poverty. As the many and varied examples in this book will vividly demonstrate, those basic issues of injustice, oppression, and poverty may take a multitude of forms. By reading the vignettes which present a wide array of insights into the life of the poor and the oppressed, a burden will, in some respects, be placed upon you to respond. The burden is to respond in such a way that you reflect the call the Jesus has upon your life to love your neighbor, perhaps in ways you have not contemplated in your wildest dreams.

Like a Ton of Bricks

Reading the words of Jesus in Matthew 25:31-46 should be a chilling and sobering experience—it should provide a wake-up call to us. However, I don't think it is such an experience for many individuals reading this text. Yet, if one were to actually take Jesus at His word, the message of that passage should hit us like a ton of bricks; no, really, it should. Try it. Read the following text from the Gospel of Matthew as if Jesus really meant what He said.

> 25:31 "When the Son of man comes in his glory, and all the angels with him, then he will sit on his glorious throne. 32 Before him will be gathered all the nations, and he will separate them one from another as a shepherd separates the sheep from the goats, 33 and he will place the sheep at his right hand, but the goats at the left. 34 Then the King will say to those at his right hand, 'Come, O blessed of my Father, inherit the kingdom prepared for you from the foundation of the world; 35 for I was hungry and you gave me food, I was thirsty and you gave me drink, I was a stranger and you welcomed me, 36 I was naked and you clothed me, I was sick and you visited me, I was in prison and you came to me.' 37 Then the righteous will answer him, 'Lord, when did we see thee hungry and feed thee, or thirsty and give thee drink? 38 And when did we see thee a stranger and welcome thee, or naked and

clothe thee? 39 And when did we see thee sick or in prison and visit thee?' 40 And the King will answer them, 'Truly, I say to you, as you did it to one of the least of these my brethren, you did it to me.' 41 Then he will say to those at his left hand, 'Depart from me, you cursed, into the eternal fire prepared for the devil and his angels; 42 for I was hungry and you gave me no food, I was thirsty and you gave me no drink, 43 I was a stranger and you did not welcome me, naked and you did not clothe me, sick and in prison and you did not visit me.' 44 Then they also will answer, 'Lord, when did we see thee hungry or thirsty or a stranger or naked or sick or in prison, and did not minister to thee?' 45 Then he will answer them, 'Truly, I say to you, as you did it not to one of the least of these, you did it not to me.' 46 And they will go away into eternal punishment, but the righteous into eternal life."

If you are like most of us when you read this, you saw yourself first as belonging to the *sheep* (vs. 34). Then you identified yourself with the *righteous* (vs. 37). So far, so good. You placed yourself right where you think you should be, on Jesus' right hand ready to *inherit the kingdom* (vs. 34). Wait! There is a caveat! This is the chilling and sobering part. According to Jesus, you would have actually have done something to be counted among the *righteous sheep*. You must have: given food to the hungry, given drink to the thirsty, welcomed a stranger (vs. 35), clothed the naked, visited the sick, or visited a prisoner (vs. 36). Hmmm. Have you ever done any of those things? Oops; if not, can you even conceive of yourself as being among the *goats* (vs. 32)? I would hazard a guess that, probably not. I would suggest that you cannot even conceive of yourself as being among the *goats*. Yet, if we take Jesus at His word, that could very well be the place some who are thinking like you and me may find ourselves.

If we learn anything about the Kingdom of God as Jesus presents it, we had better learn that the Kingdom is surprising. Clearly, the *goats* who are asking the question in verse 44 are caught off guard by the nature of the Kingdom. They never saw Jesus hungry or thirsty or as a stranger or naked or in prison. Jesus so closely identifies Himself with the poor and the oppressed here that one must realize the need to act on behalf of them. It hits like a ton of bricks, doesn't it? I'm not sure where I heard it or read it, so I can't give credit, but I remember the catchy phrase that, "Jesus is not *for* the poor, rather, He is *of* the poor." In Matthew 25:31-46, Jesus is the poor—the poor are Jesus. If you do not help feed the poor of this world, if you ignore the plight of the oppressed, you are doing the very same toward Jesus, and you fit the pattern of how He describes the *goats*.

The Design of This Book

This book brings together research, information, insights, pleas, and analysis from a variety of sources with the goal of creating easily digestible vignettes and summaries that vividly relate the state of the poor and the oppressed throughout the world. Each short piece is a self-contained unit. While the units are organized around the general topic of a chapter, the specific focus of each brief segment, along with the geographical setting, will vary within the topical framework. You may encounter a description of the horrendous water sanitation conditions in rural Malawi, and in the next reading you might come upon an analysis of water security in Kyrgyzstan. In that sense, the structure of this book is not unlike the lives of the poor and the oppressed—it's chaotic as one sifts from one geographical setting to another. Injustice toward the poor and the oppressed is also chaotic. Poverty is chaotic; it is overwhelmingly chaotic. I felt that presenting a smooth, organized and logically developed waltz through the world of the poor and the oppressed would somehow distort the sense of their chaotic lives. Thus, while following along a broad topic, I wanted to, at the same time, capture the disjointed bedlam that most often constitutes poverty and injustice among the poor and the oppressed.

I have attempted to draw upon a wide range of materials that one might not normally encounter unless one specifically set about with the task of garnering information on the topic. I have endeavored to keep each unit brief, not drawing out the conversation too long, although oftentimes it certainly could be much expanded upon. My goal in doing this was to keep the reader's attention focused upon the issue at hand, if only for a brief period. I, myself, am attracted to this style of presentation and I enjoy books constructed with brief and easily digestible portions. While the individual units are brief, hopefully, longer periods of reflection, incubation, prayer, and actual changes of behavior will be the result.

How Does One Find Out About the Poor and the Oppressed?

What would be the ideal way to learn about the poor and the poverty and the injustices that have control over them? Where does one find the oppressed? The ethnographer in me says that the answer would be to go and live among them *a lá* some of the famous anthropologists you may have heard of, e.g. Margaret Mead, Franz Boas, or Bronislaw Malinowski. Well, maybe you've heard of Mead.[1] But the point is, that *is* the way to really get insight into the lives of people. Yet, how many of us, even if altruistically motivated to learn about the poor and poverty, will go and play the part of the anthropologist by picking up and moving to some horrendous place to live for what would surely be a very miserable period of time? Yes, the best way to learn about and understand the poor and the oppressed would be to do some *deep hanging out with them*.[2] It almost seems to be the case that our particular culture breeds within us a gene in our DNA which prompts us *away* from the poor. Normative behavior in our American culture is to cross the street in order to avoid, rather than engage, the poor person who may be in need and presents an unlovely appearance. Thus, while I call the anthropologist in you to hang out with the poor, on another, deeper level, I also implore the Good Samaritan within you to engage your neighbor who is in need—wherever in the world that neighbor may be.

Rich Issues of Poverty

This book presents a concise and readable presentation of information gleaned from a wide array of sources that address rich issues of poverty and injustice throughout the world. I hope this book will function as a catalyst, prompting you into actual fieldwork sometime during your life. My fondest hope would be that, as a result of reading this book, you would, in fact, engage the poor of the world via fieldwork, *i.e.* participation in their lives, that could involve any number of scenarios, *e.g.* relief or development work, teaching, face-to-face philanthropy, construction, orphanage work, inviting a poor person to dinner, tutoring kids, etc. In a sense, as Jesus seems to have intended, it means you would become a neighbor to them. As Shane Claiborne has observed, "It is a beautiful thing when folks in poverty are no longer just a mission project but become genuine friends and family with whom we laugh, cry, dream, and struggle."[3]

How Are You With Numbers?

I'm just okay with numbers. I'm a little better with words. On the other hand, my wife, Pat, is better than me in both domains. She works crossword puzzles at a dizzying pace, and she actually liked her statistics class that she took at the University of Minnesota—enough said. While I can get along with numbers, my ego was recently bruised a bit when I read about Ai, the thirty year old chimp who can, more quickly than most humans, tap randomized numbers in sequential order on a touch-sensitive computer screen, especially when the numbers appear for only a fraction of a second and are then covered over with a white box.[4] When a chimp beats you at numbers, you really experience a new level of humility.

The reason I mention numbers is to prepare you just a little for what is an important aspect of this book—numbers. As one attempts to get a handle on what conditions are really like for the poor and oppressed people of the developing world, statistical data can be a pretty good lens through which to view regions, nations, and people. This might be particularly true if you are unable to get there and see things for yourself. However, you mustn't merely gloss over the statistics, facts, and data. Rather, as you read this book, try to synthesize and internalize the numbers. While it is easy to throw out big numbers and lots of statistics, it is very challenging to make those numbers truly meaningful. When I say that 30,000 children die every single day from preventable causes, I think I understand that the scope of the reality behind that figure doesn't easily sink in for most of us. It is a shocking figure, and shocking figures are such that we may loose the significance of the lives, or in this case, the deaths which are a part of that statistic. Shocking figures should shock us, but they usually don't.

Hopefully, this book will change you, and I suspect the numbers cited herein could go a long way to helping elicit that change. But, in order for that to happen, one needs to internalize the data. The numbers must become people, and those people must become a part of our consciousness. As it has been noted, "the experience of suffering . . . is not effectively conveyed by statistics or graphs. In fact, the suffering of the world's poor intrudes only rarely into the consciousness of the affluent, even when our affluence may be shown to have direct relation to their suffering."[5]

Culling Information Which Changes Your Life

The published literature from which one could draw information about poverty, the state of the poor, human development, social injustices, and a host of related topics is immense. My goal in writing this book has been to cull a manageable amount of information for you that will enable you to better understand and relate to the biblical call for justice. Being aware of injustice is a good start to pursuing justice.

Naturally, one of the hazards of such a book is that the data, the statistics, the numbers may soon be dated. On the other hand, the principles of poverty and oppression within this volume will, most likely, not quickly become outdated. The *oppression under the sun* (Eccl. 4:1) from which the poor suffer is not going to quickly evaporate from the scene. While you may have a hand in pushing back injustice against the poor, you will not eliminate it. Yet, you are not called to eliminate it. You are called to the principles inherent in the Kingdom of God. Loving your neighbor as yourself is a calling for those who wish to pursue justice as it is laid out by Jesus. That becomes a challenge when one is hit with the realization, or should I say, the revelation, that the poor Buddhist child in Myanmar is your neighbor. Indeed, our neighbor is a far-reaching notion, as far as the ends of the globe, for as it has been noted, our neighbor is "also that subsistence, peasant farmer in Sichuan Province in China, that HIV-Aids infected mother of eight in Lusaka, Zambia, or that penniless family trapped in the *favela* in Rio de Janeiro."[6]

The Goal is Not to Make You Feel Guilty

Please realize, the objective of this book is not to make you feel guilty. You cannot help it that you were born rich; and yes, if you are reading this book, then you are rich. Americans *must* be able to see themselves as rich when compared to the rest of the world; because we are. But then, it is also incumbent upon us to read ourselves into all those New Testament passages that talk about the rich. As I have remarked elsewhere regarding the parable of the Rich Man and Lazarus (Luke 16:19-31), "If you don't see even a little bit of the rich man in yourself and in your country, you are probably not very authentic in your introspection."[7] Feeling guilty is not the correct response to reading this book. On the contrary, one should feel a sense of thankfulness. However, beyond that, far beyond that, there must be a sense of proper response toward the poor. In the parable, the rich man was not oppressing Lazarus, however, he was neglecting Lazarus. This book may be somewhat dangerous in that, knowing what you know after reading it, you better not go back to your comfortable pattern of simply looking past the poor, or like the rich man in the parable, neglecting the poor. Oh, don't come crying to me by saying that you are not neglecting the poor. We all tend to neglect them. That's where I hope this book has an impact on you and on me. I hope that we will change our patterns of behavior—how you live your life and how I live mine. Lazarus is within the pages of this book, and Jesus' point seems quite clear—don't neglect the poor.

Should Christians See Things Differently?[8]

One might ask oneself, should Christians have a different view and understanding of the poor and the oppressed than the rest of the world? That is, should we see things differently? Norwood Russell Hanson in his book, *Patterns of Discovery*, raises a very interesting and well-known question from a scenario he created. He writes,

> Let us consider Johannes Kepler: imagine him on a hill watching the dawn. With him is Tycho Brahe. Kepler regarded the sun as fixed: it was the earth that moved. But Tycho followed Ptolemy and Aristotle: the earth was fixed and all other celestial bodies moved around it. *Do Kepler and Tycho see the same thing in the east at dawn?*[9]

Of course, the answer from Hanson's position is "No, they don't see the same thing." To fully appreciate the wit and the profundity of this scenario, one must recognize the utter separation of understanding between the two gifted astronomers. There they are upon the hill. Kepler sees heliocentrically; Brahe sees geocentrically. Yes, of course, they have received the same retinal image through their eyeballs as they looked out at the scene. But as someone has said, and I haven't been able to track down who said it first, "eyeballs are blind." People are able to "see," but a digital camera is blind. The difference between the two observers, Kepler and Brahe, is interpretive; they both have the same visual data, and yet, they see things (*i.e.* interpret things) differently.

The Kepler/Brahe story was originally set in the context of Hanson discussing the notion of observation. He would, later in the book, develop an argument against the idea of what is called theory-free observation. Hanson's point was that there are no theory-neutral observations. We all come to our observations with the baggage of experience, belief, and presupposition. While Kepler and Brahe were looking at the same object, they each came to that experience with their own baggage. For Kepler, the sun was coming into view as the earth was turning on its axis. Contrarily, Brahe saw the sun as it was starting to make its daily trip around a stationary planet. Thus, for Hanson, "Seeing is not only the having of a visual experience; it is also the way in which the visual experience is had."[10]

In his book, Hanson was attacking a two-staged model of seeing. This Two-Staged Theory presumes that seeing involves two distinct things. First, the raw perception or data, i.e. photons hitting rods and cones in the retina. Second, it also involves the *interpretation* of that physical perception. Hanson goes on to argue that there is no seeing apart from interpretation.

I suppose, at this point, one might comment, "While this whole thing is wildly entertaining, what does it have to do with the poor and the oppressed?" I have one word for you, "analogy." For just as Kepler and Brahe see things differently in Hanson's little story, so also should Christians see things differently from non-believers. While Christians have the same retinal images as everybody else, we had better see differently. For as Hanson so cleverly put it, "There is more to seeing than meets the eyeball." It is the interpretive lens of Scripture that enables us to see in such a way that we not only perceive the photons of injustice upon our retinas, but we are also able to interpret the sight and subsequently initiate behavioral change based on the interpretive model of Christ's Gospel. We need to see the poor and the oppressed and process those images with the mind of Christ.

Who are the Poor and the Oppressed?

The Old Testament speaks often of the poor, the needy, the afflicted, and the humble. Legal codes within the Hebrew Bible address and regulate the treatment of the poor. These texts aim at protecting the well-being of the downtrodden, oftentimes through avenues such as the redistribution of resources, fair treatment of workers, and limiting debt servitude. In the writings of the prophets one finds the poor being exploited, usually by rich landlowners or political power brokers. In wisdom texts, particularly Job and Ecclesiastes, those in poverty are portrayed as being exploited victims of economic and poltical chicanery. The psalms frequently present the special concern which the Lord has for the poor (see, for example, Ps 72:13-14; 82:3-4; 113:7). In the New Testament, it is the Book of James which most closely reflects the classical Old Testament prophets in its view of the poor and the oppressed.[11] However, throughout the entirety of the New Testament, the poor and the oppressed (generally, the Greek term *ptōchós* is employed) are visible— whether in Paul's stress on empowering the weak (2 Cor 12:9-10) or in the Synoptic Gospels where there is constant interest in accepting those who are marginalized.

Yet, we know that the poor and the oppressed are of infinite value, made in the image of God (*imago Dei*) even though they are despised by the world's system. It is these who we on the rich side of the world tend to merely glimpse as we transverse our way through life. It is these who we, while perhaps not despising them, tend to neglect them. Unfortunately, our knowing better does not necessarily result in our doing better. One step forward may be to read about them, to get to know what struggles they have and what their life is like, with the anticipation that we might better enact the teachings of Christ among them.

Laced With A Few Reflective Thoughts and Some Prayer

How does one bring the mind of Christ to the table when smacked in the face with the picture of the poor and the oppressed throughout the world that is presented in this book? Peppered throughout the data, information, statistics and reports are brief respites of reflection, challenges for response, and some prayers. As I read through some of my early drafts, it became quite clear to me that the data demands much reflection and urgent responses on behalf of the reader. I like books that prod one to action. I have been influenced by some of the writings of Foster, Yancey, Mother Teresa, and others in which challenges to my behavior were made. Therefore, I challenge you to consider a new praxis for your Christianity as you read about the poor and the oppressed from your view on the rich side of the world. As followers of Jesus we are compelled to do something beyond the commonplace. We are called, as His disciples, to be servants. Washing feet is a dirty business, yet that is the Master's call to us. We, who live and perceive life from the rich side of the world are to garner our resources and become servants to the poor and oppressed.

NOTES

1. Margaret Mead was probably one of the two or three best-known females in America during the 1950s, 60s and 70s. Her famous study of girls growing up in Samoa was read by virtually anyone taking a college anthropology class during those decades.

2. "Deep hanging out" is a handy phrase coined by Stanford University anthropologist, R. Rosaldo (1993), and popularized by Princeton's Clifford Geertz. It nicely captures the ethnographic methodology of spending time with people in order to find out about their lives.

3. Shane Claiborne, *The Irresistible Revolution* (Grand Rapids, MI: Zondervan, 2006), 128.

4. M.Springer, "Champ Chimp," *Scientific American Mind* (August/September 2006): 12-14.

5. Paul Farmer, *Pathologies of Power: Health, human Rights, and the New War on the Poor* (Berkeley: University of California Press, 2005), 31.

6. Richard Gibb, *Grace and Global Justice* (Paternoster Theological Monographs. Waynesboro, GA: Paternoster, 2006), xv.

7. W. R. Brookman *Grinding the Face of the Poor: A Reader in Biblical Justice* (Minneapolis: North Central University Press, 2006), xv.

8. Adapted from Brookman 2006, xviii.

9. N. R. Hanson *Patterns of Discovery* (London: Cambridge University Press, 1958), 5.

10. Ibid., 15.

11. T. D. Hanks *God So Loved the Third World*. trans. J.C. Dekker. (Maryknoll, N.Y.: Orbis Books, 1994).

CHAPTER 1

The Rich and the Poor Together

Embarrassing Relationships

On a teaching trip to India, Duncan Forrester, Professor of Theology and Public Issues at the University of Edinburgh, had an encounter with a beggar by the name of Munuswamy. The man was in a horrible state—he was a leper with nothing but a claw for a hand, and he was missing most of his toes. The beggar had a regular spot on a bridge over which the professor regularly crossed near the college at which he was teaching. On occasions, Forrester tried to engage the man with the little bit of Tamil that he knew at the time, and he remarks, "I hoped that one day I would have the language and the courage to become a friend of Munuswamy." Forrester recalls his situation with the man.

> And then I began to encounter the reality of the 'great gulf' between Lazarus and the rich man that ultimately became the unbridgeable chasm between the rich man and Lazarus. . . . Munuswamy with his broken life, his physical frailty, his illiteracy, his poor self-image lived in a different world from mine. I lived in a cosmopolitan sphere of security, opportunity, excitement, health, independence, respect— and also in the world of consumerism, where people are regularly measured by the size of their purse, and high levels of consumption are admired. Munuswamy lived in the tiny, circumscribed world of the railway bridge and his little mud hut, full of uncertainties about survival, dependent on the alms of others, his life a constant humiliation . . . for all that Munuswamy and I belonged to the opposite ends of the scale of global material inequality.
>
> The Munuswamy I met all those years ago is probably dead by now, life-expectancy in India being what it is. But if I went back to Madras today, I would find his place taken by some other Munuswamy, whose story would be very similar.[1]

Forrester's heart and mind were wrenched. He agonized over the proper way to react in such a relationship.

> I feel I must do something for Munuswamy. But nothing I can do will put the relationship right. Whatever I do, I feel rotten. Anything I do is simply a personal act which as best may ease Munuswamy's lot for a moment. The very act of giving underscores the inequality between us. Charity, alms, doles-out do not establish neighbourliness, friendship or equality. Indeed, they often make things worse, especially if they are impulsive, patronizing, ill-considered. And even if I were to help Munuswamy in a serious way, how many hundreds of thousands of beggars are there in Madras; do they not deserve help as well?
>
> The relationship (if one may call it that) between Munuswamy and me is so structured as to make virtually impossible an authentic, caring friendship between us. I am tempted to give Munuswamy a paltry sum to go away and terminate the embarrassing relationship.[2]

The problem is succinctly stated. As we glimpse the poor from the rich side of the world, it is an embarrassing relationship that we have with them. And yet, we know we have a commonality one with another. It shouldn't be such an embarrassing relationship. We who glimpse such a poor person, a beggar like Munuswamy, should take a measure of solace in that the rich and the poor do have relationship. As the Text notes, "Rich and poor have this in common: The Lord is the Maker of them all" (Prov 22:2).

Who is My Neighbor?

Have you ever noticed that rich people and poor people usually don't live side by side? Oh, I suppose that one could cite some cases of the wealthy and the poor working together and living in close proximity. Yet, they may not, even in those cases, be morally or spiritually affected by the stark contrast between them. However, for most people, at most times, in most places, it is a very rare thing for the wealthy and the poor to intermix.[3] There is, without a doubt, a reality to economic/spatial segregation. That is, there tends to be a separation of space between individuals that correlates to economic wellbeing. In the traditional use of the word, rich and poor are rarely *neighbors*. That is to say, they do not generally live next to or near each other. Yet, one need not necessarily run out, sell one's house, and move into an economically depressed neighborhood as the only means of becoming a neighbor to the poor.

Of course, one of the all-time classic questions is when the expert in the law asked Jesus, "Who is my neighbor?" We are informed that this question arose out of his trying to justify himself (Luke 10:29). However, even beyond that, the question betrays a bewildering lack of understanding the notion of love. With Jesus' reply, we learn that neighborliness doesn't necessarily have a spatial component—one does not need to live next or near to someone to be that person's neighbor. The heart of the matter actually has to do with the lawyer's initial question to Jesus which, by the way, was an excellent one—"What must I do to inherit eternal life?" Jesus answered that question with the acuity and deftness that one often finds in his remarks; he answers the question with a question.

"What is written in the Law? How do you interpret the answer?"

Give credit to the lawyer. Put on the spot by Jesus, he came up with a very good answer, and Jesus gave him praise for it. The expert in the law quoted Deuteronomy 6:5 and Leviticus 19:18—"Love the Lord your God with all your heart and with all your soul and with all your strength and with all your mind" and "Love your neighbor as yourself." Yet, the lawyer was really attempting to play at semantics; he wanted a crisp, clean definition of neighbor—however, the point is love.

We certainly know that there are many "inequalities that impede a proper relationship"[4] between the rich and the poor. Physical, spatial separation into *neighborhoods* is certainly one of those impediments. However, we on the rich side of the world, can, astonishingly, be neighbors to the poor and the oppressed even if they reside across the globe. One vehicle to bridge that impediment is love.

"What must I do to inherit eternal life?"

"Love God. . . . Love your neighbor as yourself."

"Who is my neighbor?

"A man was going down from Jerusalem . . . and a Samaritan took pity on him."

In the parable of the Good Samaritan, Jesus confronted the lawyer with the notion of love even after the expert in the law, himself, had already signaled love as *the* key factor in inheriting eternal life (Love God, love your neighbor). Over the years, much has been written about the notion of Christian love. In a chapter discussing the biblical concept of love, Stassen and Gushee, in their stunning book, *Kingdom Ethics*, nicely summarize some of the traditional Christian approaches to what the New Testament refers to as *agápe*. Setting the scene for the centrality of love within God's kingdom, they write:

> Victor Furnish says, for Jesus the love command functioned as 'the herme-neutical key to the law's interpretation' and was 'an integral part of his procla-mation of the coming Reign of God.' Jesus understood the imminent reign of God as establishing 'God's own sovereign power, justice, and mercy. . . . God's reign is thereby understood as the rule of love.'[5]

They go on to note that in 1932 Anders Nygren[6] wrote about this New Testament concept of love (*agápe*) and couched it in the framework of what he called "sacrificial love." This phrase caught on and became immensely influential as Nygren's work "has become a classic and has profoundly shaped both scholarly and popular Christian understanding of love."[7] Yet, it is pointed out that sacrificial love, as a defining notion of Christian love, *agápe*, has a number of liabilities or criticisms that have been noted.[8]

Stassen and Gushee further discuss love as taking the forms of mutual love,[9] delivering love,[10] and equal regard.[11] Love as equal regard is highlighted because, "as a definition of *agápe*, has the advantage that it fits well with the struggle for justice."[12] Indeed, it seems that love as *equal regard* has largely replaced *sacrificial love* among Christian ethicists as the prevailing notion of what *agápe* actually represents.[13]

Regardless of what nuance one prefers in defining the New Testament word, *agápe*, it is the parable, itself, that keeps me coming back to that wonderful lawyer, caught in the crosshairs, as Jesus explains who our neighbor is. I wonder, "What was he like after his encounter with Jesus? What should I be like after my encounter with Jesus?"

As we contemplate how we, who are on the rich side of the world, should interface with our poor and oppressed neighbors who may well be on the other side of the world, we may very forthrightly ask, "What can, what ought, I as an individual to do?...If we are people of faith, we know that faith must become active in love, and that turning away from need when we are capable of helping is a denial of our faith."[14] While we are capable of helping in a variety of ways, I firmly believe that one effective avenue that we on the rich side of the world have tended to overlook is prayer. Please continue by immediately reading the following vignette.

Leveling the Playing Fields

The world is a very inequitable place; inequities abound. You are probably familiar with the idiom, "to level the playing field." Of course, that phrase carries the concept of creating equity. I'm not sure of the origin of that particular idiom, nor am I going to spend time trying to run it down for your benefit. I'll just hypothesize that it came out of either soccer or American football since a sloping field in either of those two sports would create quite an unfair advantage for one side or the other, at least for one half. I suppose it could have come from other sports played on a field, baseball for instance. But it doesn't fit as well for baseball since the teams are always trading places each inning. Or, perhaps, it may have come out of cricket. I don't know, but some sport that uses a field is the setting for that idiom. I came across that phrase while reading a World Bank report that focused on equity and development, and it got me thinking a bit about inequity.[15]

Inequity is seen as unfairness. Think about the following scenario.

Consider two South African children born on the same day in 2000. Nthabiseng is black, born to a poor family in a rural area in the Eastern Cape province, about 700 kilometers from Cape Town. Her mother had no formal schooling. Pieter is white, born to a wealthy family in Cape Town. His mother completed a college education at the nearby prestigious Stellenbosch University.

On the day of their birth, Nthabiseng and Pieter could hardly be held responsible for their family circumstances: their race, their parents' income and education, their urban or rural location, or indeed their sex. Yet statistics suggest that those predetermined background variables will make a major difference for the lives they lead. Nthabiseng has a 7.2 percent chance of dying in the first year of her life, more than twice Pieter's 3 percent. Pieter can look forward to 68 years of life, Nthabiseng to 50. Pieter can expect to complete 12 years of formal schooling, Nthabiseng less than 1 year. Nthabiseng is likely to be considerable poorer than Pieter throughout her life. Growing up she is less likely to have access to clean water and sanitation, or to good schools. So the opportunities these two children face to reach their full human potential are vastly different from the outset, through no fault of their own.[16]

Certainly, in the preceding scenario, one can see theological, economic, societal, and philosophical issues and questions arising out virtually every line describing the circumstances of Nthabiseng's situation compared to Pieter's. However, one must also be cognizant of the fact that while statistically it would seem Pieter will, in all likelihood, have a much better life ahead of him, that's not a given. Perhaps Nthabiseng will become a world-class poet who inspires millions of people with her vividly written verses describing the human struggle. Maybe Pieter will become a drug addict and kill somebody while trying to steal $20 for his habit. This line of reasoning reflects an aspect of equality that pits the measure of opportunities against what are called actuals. That is, from "an equity perspective, the distribution of opportunities matters more than the distribution of outcomes. But opportunities, which are potentials rather than actuals, are harder to observe and measure than outcomes."[17]

Yet, the seemingly inequity of the situation pains us. Part of the pain is that when it comes to equity, we on the rich side of the world have been afforded, what appears to be on the surface, a huge advantage in this world. The playing field seems to be slanted in our favor. Is it even possible to level the playing field even if we really wanted to do so, or will the playing field always be uneven? The intuitive answer is that it will always be uneven. The Scriptural answer is also that it will always be uneven. It may cause a theological quiver down your spine, but it seems that God, in His sovereignty, has created a playing field that is not level—at least in regards to worldly measures of things like education, wealth, comfort, etc., etc.

It would seem that the objective, the task if you will, for the person on the rich side of the world is not to level the playing field with the goal of eliminating inequities. That would likely be an unachievable objective. Rather, the question is, given existing equities, what are the best responses within the framework of the Kingdom of God? If one has seriously considered the nature of the Kingdom of God as it was described by Jesus, one is quick to realize that something is amiss. The Kingdom is all out kilter. At least it is out of kilter with what we would expect it to be. In that sense, it reminds me of a certain Seinfeld episode in which Jerry and George are talking about "the opposite—it's a world in which things are opposite of what one expects. Down is up, black is white, etc. In the episode, George decides to do exactly the opposite of what he thinks he should do, his natural inclinations, in any given situation. After that, everything seems to be working out for him. While it's a poor and rather immature metaphor, that example actually does capture a bit of the nature Kingdom of God. God's Kingdom has been aptly described as *The Upside-Down Kingdom*, and in his book with that title, Donald Kraybill describes some of basic notions of Kingdom. He uses the imagery of two ladders.[18]

> To sharpen the issue we can think of two ladders side by side—one representing the kingdom of God and the other standing for the typical kingdoms of this world. An inverted or inverse relationship between the two ladders means that something at the top of one ladder is at the bottom of the other ladder. An object highly valued on the one ladder is on the bottom rung of the value system of the other. . . .
>
> The gospels suggest that the Kingdom of God is inverted or upside down when compared with the conventionally accepted values, norms and relationships of ancient Palestinian society and of modern culture today. This does not mean that the kingdom is geographically or socially isolated from the center of society. This is not a plea for social avoidance or withdrawal. Neither does this perspective assume a church-world split with the social territory neatly staked off into two separate plots of ungodly and holy ground. Kingdom action doesn't take place outside of the societal ball park. It's a different game played in the middle of the old ball park. Kingdom players follow different rules and listen to a different coach. Patterns of social organization which are routinely taken for granted in modern culture are questioned by kingdom values. Kingdom ways of living do not mesh smoothly with the dominant society. In fact they may sometimes appear foolish. The kingdom way often elicits responses of surprise and astonishment from the secular audience.[19]

Thus, the question remains, what are the best responses to an playing field that is not level given the nature of the Kingdom? How are we who live on the rich side of the world supposed to respond to those people who are incased within poverty? I must report to you that there is not a good, simple answer to the question. There is not a formula that you can write down or memorize in order to put it into play in any situation. But remember, you are working in the Kingdom of God, that wonderful Kingdom that is topsy-turvy. While the playing field is not level, the characters upon the playing field are all equal. How does one level the playing field? In fact, one can level it by recognizing absolute equality with the poor of this world. As Dallas Willard has observed,

> Only if we believe with our whole being in the equality of rich and poor before God can we walk in their midst as Jesus did, unaffected in our personal relations by the distinction.[20]

Perhaps a first step toward leveling the playing field is exactly that, fully realizing that there is no distinction before God and living our life after that manner.

> Our problem is not primarily with how we see the poor, but with how we see ourselves. If we still think and convey by our behavior that in some way we are fundamentally different and better as persons from the man sleeping in the discarded boxes in the alley, we have not been brought with clear eyes to the foot of the cross, seeing our own neediness in the light of it. We have not looked closely at the lengths to which God had to go to reach us. We have not learned to live always and thankfully in the cross's shadow.[21]

As Proverbs 22:2 so aptly puts it, "Rich and poor have this in common: Yahweh is the Maker of them all." Indeed, The Lord, the Holy One of Israel, has created the rich and the poor, and the common ground that we share should incite us toward positioning ourselves at the foot of the cross.

Try this prayer. "Lord, You make the rich and the poor, without distinction, and I want to be able to so identify with the poor that I would, indeed, not see any distinction between me and the poor man, wherever he may be. In the normal course of my worldly affairs I tend not to do this. Thus, I call upon You, Lord, to enable me to daily see my own neediness at the foot of the cross, and therefore, to identify myself fully with the poor. This isn't the sort of thing that comes naturally to me, so I ask in the name of Jesus Christ that Your Holy Spirit would be continually at work in me to change me, that I might not see any distinction between them and me in any of my dealings with the poor. I see things from the rich side of the world, but Lord, let me interact with people from the frame of reference one gains while kneeling at the foot of the cross. Amen"

That Quirky Dane

Søren Kierkegaard was a quirky Christian thinker. In my opinion, we could use more quirky Christian thinkers. Quirky thinkers just see things and articulate things in ways different from the masses; that's healthy. I wish I were quirkier.

Kierkegaard thought that for one to love another, as Jesus bids us to do, that love demands equality between the two lovers. "If there exists a great difference of wealth or power between the would-be lovers, it is hard for love not to be distorted or eroded by the inequality."[22] In speaking of Christ's incarnation, Kierkegaard spun a parable off of a fairy tale to use as an illustration of this point. It is a story of a powerful and rich prince who loved a very poor maiden. Kierkegaard's argument is that the prince really could not appear to the impoverished, swine herding girl as a regal and powerful sovereign. No! She would never love him for himself under that condition. He argued that the only way for the prince to enter into a loving relationship was to fully identify with her. Otherwise, the distance between them, the utter inequality between them, would forever inhibit a love between equals.

> The only way of enabling a loving union is for the king to descend and identify with the maiden, and share her lot, her suffering and her poverty. He must take the initiative and become equal to her if they are to be able to love one another. The king must become equal to the humblest. And this can be no play-acting, or deceit. It is not enough to have a beggar's cloak which the wind sweeps aside to reveal the royal garments underneath; it must be the true condition of the king, along his beloved in all respects.[23]

When Christ took the form of a servant in order to communicate God's love, He did, indeed, shatter the utter inequality of it all. Could Jesus' incarnation actually provide a model for his followers? That is, are we called, by the act of the incarnation to also do likewise and become a lowly servant? Kierkegaard draws it together by suggesting a tie with loving your neighbor as yourself.

> In being king, beggar, scholar, rich, poor, man, woman and so on, we do not resemble one another, for just therein lie our differences; but in being a neighbor we all unconditionally resemble one another. The difference is the confusion of the temporal existence which marks every man differently, but the neighbor is the mark of the eternal—on every man.[24]

Oh, that quirky Dane—he may just have hit on something here. Our neighbor is that loveless one, that stranger, that one seemingly unlike us who is downtrodden, and yet, we are to love that person. Yet, we can do so because, as Kierkegaard notes, we resemble that person, and Jesus has provided a model, a template. Therefore, as followers of Jesus, we too need to be suffering servants.

We Are Given Lazarus

As those who glimpse the poor from the rich side of the world, we are given a great gift from God. We are given Lazarus.[25] Of course, Lazarus represents the poor and the oppressed of this world, and they *are* a gift to us—whether we recognize that or not. And if we recognize it, there is still the question of whether we act on that or not. In the parable (Lk 16:19-31), the rich man (who represents all of us) was given Lazarus (who represents all of them). He was given a great opportunity to become a neighbor to this beggar at his gate and to love that man as he loved himself. "Søren Kierkegaard saw clearly that equality is rooted in God's gracious equal love for us, and is an implication of the divine command to love the neighbor as oneself."[26]

The First Task

Gustavo Gutiérrez has suggested that the church's "first social task is to be the church." As he wrote, "First, notions of 'justice' find their ground in Christ's love. . . . Caring for the poor is based on the action of Christ, who, though he was rich, yet for our sakes became poor (2 Cor. 8:9). Forgiving, reconciling, restoring, redeeming, including—all such terms capture aspects of Christ's own ministry and his ultimate work on the cross."[27]

What do you think, is the Church successful in its first social task? How effective are you, personally, at acting on behalf of the poor? As Christ became poor, it is a mystery that our caring for the poor is caring for Him (Mt 25:31f). Yet, some within the church recoil at hearing something like the "first social task." They perceive social gospel as something other than what the church should be doing, yet I'm not positive that Jesus would agree.

The Rich Need to Develop Some Listening Skills

Have you noticed that listening skills are considered very important to have in the corporate world? Fortune 500 companies pay huge amounts of money in order to have their executives become better at listening to people. In cases where there is desired communication between the rich and the poor, what do you think is necessary for there to be good interchanges? In the discipline of discourse ethics it is noted that a particular responsibility that powerful individuals have is to develop good listening skills.[28] One might look to the parable of the Rich Man and Lazarus (Lk 16: 19-31) as an example of a communication problem. There wasn't any listening going on there. The rich man, seemingly, did not engage Lazarus. But, can one really blame the rich man? It would definitely seem to be the case that, "it is not easy for people, however intelligent and sympathetic, to attend to the weak, the poor and the excluded."[29] Think about it for a moment; are you engaging the poor? That is, are you listening to the poor? While there are exceptions, my gut-level guess would be, of course not—because it is not an easy or natural thing to do.

It has been suggested that in order for us rich to listen, we need to experience "a change of direction and of priorities, and of self-understanding. It calls for intellectual humility before the complex truth. It demands breaking through some pretty stubborn and resistant social and intellectual barriers, because one cannot attend to people from a distance."[30]

May I repeat a portion of that last sentence? *One cannot attend to people from a distance.* I don't believe the distance is necessarily geographical distance; it may well be the distance of separation when one fails to listen or engage. Nor does proximity, in any way, guarantee the fine honing of listening skills. After all, Lazarus was right outside the home of the rich man, at the gate to his estate. If we (rich) truly wish to eliminate the distance, we (rich) must develop our listening skills. Do you really want to listen to the poor? Here are a few things they have to say:

> *When my husband died, my in-laws told me to get out. So I came to town and slept on the pavement.*[31]
>
>   middle-aged widow, Kenya 1966

> *Poverty is humiliation, the sense of being dependent, and of being forced to accept rudeness, insults, and indifference when we seek help.*[32]
>
>   Latvia 1998

> *They reproach me for beating my children. But what should I do when they cry when they are hungry? I beat them to make them stop crying.*[33]
>
>   a poor mother, Armenia 1999

> *Poverty is pain: it feels like a disease. It attacks a person not only materially but also morally. It eats away one's dignity and drives one into total despair.*[34]
>
>   a poor woman, Moldova 1997

What kind of listening skills do you have? Do you hear and comprehend the voices of the poor and the down-trodden? Sadly, it is especially painful to be a good listener as the poor speak, and we should readily admit that in our everyday lives, we on the rich side of the world tend not to be good listeners.

The Richest and the Poorest: The Scope of the Disparity

Just in case you weren't aware, there is a huge disparity between the rich and the poor of the world. If you were to take the richest 5% of the world's people and compare them to the poorest 5% of the world's population, you would see that the rich would have 114 times the income of poor. The ultra-rich, i.e. the top 1% have as much as the poorest 57% of the people on the planet.[35]

Opting for the Poor

Liberation theology elicits a wide range of opinions. This doesn't surprise me because liberation theology has produced a wide range of propositions. Like any type of theology, one can find the positive and the negative in it. Poor Catholics in a Third World environment tend to find much that is attractive in it, and rich Protestants in the First World tend to find elements that are threatening. With its origin in Latin America during the 1960s within a historical context of horrendous economic and political oppression, liberation theology had the lofty goal of attempting to concretely apply Christianity from the standpoint of the exploited masses of people. Of course, many who view the poor from the rich side of the world were uncomfortable with liberation theology because of the influence Marxism had upon it. Frankly, I don't think God much cares if a person is a

Democrat, Republican, or Marxist, and I suppose such a sentiment expressed in writing will get one labeled as a Marxist or as an advocate of the entire liberation theology agenda.

All that aside, what does come out of liberation theology is the notion of "a 'preferential option for the poor,' which is aimed at challenging and overcoming the structures of oppression and exploitation, the processes which condemn so many to squalor, illiteracy, poor health and early death."[36] If the Church is to be working and active within a historical praxis, what are the theological implications of millions and millions of poor people who live in what can only be described as dehumanizing conditions? It seems to me that Jesus practiced a kind of preferential option for the poor, and I would surmise that His expectation for his disciples (you and me) would be to do the same. And "doing" is a key concept within liberation theology—it has an emphasis on practice (praxis) rather than theory (theologizing). In writing about this theology of liberation, one champion of the cause, Gustavo Gutiérrez, advocated that, "the Christian community profess a faith which works through charity. It is—at least ought to be— real charity, action, and commitment to the service of others. Theology is reflection, a critical attitude. Theology follows; it is the second step."[37] Thus, the point is that theology must face the problem of historical situation, namely the existence of untold millions of poor, destitute, and oppressed people, and it must respond first by praxis and then, and only then, by theologizing.

Are We Really for the Poor?—A Valid Question

Although just about anybody in the Church, when asked, would say that they are definitely "for the poor," theologian José Miguez Bonino asks a valid question about that. "Are we really for the poor and oppressed if . . . we fail to say *how* we are 'for them' in their concrete . . . situation."[38] It is very easy and comforting to be a champion for the poor in an abstract way. How might you and I demonstrate or articulate how we are for the poor? Could you create, right now, off the top of your head, a list of five ways you are "for the poor" in their concrete situation? I double-dog dare you to get out a pencil and paper and write down, or at least try to write down, a list.

A Lesson for Hermas, You, and Me

Quick! What was the most widely-read piece of Christian literature outside of the Bible by believers in the second and third centuries? What piece of literature was widely used in the churches throughout the Mediterranean world to edify and encourage believers in the early Christian communities? Long pause . . . long pause. . . . Don't worry; very few of us moderns can answer that question. However, if any Christian in the early Church had been asked that question, there would have been no long pause, no hesitation—the answer is certain, *The*

Shepherd of Hermas would have been the response. You're reaction may well be, "What? I've never heard of it!" It's probably fair to say that most western Christians are not familiar with that ancient work which was so widely known among the ancient believers.

Think for a moment about what might be considered modern counterparts to this ancient phenomenon. There certainly are pieces of Christian literature which function to help build up people in the Church. There are all sorts of books that are used in the church—that many Christians read and enjoy in their spiritual journey. If you were to brainstorm with your small group at church, you would probably come up with a fairly long and interesting list. For instance, think of some popular Christian books that are used in Sunday School classes or in mid-week small group gatherings. Surely the writings of Billy Graham have been popular with many moderns. Books such as Philip Yancey's *What's So Amazing About Grace?* or Richard J. Foster's *Celebration of Discipline* have been popularly used in this sense. The point is, there is a corpus of non-canonical literature which functions to uplift, edify, challenge, and instruct people of the Church. Modern Sunday School types of activities were also a part of the ancient church, and the reading, citing, and discussing of the *Shepherd of Hermas* was extremely common in the early church.

My hunch is that you have never read anything from the *Shepherd of Hermas*. But, it's a new day; below is a passage from it— actually it's a parable. Go ahead; give it a read. See what you think.

*Like the Vine and the Elm, So is the Relationship
Between the Rich and the Poor*

While I was walking in the field and considering an elm tree and a vine, reflecting on them and their fruits, the shepherd appeared to me and said, "Why are you asking yourself about the elm tree and the vine?" "I am thinking, Lord," I replied, "that they are extremely well suited for one another." "These two trees," he replied, "symbolize the slaves of God." "I would like to know," I said, "what these two trees you are speaking about symbolize." "You see," he said, "the elm and the vine?" "I see them, Lord," I replied. "This vine," he said, "bears fruit; but the elm is a tree that does not. Yet if this vine did not grow up onto the elm, it could not bear much fruit, since it would be lying on the ground, and the fruit it bore would be rotten, since it would not be clinging to the elm. And so, when the vine attaches to the elm, it bears fruit both of itself and because of the elm. And so you see that the elm also gives much fruit—no less than the vine, but rather more." "How does it bear more, Lord?" I asked. "Because," he said, "it is by clinging to the elm that the vine gives an abundance of the good fruit; but when it is lying on the ground it bears just a little rotten fruit. And so this parable applies to the slaves of God, the poor and the rich." "How so, Lord?" I asked. "Explain it to me." "Listen," he said, "The rich person has money, but is poor towards the Lord, since he is distracted by his wealth. The prayer and confession he makes to the Lord are very small—weak, small, and of no real effect. And so, when the rich person depends upon he one who is poor and supplies him with what he needs, he believes that by helping the one who is poor he will find his recompense before God. For the poor person is rich in his petition and confession, and his petition has a great effect before God. And so the rich person supplies everything to the one who is poor, without hesitation. And then the poor person, having his needs supplied by the one who is rich, prays to God and thanks him for the one who has given him what he needs. And that one becomes even more eager to help out the poor person, so that he may lack nothing in his life. For he knows that the petition of the poor person is acceptable and rich before the Lord. And so both accomplish their work. The poor person works at his prayer in which he is rich and which he received from the Lord; and he gives it back to the Lord who supplied it to him in the first place. So too the rich person does not hesitate to supply his wealth to the poor person, since he received it from the Lord. And this is a great and acceptable thing to do before God, because the rich person has gained understanding by his wealth and has worked for the poor person out of the gifts provided by the Lord, and he has accomplished his ministry well. And so, people may think that the elm tree bears no fruit; but they neither know nor understand that when a drought comes, the elm nourishes the vine by holding water; and the vine, since it has an undiminished supply of water, produces fruit for two, both for itself and for the elm. Thus also those who are poor who pray to the Lord on behalf of the rich bring their own wealth to completion; and again those who are rich and supply the poor with what they need bring their souls to completion. Both then share in an upright work. And so the one who does these things will not be abandoned by God, but will be recorded in the books of the living. Happy are those who have possessions and understand that their riches have come from the Lord; for the one who understands this will also be able to perform a good ministry.[39]

Did you like it? If you did, you may wish to read more of the *Shepherd of Hermas*; it's filled with parables like the one above! In the parable you just read, the teaching point centers on the relationship that exists between the rich and poor of this world. That relationship is, of course, timeless. It goes back into the earliest antiquity of the Church, and it continues right up into the 21st century. I pray that we not too arrogant in our modernity to think that we cannot learn something from such ancient wisdom and Christian exhortation. Here, in this extremely archaic document, probably written somewhere about 110-140 A.D.,[40] we find moral instructions for those Christians of the fledgling Church. The rich are implored to give generously and establish an interdependence with the poor. What a great notion. So also ought *our* lives be lived in such a way that a symbiotic relationship with the poor and the oppressed be a fundamental part of the way in which we live our life. The centuries have changed nothing. We are like the elm; they are like the vine.

Jesus, the Poor, and You

The public ministry of Jesus began with him reading aloud for all to hear a text from the prophet Isaiah (61:1-2).

The Spirit of the Lord is on me,
Because he has anointed me
to preach good news to the poor.
He as sent me to proclaim liberation to the prisoners
and recovery of sight to the blind,
to liberate the oppressed,
to proclaim the year of the Lord's favor.
                                        (Luke 4:18-19)

On this particular occasion, in a little synagogue in Nazareth, things probably started out as a normal, if uneventful, Sabbath gathering. After all, in the first century, Nazareth was a small and rather quaint place—really, only a village. It occupied less than 10 acres and therefore one can extrapolate that it had a population of probably not more than about 400 people.[41] It was a quiet, unimportant place. It's not the kind of place one would expect the eschatological turning of a page to happen, and yet, that's exactly what happened that fateful day when Jesus announced to the people contently sitting there that, "Today this scripture is fulfilled in your hearing." What had happened? All of a sudden, in the flurry of the moment, Jesus had announced that "the year of the Lord's favor" had arrived. This was more than a jubilee year such as had been established in the Torah (Lev 25:10); it was the announcement that the Kingdom was now among them (us).

However, you must remember, Jesus wasn't just announcing it to just the few people who were sitting there that day. He was announcing it to you and to me—even though we are sitting here in the 21st century. Yet, the profundity of His announcement not only escaped the audience who sat there in the synagogue on that day in the year 27 A.D.;[42] it tends also to escape us.

This was the event that commenced Jesus' public ministry, and however one wants to interpret this event, one cannot escape the text of Scripture by which Jesus chose to make the proclamation. The text is riddled with the liberating news of Isaiah—the poor, the prisoners, the blind, and the oppressed are the ones with whom Jesus "cast his lot."[43] Not only was his mission centered upon the proclaiming and liberating foretold by Isaiah, but he identified himself as one of them by the way in which he lived his life among us.

It as been asked, "How much is the oppression and poverty of our modern world the business of the community of believers in Jesus?"[44] The message I clearly sense when reading the words of Jesus is that, not only is it our (my) business, but it is our (my) obligation to aggressively confront oppression and poverty.

NOTES

1. Duncan Forrester, *On Human Worth* (London: SCM Press, 2001), 2-3.

2. Ibid., 3.

3. John Philip Wogaman, "Towards a Method for Dealing with Economic Problems as Ethical Problems," in Dietmar Mieth and Jacques Pohier (eds.) *Christian Ethics and Economics: The North-South Conflict* New York: Seabury Press, 1980), 80.

4. Forrester, *On Human Worth*, 173.

5. Glen H. Stassen and David P. Gushee, *Kingdom Ethics: Following Jesus in Contemporary Context*. (Downers Grove: InterVarsity Press, 2003), 327.

6. Anders Nygren, *Agape and Eros* trans by Philip S. Watson. (Philadelphia: Westminster Press, 1953).

7. Stassen and Gushee, *Kingdom Ethics*, 328.

8. Ibid., 329-30.

9. Daniel Day Williams, *The Spirit and the Forms of Love* (New York: Harper & Row, 1968).

10. Stassen and Gushee, *Kingdom Ethics*, 333.

11. Gene Outka, *Agape: An Ethical Analysis* (New Haven: Yale University Press 1972).

12. Stassen and Gushee, *Kingdom Ethics*, 332.

13. Stephen J. Pope, "Proper and Improper Partiality and the Preferential Option for the Poor." *Theological Studies* 54 (1993), 242-71.

14. Forrester, *On Human Worth*, 173.

15. World Bank, *World Development Report 2006, Equity and Development* (New York: Oxford University Press, 2005).

16. Ibid., 1.

17. Ibid., 4.

18. Donald B. Kraybill, *The Upside-Down Kingdom* (Scottdale, PA: Herald Press, 1978).

19. Ibid., 23-24.

20. Dallas Willard, *The Spirit of the Disciplines* (San Francisco: HarperCollins Publishers, 1988), 209.

21. Ibid., 211.

22. Forrester, *On Human Worth*, 147.

23. Ibid., 147-48.

24. Søren Kierkegaard, trans., David Swenson *Works of Love*. (London: Oxford University Press, 1946), 72.

25. Forrester, *On Human Worth*, 98.

26. Ibid., 251.

27. Rollin G. Grams, "From Being to Doing: The identity of God's people as the ground for building a Christian social ethic." *Transformation* 18 (2001), 157.

28. Forrester, *On Human Worth*, 12.

29. Ibid., 15.

30. Ibid.

31. Narayan, et. al., *Voices of the Poor: Can Anyone Hear Us?* (New York: Oxford University Press, 2000), 255.

32. Ibid., 30.

33. Ibid., 238.

34. Ibid., 2.

35. United Nations Development Programme, *Human Development Report 2003* (New York: Oxford University Press, (2003), 39.

36. Forrester, *On Human Worth*, 156.

37. Gustavo Gutiérrez, *A Theology of Liberation: History, Politics and Salvation* (London: SCM Press, 1978), 9.

38. José M. Bonino, *Revolutionary Theology Comes of Age* (London: SPCK 1975), 148.

39. Bart D. Ehrman, ed., *The Apostolic Fathers* (Cambridge, MA: Harvard University Press, 2003), 309-315.

40. Ibid., 169.

41. Eckhard Schnable, *Early Christian Mission* Volume 1 (Downers Grove, Il: InterVarsity Press, 2004), 229.

42. Luke 3:1-2 sets the time as the fifteenth year of the reign of the Emperor Tiberius.

43. T. D. Hanks, trans. J.C. Dekker, *God So Loved the Third World* (Maryknoll, N.Y.: Orbis Books, 1994), 110.

44. John C. Haughey, ed., *The Faith That Does Justice*. Woodstock Studies 2 (New York: Paulist Press 1977), 265.

CHAPTER 2

The Nature of Poverty

The Fractal Nature of Poverty

Poverty is extremely complex; in that sense it might well be described as being fractal. Now, *fractal* may be a term with which you are unfamiliar, but I think it may be immensely useful to describe the complexity of poverty. I had heard the term "fractal" used before, and I knew that it was associated with geometry; yet, beyond that, I really had no understanding of even the rudiments of the concept. Fractals were foreign to me. My world of geometry was, at the time, pretty Euclidian. In fact, my entire view of life may be, oftentimes, too Euclidian—too simplistic, too limited, too neat. As I am constantly discovering, the world is an incredibly complex place. If I've learned anything from reading about the physical universe, cultural studies, or some topic like poverty, I have learned that we do not live in a simple, structured, neat place.

On one occasion, quite some time ago, I came across a reference to fractals in a book I was reading, and I felt compelled to find out a bit more about the topic. After a quick trip to the library I secured a copy of the bibliographic source noted in that book, and I set out to read about fractals from the horse's mouth, so to speak. It's seems the person to read on fractals is a fellow by the name of Mandelbrot. In his work *The Fractal Geometry of Nature*, I came across a chapter with the enticing title, "How Long Is the Coast of Britain?" What at first seemed to me like a fairly straightforward question, in fact, developed into a labyrinth-like maze of massively complex considerations.

To express simply and concisely the essence of fractal geometry is no easy task. And, I suspect, that you would rather that I didn't exhaust myself trying. So I won't—exhaust myself that is. Please be patient as I attempt to illustrate the concept. It will be quite worth it for the concept provides some interesting and original analogies for thinking about, of all things, poverty.

I think Mandelbrot's example of the measuring of the coastline of Britain is a good way to get a handle on fractals. Here's how it works.

If someone gave you the task of measuring the coastline around Britain, how would you do it? You could, I suppose, take a couple of yardsticks and start by placing them end-to-end. By doing this around the entire coast you would ultimately arrive at a total distance around the place. But now suppose you did the same thing, this time with a twelve inch ruler. Would you get the same distance? No, you wouldn't. As you walked around the second time, measuring with the one-foot ruler you would be able to fit that measuring device into some nooks and crannies into which the yardstick would not have fit. As you came to some jagged rocks you would be able to be more precise with the one-foot ruler than you had been with the yardstick. Now, suppose you did the measuring again—this time with a six inch ruler. And again, what if you did it again using a one-inch ruler. You see, every time you measure, even avoiding all human error, your measurements will differ. What if you used a microscope and measured the coastline in microns? Mandelbrot makes the argument that, in fact, the coastline of Britain is infinitely long because you can always measure at a higher magnification. This is where Euclid goes out the window because his nice, neat shapes like circles and squares don't very often represent nature. Indeed, if the coastline of Britain were a Euclidean shape you could ultimately get your results converging fine enough so that the Euclidean straight-line measurements would, for all practical purposes, give you the length of the coastline of Britain. But Euclidean thinking doesn't really deal well with the reality of nature. Most things in nature approximate coastlines, not circles and squares.[1]

So it is that I would argue that poverty is akin to the coastline of Britain, that is, it's fractal. It's huge, and it's complex. It's difficult to measure, and even at that, you can always measure in a more refined way. Poverty is fractal, not Euclidean. That will probably become clear to you as you read the array of vignettes within the body of this book as they look at poverty from many different angles. You will, in all likelihood, as you work your way through the vignettes in this book, discover aspects of poverty you had not even thought of before. You will also readily see that poverty is very, very complicated and no single study will ever envelope the entire scope of it.

Imaginary Numbers of Deaths and Bono

Every day, every single day of the year, something very extraordinary happens in the world. Every day about 30,000 children who are under the age of five die from easily preventable causes.[2]

Now, take 30,000 children a day who *will die* and multiply that by 365 days in the year. The product is 10,950,000. The previous two sentences should have made you sit back in your chair a bit. If they didn't—if those two sentences didn't make you tighten up just a bit as you read them—you might want to consider the possibility that there is something wrong with the way you view the world. Those seem to be nearly imaginary numbers! Of course, the notion of imaginary numbers is quite mind numbing to most of us. One might even react by suggesting that those numbers can't possibly be correct. You might be right; they may be a tad low.

While there are plenty of days I just don't feel like listening to a rock-concert, there are those days when a quote from Bono seems appropriate.

What is happening in Africa mocks our pieties, doubts our concern, and questions our commitment to that whole concept. Because if we're honest, there's no way we could conclude that such mass death day after day would ever be allowed to happen anywhere else. Certainly not in North America, or Europe, or Japan. An entire continent bursting into flames? Deep down, if we really accept that their lives—African lives—are equal to ours, we would all be doing more to put the fire out. It's an uncomfortable truth.[3]

Bono is correct, but only partly so. That's because it isn't *just* a case of African lives being lost for no good reason. Of the 30,000 kids dying every single day, half of them are on the African continent. The other half is spread all over the place, but almost always in contexts of poverty. Bono is probably right, however, in saying that we almost certainly wouldn't allow such a thing to happen in North America, Europe, or Japan. The phrase he uses, "What is happening . . . mocks our pieties," jars us to introspection—it is, as he said, "an uncomfortable truth."

Indeed, does the Christian West, do we who view the poor and the oppressed from the rich side of the world, have an apt reply to what is happening? If not, perhaps we pious Christians whose piety is being mocked by this scandal of needless death should develop a response, and I highly suggest that our response needs to be behavioral, not cognitive. While this book is designed to inform, *i.e.* provide some cognitive awareness of what life is like for the poor and the oppressed, the larger goal is to incite behavioral changes, to rouse a new praxis of biblical justice among the poor and the oppressed by people who are followers of Jesus.

Addis is Like a Salvador Dali Painting

My first impression of Ethiopia was based upon our arrival in the Addis Ababa airport. It was about the most confusing scene I have ever experienced. Yet, by some inexplicable breach of Murphy's Law, all of our baggage did arrive, and my wife, daughter, and I all got through customs. Then, exiting the airport, we entered an altogether different world. It was a world for which I was not fully prepared.

The wonderful thing about Addis is that the city gives you new and memorable impressions every day. It's one of those cities that is impossible to describe to people—one really needs to be there because words just don't work well enough to paint an accurate picture of the place. I guess that's because the city is actually like a Dali painting; it's surreal.

And there you are, in the middle of this surreal painting, and unreal things are all around you. I spent four months in that city during the spring of 2000. The first thing I would like to say about Addis Ababa is that I don't believe that anybody knows how many people live there. Yes, I know you can *google* Addis and find that the population is such and such or so and so. But please believe me; those numbers, whatever they happen to be, aren't accurate. I would like to go on record as saying that nobody, no institution, no government, nothing and no one is capable of counting the people of Addis.

One of the fun things I discovered early on during my stay in Addis is that the streets don't have names. Getting directions to go somewhere was another part of that surreal experience. My hosts and their friends who had lived in the city for years simply created their own names for streets in order to pass on directions of how one moves from point A to point B through the city. Perhaps things have changed in the time since I've been there and they have some street signs, but I doubt it. It seems street signs were taken down during the years of the repressive Marxist regime (1974-1991). After all, if they can't find your street, they can't find you.

By interesting coincidence, the morning after I started writing this particular section about Addis, I noticed the following headline in my daily newspaper— "Judges convict former dictator of genocide after a 12-year trial."[4] The article was a short piece from the Associated Press that explained how the former dictator of Ethiopia during those Marxist years, a despicable fellow by the name of Mengistu Haile Mariam, was just found guilty of genocide at the conclusion of a protracted trial which has lasted for twelve years. Yet, Mengistu was found guilty in absentia as he fled to Zimbabwe after his overthrow in 1992. Since then he has quietly remained in near total seclusion under the protection of Zimbabwe's strongman, dictator Mugabe.

Another of the many surreal experiences I had in Addis was the day I went to the Sheraton Hotel which is located somewhere in the city. It was the most extreme example of opulence across the street from poverty I have ever seen. The *Sheraton Addis* is a luxury hotel on par with any other ultra-luxury hotel in the world. Yet, within the confines of the city of Addis, there really is no appropriate place for such an entity, and so, literally across the street, one sees the slums and poverty of the city. It is a surreal picture.

Whatever the population of Addis is, a UN HABITAT survey of the city estimates that "less than 10 per cent of that city's inhabitants live in non-slum areas."[5] What does it mean that 90% of everybody in a city lives in slum conditions? Is that even fathomable for you to think about what life is like for the millions and millions and millions of people whose entire existence, from birth to death, is within that context of that single, slum-ridden city?

My feeling is that every American should spend a few months in Addis. In fact, I would advocate (somewhat tongue in cheek) that our government should subsidize everyone to be able to go. I think that would actually be money very well spent. It would be a mere sliver of our defense budget for a given year, and it would literally change everyone's view of the world. You can't put a price tag on something like that. Addis Ababa is a great city to use as an example of the sort of chaotic environment in which most the poor and the oppressed around the globe live their lives.

Clothes Make the Poor Man

Mark Twain once remarked, "Clothes make the man. Naked people have little or no influence on society." The first sentence of that quotation is fairly well known. The second part is not so often quoted, nor is it widely known. Yet, while the saying is witty, as is most of what Mark Twain said, the sad fact is that a large number of people throughout the world are, for all practical purposes, quite naked.

A 20th century Rabbi by the name of Eliyahu Lopian quipped that, "When someone is dressed in a manner that shows he is wealthy, people will usually greet him with much respect. If someone else comes along who is dressed in rags, many people just ignore him. Even if someone were to greet him, it would usually be in a perfunctory manner, done out of a feeling of obligation. But this is based on falsehood. Who are you greeting—a human being or his style of clothing?"

The clothing one wears definitely impacts the perception of the individual by those people who encounter him or her. People are judged according to their clothes. Yet, we are admonished (James 2:2-4) to avoid such judgments. As the text reads,

> Suppose a man comes into your meeting wearing golden rings and fine clothes, and a poor man in shabby clothes also comes in. If you show special attention to the man wearing fine clothes and say, 'Here's a good seat for you.' But say to the poor man, 'You stand there' or 'Sit on the floor by my feet,' have you not discriminated among yourselves and become judges with evil thoughts?

Sadly, even young children are not exempt from this type of judgmental discrimination as people look at the rotten, filthy clothing worn by kids in poverty. In a number of PPA studies[6] it's oftentimes the children who complain about the stigma of wearing torn and ragged clothing. They experience, on a daily basis, the brunt of judgment against them based on the garments they wear.

> In Georgia children who wear old, patched clothing to school are often cruelly taunted, which becomes another reason for their parent to keep them home from school or to enroll them a year late in the hope that their situation may improve. Some Tbilisi youth admit to avoiding university classes because they are humiliated at the daily prospect of appearing dirty and poorly groomed in front of others.[7]

We who are viewing things from the rich side of the world have the powerful tendency to see the clothes and have *that* influence our view of the person.

The next time you see someone dressed shabbily, please remember what Rabbi Lopian said, "Who are you greeting—a human being or his style of clothing?"

Poverty is More Complicated Than You Think

There are not simple answers to many of the questions about poverty. A good lesson to learn is that the poor, themselves, are generally more astute than those of us who are not poor at getting to the root of some of the issues. Poverty has been described as being very multidimensional. "The persistence of poverty is linked to its interlocking multidimensionality: it is dynamic, complex, institutionally embedded, and a gender— and location-specific phenomenon."[8] While poverty is undoubtedly complex and multidimensional, the lowest common denominator, ever-present in the equation, would always seem to be hunger. Beyond that, however, what the rich of this world probably don't recognize full-well enough are the psychological aspects of poverty. That is, whatever you think about poverty, you almost assuredly do not comprehend the scope and impact that "powerlessness, voicelessness, dependency, shame, and humiliation"[9] have upon the poor. Yet, the poor will speak to us very directly about such things.

The poor also speak of the role of the government and how ineffective it is in addressing their state of poverty. They report how "their interactions with state representatives are marred by rudeness, humiliation, harassment, and stonewalling."[10] How hard it is for us, who have so much, to identify with the poor. After all, when we are met with such obstacles, we tend to overcome them. It is amazing what money can overcome.

Being Poor in Uganda or Being Poor in Cameroon

In Uganda there are different labels or categories of people who are viewed as poor. In a study done to assess poverty in that country, various women's groups were asked to participate in a project designed to better understand how the system of poverty worked.[11] The women indicated that there are three levels of poverty for poor people.

> The poor are described primarily as laborers who work on other people's land or on boats in exchange for food or cash, but who live in a hut on their own tiny patch of land. The poorest have no housing, but work for food and live on the land of the rich. The fully dependent include single mothers, disabled persons, and the elderly who have nothing and cannot work, and so depend entirely on state services or assistance from others.[12]

One PPA study done in Cameroon[13] found that poor people there distinguish themselves from those who are not poor by some basic criteria. Among those factors most often mentioned one finds: a feeling of powerlessness and the inability to have their voices heard, fewer meals, little or no cash and a greater percentage of their "meager and irregular income spent on food."[14]

Internalized Deception Among the Poor

Living in abject poverty does oftentimes seem to create a particular mental condition which has a horrendous effect among the poor. That condition is a perception of blame, and the poor tend to see themselves as the cause for their own poverty. In a study done in Tanzania, it was found that the poor people of the community in which there was a World Vision development project underway perceived themselves as the problem.[15] Causes such as ignorance, laziness, lack of entrepreneurial spirit and lack of community spirit were seen by those within the community of the poor to be their fault. This is quite contrary to the views of the World Vision staff working at that site who saw injustice as, perhaps, the major root cause of the poverty.

Mental frameworks of perception are difficult to change, even under the best of conditions. Serious prayer for the poor should include petitions for them to be loosed from this "mental web of lies that the poor believe and, by believing, disempower themselves."[16]

It's a New World!

When the former Soviet Union fell, one of the newspaper headlines I remember seeing was, "It's a New World!" Indeed, it is a new world in a variety of ways, however, it's not all good. Things in the regions of the former Soviet bloc are not so rosy with regards to the economic situation many people found themselves in for the first time in their lives after the collapse of communism. A new poverty has wrapped its tentacles through the former Soviet empire, and countless numbers of people have found that they are engulfed by conditions they had never faced before. "In the former system, poverty was ascribed to laziness and incompetence, and poverty was often associated with criminality. Poverty was mainly perceived to be a result of personal failings or evidence of undesirable family traits and upbringing."[17] Now however, although they may be steeped in poverty, people feel forced to maintain a façade of economic well-being in order to avoid the sigma of the previous cultural perceptions about those who are in poverty.[18] Poverty has produced a humiliation under which the people are suffering. For example, a "former university lecturer in physics from Tbilisi reports that he was compelled to take a job as a chauffeur in order to support his family. He found work in another city so that he would not have to suffer the humiliation of having people he knew see him driving. . . ."[19] This exemplifies the extreme psychological impact poverty has upon people who grew up under the old Soviet system. That's another very powerful aspect to the nature of poverty; it produces humiliation for those who live in grasp of its tentacles.

The Nasty, Multifaceted Nature of Poverty

Poverty is nasty; even the wealthy can appreciate that as fact without ever having experienced it themselves. After all, don't you think it's nasty even though you are wealthy? If you don't think you are wealthy, you are deluding yourself. I always tell my students, "By the mere fact that you are in college, you are very wealthy compared to most of the rest of the people in the world." Even the poorest Americans are quite wealthy compared to the rest of the world. More than half of the world's people live on less than $2 per day.[20] If you make (or spend) more than $730 a year, you are wealthy.

How would you feel toward poverty if you were enveloped by it throughout your entire life, with no reasonable expectation that anything would ever change?

Poverty Means . . .

A poor woman in Cambodia once said, "Poverty means working for more than 18 hours a day, but still not earning enough to feed myself, my husband, and two children."[21] If you had to write out a definition of poverty, how would you construct it? What phrases would you use to describe it? Want a not-so-fun exercise? Complete this sentence—Poverty means. . . . That's actually a pretty difficult thing to do for someone who merely glimpses the poor and the oppressed from the rich side of the world. That is, when it comes to defining and understanding the chaotic entanglement which is poverty, the people who seem to have the clearest and most accurate insights are those who are themselves mired in the befuddling chaos of poverty.

The Center is Shifting—It's Moving from Asia to Africa

In both East Asia and in South Asia solid gains have been made in reducing the number of people in poverty over the past several decades. It is well known that the center of poverty has traditionally been located in Asia as about two-thirds of people in extreme poverty across the world live in Asia. However, that center is shifting. Not only has the number of people in poverty in Asia been reduced, but the economic growth in that region has also been steady. It's safe to say that now the center of poverty is moving toward Africa. As David Dollar of the World Bank has noted, "It is still the case that two-thirds of the extreme poor live in Asia, but if strong growth there continues, then global poverty will increasingly be concentrated in Africa."[22] Sub-Saharan Africa is an economic train wreck. In the two decades from 1981-2001 that region actually faced a double whammy as it had negative economic growth *and* an increase in the number of people living in extreme poverty. In 1981 41.6% of the population (164 million people) lived in extreme poverty while in 2001 46.9% (316 million) found themselves to be in that predicament. The really bad news is that this trend continues to this very day.

A Place You Don't Hear Much About

Browse the newspaper. Listen to the radio. Watch the nightly news. Do all these things regularly, and you still won't hear much about the Central African Republic. That's why I was pleasantly surprised the other day when I opened the newspaper and found an Associated Press article on this beleaguered country.[23] The place, to be sure, doesn't get much press. After all, it's not a vacation spot, and while there is fighting there, nobody notices. Let's face it, not only is the Central African Republic a place we don't hear much about, it's a place we don't care much about.

However, there is a place where the Central African Republic shows up and gets its fair share of press—that's in the index of World Development Indicators.[24] Pick an indicator, any indicator—mortality, child immunization rate, percentage of population living on less than $1/day, or any of several dozen other measures of a difficult life, and you will find the Central African Republic prominently near or at the bottom of the list. Mortality? One way to gauge mortality is with the Life Expectancy at Birth measure—how long can one expect to live if born in a particular country. The high 70s is pretty good. Several countries are at 80 years of age or over (Australia, Canada, France, Japan, Norway, Switzerland).[25] On the other end of the spectrum, life expectancy in the Central African Republic is 39.[26] How about another measure? Let's take the Child Immunization Rate. When one measures the percentage of children (ages 12-23 months) who are immunized for measles, the Central African Republic is tied with Nigeria as the lowest rated country in the world. Both those nations have a mere 35% of their kids immunized against measles.[27]

Another indicator is poverty. There are, of course, a number of ways to measure poverty. One is to use the International Poverty Line and determine the percentage of the population which earns less than $1 a day. In the Central African Republic, two-thirds (66.6%) of the population lives on less than $1 per day.[28] What one sees in indicator after indicator in the World Bank's latest data is the appearance of the Central African Republic near the bottom of every list. On top of all of that, it's a place where rebels run rampant.

The northern part of the country is mired in incredible poverty. Consider the conditions there as described in a recent Human Rights Watch report.

> There are no tarred roads or electrified towns, and schools and medical facilities are primitive and understaffed, if functioning at all. In many villages, there are no water pumps to provide clean water. In the most remote areas of northern CAR, state structures are virtually non-existent—there are no police officers, administrative officials, teachers, or health professionals. There are almost no development projects in many parts of the north, in contrast with southern

CAR, where the donor community and the World Bank are supporting large-scale development initiatives.[29]

Conflict is everywhere as rebels fight against government forces. "The conflict has displaced at least 220,000 people, but with arson the primary weapon and major battles rare, it's quiet a war that doesn't grab the headlines—or aid."[30] Actually, the latest UN figures put the total of displaced people at 280,000;[31] but who really cares once you're past a quarter of a million? And so it is that the Central African Republic stays out of the headlines and out of the limelight of humanitarian crises that those of us on the rich side of the world hear about now and then.

Large Islands of Chaos

Speaking of the Central African Republic, one might well describe that nation as one of the "large islands of chaos," a phrase used by Paul Collier in his book, *The Bottom Billion: Why the Poorest Countries Are Failing and What Can Be Done About It* to describe countries caught in a variety of traps which stymie development.[32] In the book he tells the story of his visit to the CAR in 2002. He writes,

> at the airport I was met by a crew from the national television station as if I were a celebrity. That also tells you something—that nobody visits the Central African Republic. When I settled into discussions with the government, I asked them a question that I always ask when advising a government, because it forces people to get concrete and also serves as a measure of ambition: which country did they wish to be like in twenty years' time? The group of government ministers discussed it among themselves for a while, then turned back to me with the answer: Burkina Faso. Burkina Faso! In fact it was not a foolish answer by any means. The two countries share some important characteristics, and Burkina Faso has been doing abut a well as possible given those conditions. But it remains dirt poor. That the realistic horizon of ambition for the Central African Republic in twenty years should be to get where Burkina Faso now is speaks of despair.[33]

Doesn't it seem that despair is an earmark of the poor and the oppressed around the world? As one glimpses the masses of people steeped in poverty or injustice, wherever they may be, one senses the sinister presence of despair—of a hopelessness. The Future is not something to which they look forward. On the other hand, we who live on the rich side of the world tend to eagerly anticipate the future. We have exciting expectations of what the future might possibly hold for us. There are very different psychological aspects at work that separate us from them.

I wonder how you and I might be better able to identify with their despair—not with the aim that we would ourselves despair, but rather, that we, like Jesus, might exude a compassion for those who do. What do you think? What are any ways for you and for me to more closely identify with someone's despair? How do we even begin to connect with, let's say, the children of the Central African Republic? Here we need to be careful, because most certainly there is a cost in more fully identifying with the poor and the oppressed.

Talk About Being Fatalistic

The poor often self-describe their situation as one of hopeless; they tend to be very fatalistic. What kind of psychological impact would living in a constant state of hopelessness or chronic fatalism have on a person's life? I'm sure studies have been done, but frankly, I thought it would be too depressing to investigate that. So I didn't.

In rural India the proportion of the total population which lives in extreme poverty, marked by chronic malnutrition and hunger, typically swings between 40% to 60%. A major determiner of this variation is the weather that can drastically impact food production and consequently food prices. As the poor often describe it, their fatalism stems from the belief that they really do not have any significant measure of control over their life.[34]

The Vicious Cycles Which Engulf the Poor

There is a well-established relationship between the real economic growth of a nation and its Human Development Index (HDI). One impacts the other to the point of creating a vicious cycle of sorts. Poor human development will lead to a decline in economic growth, and a decline in economic growth will lead to poor human development. Breaking out of such a cycle is crucial if a country will have any hope of reaching one or more of the MDGs.[35]

The HDI is a three dimensional measure which combines elements of 1) living a long and healthy life, 2) education, and 3) standard of living. Performance in each of the three elements is express as a value between 0 and 1. The HDI is then calculated as the simple average of the three elements. Can you guess which countries are very high on the HDI? See below.[36] How about the countries with the lowest HDI, can you guess the bottom of the heap? See below. [37]

Left Behind

While in some areas of the world improvement is being made in those factors that determine a nation's HDI, there are many places and people who are being left behind. Sub-Saharan Africa is in a horrible situation, and the masses there are caught in vast and extreme poverty. It is a region in which there is no progress being made. At best, there is stagnation. Even as a whole, the continent faces enormous obstacles. One out of every two Africans lives in acute poverty. One-third of all Africans suffer from chronic hunger. Approximately one-sixth of children there die before they reach the age of five. These numbers are about the same as they were ten years ago. A dent has not been made in development improvement among the poor of Africa. [38]

What Would Happen if the Poor Complained?

Historically, the response of the rich to the poor has been one of resignation to the hopelessness of the situation. After all, we are, for the most part, unable to do anything—that is, anyway, what we have come up with as our most common excuse. Indeed, the scope of the problem *is* so huge that it is way beyond the ability of a few individuals to change the way things are. To a certain degree, that sentiment is correct. "Personal initiatives are hopelessly inadequate to the scale and complexity of the problem."[39] This resignation, the acceptance of things as they are, exists in large measure because most rich people, like you and me, are quite content with the status quo. In addition, the poor people of this world, those mired within poverty and oppression, are most often accepting their lot in life without question—usually without complaint. What would happen if the poor complained?

An Apt Word from the 4th Century

Have you ever read anything by Basil the Great (330-397)? Try the brief passage below; he has an apt word for those of us viewing things from the rich side of the world.

> The bread which you keep, belongs to the hungry; the coats which you preserve in your wardrobe, to the naked; those shoes which are rotting in our possession, to the shoeless; the gold which you have hidden in the ground, to the needy. Wherefore, as often as you were able to help others, and refused, so often did you do them wrong.[40]

A challenging exercise for you right now would be to go to your closet and count the pairs of shoes you have. I know that's something you aren't very likely to do. There are scores of ways of rationalizing why you really don't need to go to your closet to count shoes. I can hear your thinking because my thinking would probably be about the same if someone were to tell me to go count my shoes—especially if it's meant to be some sort of guilt trip—shaming me into some altruistic action. Yet, that is definitely not the case here. Basil is imploring Christians to act in love, not out of guilt. Okay, okay . . . I'm going to stop typing now and walk over to my closet. . . . There, I've done it. I rummaged through my closet, and I found ten pairs of shoes. Two pair are boots (one pair of which doesn't fit too well, so I don't wear them. There is one pair of sports sandals. Do those count? I'm wearing tennis shoes right now so they weren't in the closet, but I did remember to count them. I also found a pair of old casual shoes I had forgotten I had; they were in the very back of the closet under some blue jeans with holes in both knees. When Basil mentions shoes rotting in my possession, he wasn't too far off the mark on that pair. That reminds me, I've got a pair of old dress shoes in the basement that I had good intentions to give away. Yet, they've been in my basement for about a year and a half now. I didn't count my snow boots, after all, they are so specialized that I didn't think I needed to count those. Also, they were in the front closet, not in my bedroom closet. They don't really seem to fit the category of shoes. So, I suppose, depending on the way you count, I have twelve pairs of shoes. How many pairs do you have?

Let's Just Wait until 2165 A.D.

Without any kind of drastic change in the trends, Sub-Saharan Africa will not have universal primary education until 2129. Of course, that's only a hundred and twenty-two years from now. Only eighteen more years after that (2147), we could realize the goal of cutting the level of extreme poverty there by one half if we continue as we are. Finally, I'm sure we are all patient enough to wait until 2165, as it is predicted, to cut into the child mortality rate and reduce it by two-thirds. We know patience is a virtue, don't we? Oh, and by the way, the World Bank did not set a date for the elimination of hunger in Sub-Saharan Africa because the data shows that the situation is worsening there at such a rate that predicting the end of it is impossible.[41]

NOTES

1. Benoît Mandelbrot, *The Fractal Geometry of Nature* (New York: W.H. Freeman & Co., 1982).

2. United Nations Development Programme, *Human Development Report 2003*, 8.

3. Jeffrey Sachs, *The End of Poverty: Economic Possibilities for Our Time* (New York: Penguin Press 2005), p. xiii.

4. *Minneapolis Star Tribune* (Dec. 13, 2006), A3.

5. United Nations Human Settlements Programme, *State of the World's Cities 2006/7* (Nairobi: UN-HABITAT, 2006), 21.

6. United Nations Development Programme, *UNDP's 1996 Report on Human Development in Bangladesh: A Pro-Poor Agenda—Poor People's Perspectives* (Dhaka, Bangladesh, 1996); Centre for Community Economics and Development Consultants Society, *Report on Social Assessment for the District Poverty Initiatives Project: Baran District* (Jaipur, India: Institute of Development Studies, 1997); Hermine G. De Soto and Nora Dudwick, "Poverty in Moldova: The Social Dimensions of Transition, June 1996-May 1997" (Washington, D.C.: World Bank, 1997).

7. Narayan, et. al., *Voices of the Poor*, 45.

8. Ibid., 4.

9. Ibid., 4-5.

10. Ibid., 5.

11. Kimberley McClean and Charles Lwanga Ntale, "Turmoil in Tajikistan: addressing the crisis of internal displacement," in Roberta Cohen and Francis Madding Deng, eds., *The Forsaken People: Case Studies of the Internally Displaced* (Washington, D.C.: Brookings Institution Press, 1998).

12. Narayan, et. al., *Voices of the Poor*, 35.

13. World Bank, "Diversity, Growth, and Poverty Reduction," (Washington, D.C.: World Bank, 1995).

14. Narayan, et. al., *Voices of the Poor*, 36.

15. R. B. Johnson, *World View and International Development: A Critical Study of the Idea of Progress in Development Work of World Vision Tanzania*. Ph.D. thesis (Oxford Centre for Mission Studies, Oxford, UK, 1998).

16. Bryant L. Myers, *Walking With the Poor* (Maryknoll, NY: Orbis Books, 2006), 84.

17. Narayan, et. al., *Voices of the Poor*, 68.

18. Hermine G. De Soto and Nora Dudwick, "Poverty in Moldova: The Social Dimensions of Transition, June 1996-May 1997." (Washington, D.C.: World Bank, 1997).

19. Narayan, et. al., *Voices of the Poor*, 69.

20. United Nations Development Programme, *Human Development Report 2003*, 9.

21. Narayan, et. al., *Voices of the Poor*, 39.

22. David Dollar, "Globalization, Poverty, and Inequity since 1980," World Bank Policy Research Working Paper 3333 (Washington, D. C.: World Bank, 2004), 19.

23. Todd Pitman, "Africa's 'forgotten crisis," *Minneapolis Start Tribune*. (April 30, 2007).

24. World Bank, *2006 World Development Indicators* (New York: Oxford University Press, 2006).

25. Ibid.,120-22.

26. Ibid., 20.

27. Ibid., 104-105.

28. Ibid., 70.

29. Human Rights Watch Human Rights Watch. *The War Within the War: Sexual violence against women and girls in Eastern Congo* (New York: Human Rights Watch, 2007).

30. Pitman, 2007.

31. Agence France-Presse, "Military clash with rebels in Central African Republic." www.reliefweb.int/rwr. (April 27, 2007).

32. Paul Collier, *The Bottom Billion: Why the Poorest Countries Are Failing and What Can Be Done About It* (New York: Oxford University Press, 2007), 3.

33. Ibid., 53.

34. Foster and Leathers, *The World Food Problem* (London: Lynne Reinner Publishers, 1999), ix.

35. United Nations Development Programme, *Human Development Report 2003*, 69.

36. In 2007 rank order they are: Norway, Australia, Iceland, Canada, Ireland, Netherlands, Sweden, France, Switzerland, Japan. That's the top ten. Where is the U.S.? It's number 13.

37. From lowest rank (182) up, they are: Niger, Afghanistan, Sierra Leone, Central African Republic, Mali, Burkina Faso, Democratic Republish of the Congo, Chad, Burundi, Guinea-Bissau.

38. United Nations Development Programme, *Human Development Report 2003*, 33-37.

39. Forrester, *On Human Worth*, 4.

40. Charles Avila, *Ownership: Early Christian Teaching* (London: Sheed & Ward, 1983), 50.

41. United Nations Development Programme, *Human Development Report 2003,* 33-34.

CHAPTER 3

Is There a Magic Bullet?

The Magic Bullet

Are you familiar with the slang phrase, *a magic bullet*? The meaning of the term
is that of something which is regarded as a wonderful, magical solution or cure
to a complex problem. Some have seen what are known as the Millennium Development Goals (MDGs) as a magic bullet to cure poverty. Chapter 2 set out to
create an image of how complex and chaotic poverty is. Yet, there must be a
way out. If there could only be enough planning and effective engagement, surely all the countries world could come together, coordinate resources, and defeat
the horrendous, scandalous conditions of poverty around the globe.

The Millennium Development Goals

The MDGs play a significant enough role in the illustrations and examples in
this book that a brief introduction to them seems somewhat necessary. Something very interesting happened at the United Nations on September 6-8, 2000.
The UN held what was known as the "Millennial Summit." As a result of that
occasion, 189 countries adopted and 147 heads of state signed the Millennial
Declaration. This document articulated eight goals that the General Assembly
passed as a resolution whereby the eight goals were to be met by 2015. Appendix A is the resolution adopted by the United Nations.

The eight goals are actually organized around 18 quantifiable targets that
one can measure through 48 different indicators whereby it will be possible to
determine the actualization of each goal. Appendix B provides a list of the eight
MDGs along with all the targets and indicators associated with each goal. You
should stop after reading this paragraph and turn to Appendix B to read through
the MDGs. Since references to them are embedded throughout this book, it
would be well worth your time to take a few minutes right now to read through

those goals. After looking at Appendix B, come back and read the following section.

Flaws in the Setting of Goals

Of course, the nasty thing about goals is that, oftentimes, they are not met, and one should forthrightly reflect upon why goals are not met. William Easterly, in a rather frank, but not mean-spirited assessment of the methodology and theory behind the MDGs, challenges the presumptions behind the mega-over-the-top goal setting one finds in the MDGs.[1] There is good news, and there is bad news. The good news is that some of the MDGs are on target to be met by 2015. The bad news is that some of the MDGs are not on target to be met by 2015. As Easterly has noted,

> the West already has a bad track record of previous beautiful goals. A UN summit in 1990, for example, set as a goal for the year 2000 universal primary-school enrollment. (That is now planned for 2015.) A previous summit, in 1977, set 1990 as the deadline for realizing the goal of universal access to water and sanitation. (Under the Millennium Development Goals that target is now 2015.) Nobody was held accountable for these missed goals.[2]

With nobody accountable when such lofty goals are set, but not met, the failure to reach any such goals loses its significance. Yet, where would we be without something like the MDGs? I suspect we would not be better off in trying to reduce poverty without the goals. They certainly provide some impetus for nations, institutions and individuals to work for improvements for those people of the world who so desperately need improvement, any improvement, in their life. Yet, setting the goals does not insure their actualization, and there will be plenty of hard, concerted work to do in order to make the kind of headway against poverty and oppression that the goals anticipate in the coming years.

Failing to Reach Goals

Led by the United Nations, the nations of the world have a noble and ambitious record of setting laudable goals to reverse human development problems throughout the world. Unfortunately, there is not a very impressive history of reaching those goals and objectives. While credit must be given for the achievement or near achievement of some goals,[3] the track record is, generally, not all that impressive. For example, in 1977 the Alma Ata Declaration set the goal of achieving health care for all people by the end of the century. Sadly, after 2000, millions of individuals continue to die each year from diseases that are very treatable or even preventable.[4]

Achieving the Goal Doesn't Look Good

By 2015 the poverty rate (the share of people living on less than $1 per day) in Sub-Sahara Africa will decrease. That's the good news. However, the goal of reducing by half the number of people living at that poverty rate by 2015 will, in all likelihood, not be reached. Whereas the MDG was to reduce the rate from 44.6% of the population living on less than $1 per day to 22.3% of the population, the current projection is that it may be reduced to 38.1%.[5] Yet, that is being optimistic.

Deep Pockets

While a number of countries seem to be making adequate progress toward meeting the U.N. Millennium Development Goals by the target dates, this can be extremely deceptive in that national averages are oftentimes used. The fact is that there remain "deep pockets of entrenched poverty" even in countries that, on the surface, seem to be making good progress.[6]

We'll Know in 2010

It was back in 2000 that the Millennium Development Goals (MDGs) were set. Those goals and the baselines upon which they were established were the product of the state of affairs in the world going back to about 1990. Obviously, nothing could be done to impact the preceding ten years. However, from the time of setting the MDGs, for a period of five years, assessment was made to monitor progress. The bad new is that without changes to accelerate the rate of change for improvements, "many countries may fall short of the targets set for 2015. That is why the next few years are so important. By 2010 we will know whether the goals can be achieved."[7]

Problems in Expertville

Experts have a lot to say about poverty. Much of what they say is really good, and some of what they say isn't so good. It seems to be a mixed bag. While it is pretty easy to appreciate the hard work and impressive insights they may bring to the table, it is a little more difficult to be critical. At least it's difficult for me to be critical—after all, I'm a novice, not an expert. Therefore finding fault with the experts is, perhaps, best left to other experts. Who are the experts? There seem to be two basic groups of experts when it comes to poverty. The first group is comprised of the poor themselves. It should be no surprise that the poor and the oppressed are pretty fair experts at understanding their particular situations. Yet, one of the flaws of the second group of experts, those from government and international non-governmental agencies, is that they often miss what the first group of experts is saying.

For example, one study which addresses this issue states that,

> One of the difficulties with expert-led 'solutions' is that most experts lack knowledge of the specifics of each city or neighbourhood, and lack engagement with the local population. Foreign experts often cannot speak the language of those in the settlement where their recommendations will be implemented. These recommendations are often biased by their experience in other nations, by their reading of other 'success stories', or by their analysis of data sets that have grave limitations. What they recommend so often fails to support the kinds of local processes that benefit those with the least income, assets and political power (including those designed and implemented by 'the poor' themselves). Even if the 'experts' make the right recommendations, they often undermine the local learning processes that are essential for effective local change.[8]

In all fairness, it should be said that, "Most international agencies recognize the relevance of local processes. But it is very difficult to measure and monitor their progress. These local processes are a long way from cities such as London, Brussels and Washington DC, where so many decisions about priorities are still made."[9]

In addition, it has been suggested that, in fact, "there is no lack of nonsense statistics on levels of urban poverty."[10] This exacerbates the problem of trying to make prudent decisions in the allocation of resources even in an altruistic attempt to meet the MDGs. David Satterthwaite cites some examples of such nonsense statistics coming right out of official WHO/UNICEFF reports and a scholarly journal. For example, he addresses the following table.

Table 3.1 Example of Nonsense Statistics

Nation	% of urban population that is poor, with survey date (first survey)	% of urban population that is poor, with survey date (last survey)
Burkina Faso	6.3 (1992)	5.4 (1999)
Ghana	15.6 (1998)	6.8 (1998)
Kenya	1.5 (1998)	1.2 (1998)
Senegal	7.5 (1988)	0.9 (1997)
Zimbabwe	0.3 (1988)	2.1 (1994)

Source: Sahn and Stifel , "Progress toward the Millennium Development Goals in Africa." *World Development* 31 (2003).

Here the numbers are said to be complete and utter nonsense. "Anyone with any knowledge of Nairobi or any other urban centre in Kenya would be astonished to see that only 1.2 per cent of Kenya's urban population was considered 'poor' in 1998. . . . These are statistics that can only be produced (or believed) by people with no knowledge of Kenya."[11] Satterthwaite makes it clear that the intent is not to deceive. Rather, "most dubious statistics like this are based on dubious definition or assumptions."[12] For instance, he alludes to something like the poor urban interviewee, who when asked, "Do you have access to a latrine?" answers with a simple, "yes." The data collector, sometimes not well-trained, will mark that individual as having access to sanitation. In fact, the urban dweller may be using only a pit four blocks from his house with no provision for hand washing.

So it is that even the experts face daunting problems when it comes to fully understanding and accurately documenting aspects of poverty in any given locale. How much more do we who are simply glimpsing the poor and the oppressed from the rich side of the world face an uphill struggle to understand, identify with, and assist those in need?

A Long Time Ago, In a Place Far Away

Poverty, injustice, and oppression are seemingly a universal throughout space and time. That is, one finds countless examples of all these elements in all historical periods and in all geographical locales. For that reason, it is not a surprise that the biblical text bulges with exhortations to those who lived in antiquity to seek justice for those who were poor and oppressed.[13] Indeed, people who lived a long time ago in places far removed from us experienced what it means to be among the poor and the oppressed in a world dominated by the rich. It is certainly not simply a modern phenomenon to have people suffering from injustice. Within the ancient Church there were individuals who clamored for attention to be given towards those who were suffering from injustices, those whose life was considered to be worth less than others. One such voice, a champion for the cause of the poor and oppressed, who lived in a time long ago and a place far way was a rather interesting character by the name of Ambrose.

Ambrose of Milan (339-397) initially dealt with the notion of social and economic justice toward the poor in a brief work he wrote which was entitled, *Duties of the Clergy*. Ambrose noticed that a concept widely held in the early Church was being largely ignored by many of his contemporaries—namely, that all people had an equal right to share in the gifts of God. He observed that, in fact, even the clergy oftentimes fell prey to the human tendency to deny to the poor those things to which they had a right. Greed was the element within us that he saw as diverting us away from the biblical pleas to show mercy and justice. As he wrote:

> God has ordered all things to be produced so that there should be food in common for all, and that the earth should be the common possession of all. Nature, therefore, has produced a common right for all, but greed has made it a right for a few.[14]

Ambrose, like a number of other patristic writers, saw the good things on the earth created by God and believed they were meant to meet the needs of all people, the poor and the rich alike. However, he felt that the rich have, in fact, embezzled from the poor in that they have they have not shared with the poor. Ambrose further addressed this issue of the rich and poor in a little work entitled, *Naboth*, in which he employed the well-known story of Naboth[15] to further develop the widely held notion among the Church Fathers that the rich were merely stewards of that which also belonged to the poor. For example, John Chrysostom also echoed this thought when he wrote, "Do not say, 'I am simply spending what is mine. I am merely enjoying what belongs to me.' In reality, it is not yours but it belongs to another." He adds, "All the wealth of the world belongs equally to you and to others, just as the sun, the air, the earth, and everything else."[16]

Thus, we have another interesting take on the nature of poverty that comes from the ancient world. The question of the moment is, how can we adjust our living in order to put into play the admonitions of Ambrose and Chrysostom? Every bit of our culture fights against the notions they espouse. Greed permeates the rich side of the world in which we live. We don't see ourselves as stewards, but rather we crave the acquisition of material things. When the earliest Christian community "held everything in common" and "gave to anyone as they had need," (Acts 2:44-45) they effectively bridged that gulf between the haves and the have nots.

The New Testament certainly implores us all to practice a spirit of reckless generosity. That's just what it takes to impede the economic lure of our culture. Followers of Jesus who live on the rich side of the world must categorically embrace that reckless spirit. Because the Lord requires that we act justly (Micah 6:8), so we must live a style of life in which we perceive ourselves as stewards, not owners. That will liberate us to this clarion call to share with those who are in need. After all in the argument made by Ambrose, they have every bit as much right to the gifts of God that we posses as we do.

NOTES

1. William Easterly, *White Man's Burden: Why the West's Efforts to Aid the Rest Have Done So Much Ill and So Little Good* (New York: Penguin Press, 2006).

2. Ibid., 9.

3. For a summary of development goals attained or nearly attained by the U.N. over the last three decades see *Human Development Report 2003*, p. 31. A good example of such is the goal of the World Health Organization back in 1965 to eradicate smallpox. That goal was achieved in 1977. An example of a goal largely met, but still not totally realized was a resolution by the U.N. General Assembly to raise life expectancy to 60 by the year 2000. That goal was achieved in 124 out of 173 countries.

4. United Nations Development Programme, *Human Development Report 2003*, 29.

5. World Bank, *2006 World Development Indicators*, 2.

6. United Nations Development Programme, *Human Development Report 2003*, 3.

7. World Bank, *2006 World Development Indicators*, 1.

8. David Satterthwaite, "The Millennium Development Goals and urban poverty reduction: great expectations and nonsense statistics," *Environment & Urbanization* 15 (2003): 183.

9. Ibid., 183-84.

10. Ibid., 184.

11. Ibid., 185.

12. Ibid., 186.

13. See Brookman 2006.

14. Ambrose, "Duties of the Clergy" in *Selected Works and Letters*. Philp Schaff, ed. *Nicene and Post Nicene Fathers*. Series II Volume X. (Grand Rapids: Michigan: William B. Eerdmans, 2002),132.

15. I Kgs 21:1-29.

16. John Chrysostom in J. P. Migne ed., *Patrologiae Graeca*, vol. 61 (Paris: Migne, 1862), 86.

CHAPTER 4

Issues of Health Among the Poor

You Don't Want to Get Sick in Zacatecas

If you have done any amount of traveling, you probably know there are some places where you just don't want to get sick. The scariest experience I've had was in a remote part of Ethiopia. I wasn't sick, but my daughter, Kelly, who was nineteen at the time got quite sick. Fortunately, it was only a scare. She was sick for just a day or so, probably because of the combination of sun and some medication she was taking. But, I remember thinking as she lay under a small tree in a remote village, "This isn't good." We had gotten to the spot by donkey, and that looked like the only way back. While there was a road relatively close by, it led to remote Lalibela, and I just wasn't expecting much of a medical facility there. However, after a little rest and the villagers giving her some dirty water, she felt better. We made it back to where we were staying in Lalibela, and she had a chance to lie down. The reality of the problem of access to health care in remote regions really hit home for me on that trip. We who glimpse the poor from the rich side of the world generally don't have to deal with such problems. I live about nine minutes travel time in my 2002 Mazda from a first-class health care center where I can get about the best medical care in the world. While my travel time there seemed longer than nine minutes the day I had a kidney stone, the fact of the matter is, most of the people in the world can't get to a medical facility with such ease as I am able.

There is a remote rural area in Mexico called Zacatecas where simple transportation to the nearest doctor costs about the equivalent of a month's wages.[1] How much do you make in a month? Now consider spending that much simply to travel get to see a doctor. "In Zacatecas it is not rare to hear of families that have lost all their animals and gone into debts of from 2,000 to 5,000 pesos (US$365 to $900) due to sickness of a family member."[2] You don't want to get sick if you live in Zacatecas.

26x More Likely to Die

You live in a rich country, and yet, you may well not perceive yourself as being rich. Why is that? One reason might be that we know from our own experiences that there is a gulf between the rich and poor. Even in a clearly defined rich country, such as the United States, not everybody is rich, as least as it is defined within the American cultural standard. Actually, the defining of income inequality on the global scale, is extremely complicated, and "there is heated debate on whether income inequality is increasing between rich and poor countries."[3]

On the other hand, "inequality in child mortality has gotten unambiguously worse. In the early 1990s children under five were 19 times more likely to die in Sub-Saharan Africa than in rich countries—and today, 26 times more likely."[4]

As You Might Think, Ethiopia is Not A Good Place for Children

It's probably not a surprise to anybody that Ethiopia has one of the highest child malnutrition rates in the entire world. One study reports that about half the children there who are under five years of age are malnourished.[5] There are several leading indicators that signal various levels of malnutrition. Stunting, which is having low height for age, is one indicator for chronic malnutrition. Another indicator is wasting, which is defined as having a low weight to height ratio. Wasting is seen as indicating acute malnutrition. Finally, there is the factor of having low weight for age, known as being underweight, and it is considered to be "a general indicator of malnutrition, since a child that is underweight could be stunted or wasted, or both stunted and wasted."[6]

While we know that Sub-Saharan Africa, in general, is not a healthy place for children, Ethiopia stands out from among other African nations with regards to levels of malnutrition. For instance, Ethiopia ranks second in the highest rates of stunting and underweight children of all the Sub-Saharan countries. In addition, the "proportion of children stunted is 50 percent higher than the average for those countries."[7] When one looks at the averages for stunting, wasted, and underweight populations throughout Sub-Sahara Africa, Ethiopia clearly stands out as the champion of malnutrition indicators.

Devastating the Teachers

What happens in a developing country when two-thirds of the teachers trained each year die from HIV/AIDS? Ask the people of Zambia. 1,300 teachers died of the disease in 1998 alone. How does a country, or for that matter, how do individual people deal with such devastation? The problem is, all projections show that things will be getting worse. Those countries in Africa which are most engulfed by HIV/AIDS will lose about 25% of their workforce by the year 2020.[8]

I Don't Know Anybody with Tuberculosis;
Do You Know Anybody with Tuberculosis?

If you live in the United States, you, in all likelihood, do not know anybody with tuberculosis. My only brush with the disease came during a sabbatical leave I had in Ethiopia. The school at which I taught had a gate guard who contracted it. However, I never actually met him, yet that's as close as I ever came to anybody with tuberculosis.

Take a guess how many people die each year from Tuberculosis. No really, take a guess. "Tuberculosis kills some 2 million people a year, most of them 15-45 years old. The disease is spreading more rapidly because of the emergence of drug-resistant strains of tuberculosis; the spread of HIV/AIDS, which reduces resistance to tuberculosis; and the growing number of refugees and displaced people."[9]

It's Only 42 Million People

Without a doubt, one of the greatest detrimental variables to development in the last quarter century has been HIV/AIDS. After the initial cases were highlighted in the early 80s, the problem skyrocketed. Slightly over 10 million people worldwide had been inflected by 1990. In 2003 the number of infected reached 42 million individuals. It is thought that about 22 million people have died from the disease, and that over 13 million orphans have been created as a result.[10]

Let's Write Off Zimbabwe

What a ticking bomb we have in HIV/AIDS. It is devastating Africa. Your initial reaction to the previous sentences might be, "This is nothing new; everybody knows about it." But oftentimes we don't know the details, and rarely, if ever, are faces knit to the problem. The countries of Botswana, Swaziland, Lesotho, and Zimbabwe have rates of infection that are nearly unbelievable where, at the minimum, one in three adults have the disease. I once had a health care worker in Ethiopia tell me that we might as well write off Zimbabwe because AIDS is so widespread there. That was nearly ten years ago, and I remember being rather shocked that someone would have such a pessimistic view as to write off an entire country. As it turns out, it doesn't appear that we need to go so far as to write off the entire country of Zimbabwe. The situation there is not that bad; it's just very horrible—no need to write off the entire country because some people *will* live. That's the good news—some people in Zimbabwe will live as the infection rate seems to have stabilized at just over 20%. Yet, other nations, such as Namibia, South Africa and Zambia have rates of infection that are nearly as high (1 in 5).[11] What do you suspect is the mindset of individuals who live in such places? Can we who view the world from the rich side of the planet (where the rate of HIV/AIDS infections are tolerably low) actually identify with those masses who are, quite frankly, doomed?

She Carried the Child 10 Kilometers for Medicine

A realistic picture of life for the children in a small village in Malawi is very depressing. First of all, most of them have no parents. AIDS has decimated the population of 20-40 year olds, and grandmothers are oftentimes the key caregivers of the village children. Malaria is a scourge among those children—a preventable scourge that continues to kill over a million kids throughout Africa each year because preventable measures are not taken. Jeffrey Sachs, Director of the Earth Institute at Columbia University tells the following story of a woman he met in the village of Nthandire in Malawi.

> I asked her about the health of the children. She points to a child of about four and says that the small girl contracted malaria the week before. Her mother carried her child on her back for the ten kilometers or so to the local hospital. When they got there, there as no quinine, the antimalarial medicine, available that day. With the child in high fever, the mother and child were sent home and told to return the next day.
>
> In a small miracle, when they returned the next day after another ten-kilometer trek, the quinine had come in, and the child responded to treatment and survived. It was a close call, though.[12]

Time is of the essence when a child contracts malaria. It may move very quickly, in just a day or so, into a stage known as cerebral malaria. After that, the prognosis is not good—coma and death come very rapidly.[13] While there was a happy outcome to this particular story, that is not necessarily the norm. What is the norm would be the difficulty of getting a child to a hospital. Would you want to carry your child, literally on your back, for about six or seven miles to get treatment, only to be asked to return the following day? That's normal in the life of the poor in many parts of the world. Naturally, for those of us on the rich side of the world, we don't have to worry about that . . . or should we be worrying?

Life Expectancy: What if You Lived in Zambia?

If you had been born in Zambia your life would be very different from what it now is. First of all, you wouldn't live nearly as long as you probably will. Since you are reading this book, you are most likely American, Canadian or British. As such, you will, statistically at least, long outlive any given person in Zambia. Oh yes, if you were born in Zambia, there is a pretty good chance you can't read. I suppose the argument could be made that life is a qualitative, not a quantitative thing, and life expectancy really doesn't measure all that much. Yet, it does measure something. What do the figures below mean to you? What if you lived in Zambia? What would be your attitude toward the people at the top of the list?

Table 4.1. *Life expectancy at Birth*[14]

Country	1970-75	2000-05
Sweden	74.7	80.1
Iceland	74.3	79.8
Australia	71.7	79.2
Norway	74.4	78.9
United States	71.5	77.1
Tanzania	46.5	43.3
Côte d'Ivoire	45.4	41.0
Rwanda	44.6	39.3
Mozambique	41.1	38.1
Malawi	41.0	37.5
Zambia	49.7	32.4

Of course, there are several ways to categorize the above data. When people look at a list like the one above, some people immediately divide the list geographically. Others immediately see that some countries, those on the top of the list with the longest life expectancy, have increased that expectancy since the 70's, while those on the bottom of the list with shorter life expectancies had those expectancies decrease during the thirty year period 1975-2005. What is your opinion, do people in the top portion of this list have any type of obligation toward the people at the bottom?

The Fastest Population Growth for Three Decades

Rapid population growth can cause many problems, and wouldn't you know it, Sub-Saharan Africa is the region of the world that has had the fastest population growth for the last thirty years.[15] Whereas fertility rates have declined throughout most of the world resulting in slowing of the growth rate, this isn't the case in Sub-Saharan Africa. Unquestionably this region faces some of the most difficult, up-hill fights in overcoming poverty, and this rapid growth rate does nothing but exacerbate this situation.

> Half the world, including all of the rich world, is at or near the so-called re-placement rate of fertility, in which each mother is raising one daughter on average to 'replace' her in the next generation. The replacement rate is two children, one of whom, on average, is a girl. . . . The poorest of poor countries, by contrast, are stuck with fertility rates of five or more. On average, a mother is raising at leas two girls, and in some cases three girls or more. In those circumstances, national populations double each generation.[16]

It's not just a high fertility rate in Sub-Sahara Africa; it's a stunningly high rate. Compare fertility rates by region of the world in the following table.

Table 4.2. *Fertility Rate by Region, 2004* (Adapted from World Bank, *World Development Indicators,* Table 2a).

Europe & Central Asia	1.6
East Asia & Pacific	2.1
Latin America & Caribbean	2.4
Middle East & North Africa	3.1
South Asia	3.1
Sub-Saharan Africa	5.4

There are many reasons for the extra-ordinarily high fertility rate in Sub-Sahara Africa. "The logistical and cultural challenge of delivering family planning programs, the often poor quality of health services, ignorance about reproductive health issues, differences in economic status, and continuing gender inequality all contribute to high fertility rates."[17] Another common-sense reason for a high fertility rate is that of desired family size. Simply put, some people want to have a larger family than others, and this desired family size dramatically impacts the national fertility rate. While throughout much of the world desired family size has been slowly decreasing over the past decades, it has remained high for most Sub-Saharan African countries.[18] For instance, desired family size in Bangladesh and India has declined so that the desired number of children is 2.5 and 2.6 respectively.[19] Compare that to the desired number of children in some Sub-Saharan countries.

Table 4.3. *Desired Family Size* (Adapted from World Bank, *World Development Indicators,* Table 2e).

Cameroon	5.7
Eritrea	5.8
Niger	8.2
Chad	8.3

What are the future implications of high fertility rates for this region of the world? It's not pretty. "The population of Sub-Saharan Africa has grown from 225 million in 1960 to 733 million in 2004. The World Bank project a doubling of the population to 1.4 billion by 2050, increasing the region's share of the world population from 13 percent today to 20 percent."[20] This so-called "demographic trap" that many Sub-Saharan African countries find themselves in actually produces the poverty trap from which they have not be able to extricate themselves. For as Sachs has remarked, "High population growth leads to deeper poverty, and deeper poverty contributes to high fertility rates."[21]

The Global Burden of Disease—It Falls on the Young

When one speaks of disease, it's the children who are bearing the brunt of the burden worldwide. One study[22] has found that "three of the four leading contributors to the burden of disease worldwide are disorders that primarily affect children—lower respiratory disease, diarrhoeal disease and perinatal disorder."[23] Of course, children in the rich side of the world rarely die from such diseases. It's the kids deeply entrenched in extreme poverty who suffer from such ills and die from them. Fixing the problem is really quite inexpensive, compared to say, fighting a war in Iraq. And yet, year after year, decade after decade the same basic condition exists—poor kids get sick and die from diseases that are easily preventable. Shame on us.

The Perils of Childbirth While in Poverty

Childbirth is relatively safe for those women who are in rich countries. The same cannot be said for women who reside in poor countries. In rich countries there are usually fewer than 10 mothers who die for every 100,000 live births. However, some of the poorest countries have rates which are 100 times higher. Add to that the variable that women in poor countries will have more children, and the result is that the rate at which mothers die in childbirth may be an astounding 200 times greater than for mothers in rich countries. Why are they dying at such a high rate? "They die because they are poor. Malnourished. Weakened by disease. Exposed to multiple pregnancies. And they die because they lack access to trained health care workers and modern medical facilities."[24]

Where are the Health Workers?

In 2007, in the least developed countries of the world, the average amount spent on health care was $6 per capita. By contrast, the amount spent per person in high-income countries was $1,356. It is estimated by the World Health Organization (WHO) that it takes at least $35-40 per person to meet even the lowest level of health care. Hmmm, it seems that once again the rich get richer—in this case, through better health care—and the poor get poorer. Beyond that, the poor lose out on another level. In virtually every country, whether low, medium or high income, the poor 20% of the population does not receive anywhere near 20% of the spending. That is, the rich get more than their fair share.

Unfair spending also is reflected in the rural/urban divide. It is pretty intuitive that rural areas almost always get less. One of the things that those in rural areas get less of is access to health care workers. That is, there are fewer health workers in rural areas, and the proportion doesn't necessarily mirror the actual ratio of people in the urban setting compared to those in rural areas. For instance, in Cambodia, 85% of the population is rural, yet only 13% of health workers are located the rural areas.[25]

Women and HIV/AIDS

Women constitute a little less than half of the world's HIV/AID population. Things are different in Sub-Saharan Africa, where heterosexual activity is the main way in which the virus is spread. There, more than 55% of those infected are women. The largest at-risk group is young women who are two to four times more likely to become infected than are young men. The story is similar in both South Asia and South-East Asia where 60% infected are young females.[26]

Gross Underinvestment in the Diseases Afflicting the Poor

The great strides forward in biotechnology in recent decades are not paying much of a dividend for the poor and oppressed of this world. It seems that, compared to investment in the rich sectors of the world, very little investment has been made into technology geared toward the problems of poverty. That is to say, those diseases that most dramatically impact the poor are not getting the level of investment one might have desired. Indeed, the World Health Organization's Commission on Macroeconomics and Health called it blatant "gross underinvestment."[27]

As an example of this underinvestment, "tropical diseases and tuberculosis accounted for 11% of the global disease burden in 1999. Yet of the 1,393 new drugs approved between 1975 and 1999, only 16—just over 1%—were specifically developed for those ailments."[28] Why is it that 90% of what is spent on research and development in the health sector is geared towards the richest 10% of the world's population? Bingo! It's the market! Rich people and rich countries can pay the price of pharmaceutical research and development while poor countries and poor people are not able to pay.

How do You Define Hunger?

How do you know when you are hungry? That's actually a difficult question to technically answer, but however you describe it, you generally know it when you are hungry. How do you define someone else's point of hunger? Of course, you may simply rely on their relating to you that they feel hunger, just as you would be able to convey your feeling of hunger to someone else. Yet, there is a technical definition of hunger that has been established. It is this: hunger is consuming fewer than 1,960 calories per day.[29] Some people are calorie counters; I never have counted my calorie consumption. Usually, in the American culture, it's people who are on a diet who are counting calories. I'm quite small in build, and I have never had anything close to a weight problem. I have the type of metabolism that burns up everything I eat. Thus, I'm not much of an expert on tracking calories. I have no idea how many calories are in various foods simply because I have never had to count. But I do know that 1,960 doesn't sound like too many calories. Since, according to this definition, individuals below that magic number are hungry, they face the dilemma.

The ironic aspect of this dilemma is that there seems to be enough food to go around so that nobody in the world should need to go hungry. As the HDR 2003 notes, "If all the food produced worldwide were distributed equally, every person would be able to consume 2,760 calories a day."[30] Nobody would go hungry! Enough food is not the problem. The proper distribution of food resources is a problem. Poverty is a problem. People with enough financial resources don't go hungry. Even in areas of famine, the wealthy don't go hungry; the rich are able to procure food even in areas of scarcity because of their economic resources. Those who cannot procure food resources merely lack economic resources, and it is usually women and children who fit that category. Armies generally don't go hungry. In America, you and I enjoy a high food entitlement, or that which we are able to command given our income. The widow in Sub-Saharan Africa has a very low food entitlement because of her lack of economic resources. It has very little to do with food availability.

18% is only 799 million

"Everyday 799 million people in developing countries—about 18% of the world's population—go hungry."[31] Unfortunately, that data (from 2003) is a few years out of date. While the percentage is about the same today, the total number of hungry people has increased.

A Surplus of Food Doesn't Necessarily Mean You're Getting Enough to Eat

In some of the northern districts of Ethiopia e.g. Tigray and Ahmara, more than half of the children are malnourished. Yet surprisingly, that isn't necessarily due to a food shortage. In fact, it has been demonstrated that in Ethiopia some of the regions with a food surplus are actually regions experiencing the highest rates of malnutrition.[32] Malnutrition is a tricky business. Not only can it be correlated to something as intuitive as household income, but it has been demonstrated that unequal distribution of food within a household can be a factor.[33] The amounts of food consumed within a household "are unequal throughout the entire world"[34] For example, in South Asia men take a disproportionate amount of food resources within their own household. This is necessarily at the expense of the women and children who suffer physiologically as a result. One study has connected this to Hindu cultural traits, however the phenomenon is actually worldwide.[35] The fact of the matter is that the distribution of food within any given household around the world may be unequal, whether one looks at a peasant society in Ghana or a working class household in England.[36] Regardless of where this happens, the children suffer.

The Fight for Daily Survival

While globalization has enhanced standards of living in many parts of the world, hundreds of millions of people actually have realized economic decline at the same time that some are advancing. Poor health and hunger continue to be major factors in the lives of many people on the planet. It is estimated that about 1 billion people fight every day of their life against the nemesis of hunger and/or poor health.[37]

Widening Gaps and Disparities: Burkina Faso

I have never been to Burkina Faso. However, I have a friend who spent some time there, and he made it clear that it is not exactly a prime vacation destination. Consider what *The Human Development Report* has to say of this African nation. "One of the world's poorest countries according to the human poverty index (HPI) and GDP per capita, Burkina Faso presents sharp differences in development between its Eastern and Western regions. The East is dry, which complicates agricultural practices. The West is more humid, creating a climate suitable for cotton production. Furthermore, poverty incidence is five times higher in rural areas.

Between 1993 and 1999 malnutrition increased in all provinces. Stunting increased from 29% in 1993 to 37% in 1999, with rural areas driving the trend. In the capital city of Ouagadougou an estimated one-fifth of children suffer from malnutrition."[38]

This is exactly the type of place of which American Christians need to be fully aware. How many of us are praying about, giving toward, or going to this nation of people who are in desperate need?

A Prayer for the People in Tabe Ere

There are plenty of problems in Ghana, and naturally, the poor face a landslide of them. Meet Ziem Der. He's our neighbor—neighbor in the sense that Jesus understood the term. He's one of the poor in Ghana. In fact, he lives in one of the poorest regions of the country in a settlement called Tabe Ere. It's a region where 70% of the entire rural population lives in poverty.[39] Consider Ziem's life—here's a snapshot of his situation.

> Ziem was born in 1948, the fourth of sixteen children. His father owned land as well as sheep, goats, and cattle. Ziem's father did not view formal education as a priority for his children, and consequently only four of the siblings attended school; Ziem was not one of them. Ziem describes himself as *zung* or "blind," a metaphor for illiterate. He explains that because he is unable to read or write, he cannot get a job in town.
>
> Ziem has two wives and eight children of his own. In addition, when his brother died, he left Ziem his two wives and seven children, bringing the num-

ber of people in Ziem's household to twenty. Feeding his large family has become extremely difficult for Ziem. His wives search for firewood, which they then trade for food.[40]

So, how do you feel when you read about Ziem? Do you find yourself being able to somehow imagine what your life would be under such circumstances, or is that simply not possible? For those of us looking in on Ziem from the rich side of the world, his situation seems pretty far removed and quite unimaginable for us. Beyond his poverty, I find myself quite unable to imagine illiteracy. What would it do to me if I were illiterate? What would a life of not be able to read, anything, be like? Of course Ziem is not an isolated case. "Like Ziem, many people in Tabe Ere live in extreme poverty. Residents estimate that 80 percent of them have but one tattered piece of clothing to wear, insufficient food, no money, no shoes, and no relatives who can help."[41]

Don't' you think that it would probably be a good thing if we who are on the rich side of the world would consistently pray for the destitute who are not on the rich side—rather, they are on the poor side, in situations like the one in which Ziem finds himself? That's not meant to be a rhetorical question that the reader does not answer. Really, what sorts of obligations do he have in such a case? If Jesus is to be taken at his word, prayer is a rather potent aspect of our Christian life. Ought we not employ such a resource on behalf of someone like Ziem? I don't really know him; nor do you. However, one need only to draw upon the compassion of the risen Christ to better identify with a character like Ziem.

Cooperate with me in a prayer for Ziem and the other people of Tabe Ere who are living what might best be described as a desperate life. Read the following words of prayer with a heart that truly desires better identification with the poor and the oppressed.

Father in Heaven, while our words are generally feeble in such cases, our heart is driving us to try to articulate a prayer of intercession for Ziem. We know your heart for the poor, Lord, and as a result, we desire that our hearts might be tilted in the same direction as Your orientation towards the oppressed and down-trodden of this world as we strive to replicate Your love and concern for them. Therefore, we call upon You, Lord, to act in response to our prayer today. Bless Ziem as we humbly call him to our mind for the purpose of interceding for him. Bless him in ways that we cannot even apprehend or expect. We pray in faith, believing, that You, in Your compassion, will act on his behalf, even in this very hour we are praying. Grant him, Lord, relief from the particular burdens he has been facing lately. Keep him in good health. You, who call things into being that don't exist, create economic opportunity for him. We pray, Lord, present him with cattle. Under circumstances in which he will recognize the hand of God working in his life, bring a multitude of unforeseen blessings to his humble house.

Lord, we want to incite You to act also on behalf of the people of village of Tabe Ere. Work in and among and through them in such a way that the blessing of the Lord is realized and acknowledged by them. May we who have

everything humble ourselves before You and plead for You to act on their behalf. And help us Lord, to repeat often the essence of this prayer—not only for
Ziem and the people of Tabe Ere, but for the poor and the oppressed around the
globe. May Your Holy Spirit be at work in the world through something as
unimaginable as prayer. As we are instructed to pray with faith (Matthew
17:20), we do so now, Father. In the name of Jesus of Nazareth, hear our prayer
and act to soothe the lives of Ziem and the people of Tabe Ere. Amen.

Even in merely glimpsing the poor, as we have just caught a mere glimpse
of Ziem, I believe that we are able to directly encounter them as neighbors
through prayer and intercession.

NOTES

1. Narayan, Patel, Schafft, Rademacher, and Koch-Schulte, 47.

2. Lawrence Salmen, "The People's Voice: Mexico—Participatory Poverty Assessment," (Washington, D.C.: World Bank, 1995).

3. United Nations Development Programme, The *Human Development Report 2002*
(New York: Oxford University Press, 2002) spoke of global income inequality as being
"fuzzy and its trends ambiguous."

4. Ibid., 39.

5. See pages 5-7 of L. Christiaensen, and H. Alderman, "Child Malnutrition in
Ethiopia: Can Maternal knowledge Augment the Role of Income?"

6. Patricia Silva, "Environmental Factors and Children's Malnutrition in Ethiopia."
World Bank Policy Research Working Paper 3489. (Washington, D. C.: World Bank
2005), 6.

7. Ibid., 6-7.

8. United Nations Development Programme, *Human Development Report 2003*, 43.

9. World Bank, *2006 World Development Indicators*, 12.

10. United Nations Development Programme, *Human Development Report 2003*,
41.

11. Ibid., 43.

12. Sachs, *The End of Poverty*, 6-7.

13. Ibid., p. 7.

14. United Nations Development Programme, *Human Development Report 2003*,
262-65.

15. World Bank, *2006 World Development Indicators*, 41.

16. Sachs, *The End of Poverty*, 64.

17. World Bank, *2006 World Development Indicators*, 42.

18. Ibid., 42-43

19. Ibid., 43.

20. Ibid., 43.

21. Sachs, *The End of Poverty*, 66.

22. C. J. L. Murray and A. D. Lopez, *The Global Burden of Disease* (Boston: Harvard University Press).

23. Sheridan Bartlett, "Children's experience of the physical environment in poor
urban settlements and the implications for policy, planning and practice." *Environment &
Urbanization* 11 (1999), 65.

24. World Bank, *2006 World Development Indicators*, 10.

25. United Nations Development Programme, *Human Development Report 2003*, 8.

26. Ibid., 50.

27. World Health Organization, *Macroeconomics and Heath: Investing in Health for Economic Development*, (Geneva: World Health Organization, 2001).

28. United Nations Development Programme, *Human Development Report 2003*, 158.

29. United Nations, *Human Development Report 2002*.

30. United Nations Development Programme, *Human Development Report 2003*, 87.

31. Ibid., 88.

32. Haidar and Demissie, "Nutrition Situation in Ethiopia." *South African Journal of Clinical Nutrition* 89 (1999): 181-83.

33. Harriss, "The Intrafamily Distribution of Hunger in South Asia." in Jean Drèze, Amartya Sen, and Athar Hussai, eds. *The Political Economy of Hunger* (Oxford: Oxford University Press, 1997), 53.

34. Ibid., 58

35. R. S. Khare, *Culture and Reality: Essays on the Hindu System of Managing Foods.* (Simla: Indian Institute of Advance Study, 1977).

36. A. Whitehead, "'I'm Hungry Mum': The Politics of Domestic Budgeting" in Young, Wolkowitz, and McCullogh, eds., *Of Marriage and the Market: Women's Subordination in International Perspective.* London: CSE Books, 1981).

37. United Nations Development Programme, *Human Development Report 2003*, 16.

38. Ibid., 65.

39. Kunfaa and Dogbe, "Empty Pockets," in Deepa Narayan and Patti Petesch, eds., *Voices of the Poor: From Many Lands*, 17.

40. Ibid., 17-18.

41. Ibid., 18.

CHAPTER 5

The Economics of Being Poor

People Living on $1 Per Day

To be straightforward, there never was total agreement on the World Bank's use of the $1 a day as an appropriate scale to measure extreme poverty. Some economists saw it as not precise, but perhaps, adequate. Others refused to embrace it because they didn't see it as particularly useful. In 2008 the World Bank revised the extreme poverty line to $1.25/day.[1]

"Whatever the case, the data show that globally the proportion of people living on less than $1 a day dropped from nearly 30% in 1990 to 23% in 1999. But the story is not necessarily one of good overall progress. Rather, it is one of some countries forging ahead while others see bad situations get even worse. Much of the impressive reduction in global poverty has been driven by China's incredible economic growth of more than 9% a year in the 1990s, lifting 150 million people out of poverty."[2]

Sadly, more than half of reporting countries experienced poverty rate increases during the decade of the 90s which is continuing now for a decade into the new millennium. While we can cheer the advances in places like Brazil, Thailand, and Chile,[3] the fact remains that poverty is still winning. Indeed, using the revised extreme poverty line of $1.25/day, the World Bank currently estimates that 1.4 billion people are at or below that demarcation point. Back in 2004, when the line was still at $1, there were an estimated 984 million at or below the poverty line.[4] Thus, there are many more people living in extreme poverty now than there were in 2004.

What $1 Would Buy?

At the start of the new millennium more than 1.2 billion people (1,200,000,000) were living, if you can call it that, on less than $1 day. On top of that, another 2.8 billion humans (2,800,000,000) were living on less than $2 a day.[5] In 2008 the World Bank did revise the level of living in extreme economic poverty to

$1.25/day, yet $1/day remains the most popular notion of extreme poverty, after all, who likes to count cents? What does it mean to live on $1 a day, or even $1.25? First of all, the way in which the World Bank calculates it, having $1.25 a day to spend does not mean being able to buy what $1.25 converted into local currency could purchase. Rather, it means "the equivalent of what $1.25 would buy in the United States: a newspaper, a local bus ride, a bag of rice."

Indeed, what does it mean to live on $1 a day? Frankly, I'm not convinced that those of us within the American culture can easily understand what that means. If you think you are able to fully understand it, I might challenge you to a bit of an experiment. Go ahead; try to live on $1 a day for just one day, 24 little hours. How would one go about trying that kind of an experiment? What kind of behavior would it take for you to live for one day like someone who lives every single day of their life on $1? What would your life be like for this brief period of time? There's a scenario for you to try this which is given in the classic book *Rich Christians in an Age of Hunger*.[6]

You Do the Math

This is a simple one; no algebra is involved. Three very basic meals a day of vegetables and rice costs $2.10. You make $1.60 a day. You do the math; how much are you eating? That is the situation faced by young women who work in the Nike factories in Vietnam.[7] While the numbers have changed a bit since the 1997 study which cites this data, the bottom line (quality of life) has not changed significantly.

Econ 101: Does Economic Growth Actually Help the Poor?

In the circles of world-class economists, there is disagreement about whether economic growth actually helps the poor who live in the third world. During the decade of the 1990's the world's gross domestic product (GDP) grew at a rate of 2.5 percent per year.[8] While it seems rather intuitive to you and to me that such economic growth in the world economy would surely be a benefit to the poverty-stricken people of the world, there is, in fact, a hot debate about this. Several studies have produced widely differing opinions on this. For example, one study came to the conclusion that because "average income of the poorest fifth of society rises proportionately with average incomes," it follows that such growth, "generally does benefit the poor as much as everyone else."[9] Yet, at the other end of the spectrum, "some observers argue that economic growth tends to increase income (and asset) inequality, and that these higher levels of inequality ensure that economic growth benefits the rich rather than the poor."[10] Indeed, economist Justin Forsyth states that, "there is plenty of evidence that current patterns of growth and globalization are widening income disparities and thus acting as a brake on poverty reduction."[11]

Neither is this debate a recent one, for it was thirty-three years ago that the argument picked up when it was stated, "Development is accompanied by an absolute as well as a relative decline in the average income of the very poor." In fact, the "frightening implication is that hundreds of millions of desperately poor people . . . have been hurt rather than helped by economic development."[12] Isn't it difficult to believe that what seems to be such a straight-forward question has been so difficult to answer? Recently, a suggestion has been put forth to try to once and for all answer the slippery question by employing a new way of measuring things based on a new type of data. The new data would "focus on the low-income countries of the world; second, it should utilize the results of household budget surveys, since these surveys represent the best source of poverty information in most developing countries, and third, it should include complete growth, poverty and inequality for as many countries and time periods as possible."[13] The basic conclusion that was reached using this new data set was that, "Outside of Eastern Europe and Central Asia, there is no systematic relationship between growth and inequality; inequality may increase, decrease or remain the same with economic growth."[14] Well, that doesn't seem to help the problem!

Favoring Cows Over People

It seems as if we are living in a strange world, one in which, at least economically speaking, cows are favored over people. The European Union, through the Organisation for Economic Co-operation and Development (OECD), allocates subsidies each year. In 2000, they granted a subsidy of $913 for each cow owned by farmers in the rich countries of the European Union. At the same time, they granted a subsidy of $8 per African person in the poorest sub-Saharan region. As if that were not bad enough, Japan, in that same year, allocated a subsidy of $2,700 per cow to Japanese dairy farmers, while at the same time, granting a subsidy of $1.47 in annual aid per person in sub-Saharan Africa.[15]

Gini in a Bottle

In the *Arabian Nights*, or perhaps more popularly, in Walt Disney's *Aladdin*, one finds the story of the powerful genie (Arabic *Jinn*) who is captive in a bottle, but when released, grants his liberator three wishes. Of course, the female counter-part was Barbara Eden in the 60's sitcom, *I Dream of Jeannie*. While she played the traditional role of the genie, she granted her liberator, a NASA astronaut, an unlimited number of wishes. I always liked that show as a youngster. I even like reruns of it now, although it seems pretty hokey to me that she lived in that bottle. When one reads about poverty, human development, and the like, one oftentimes sees reference to some something called the Gini Index. What in the world is that?

The Gini Index is something entirely different from the genie in the bottle. It is a commonly used indicator that measures the degree of equal distribution of wealth. It focuses upon how much the distribution of income among individuals or families deviates from perfectly equal distribution. The formula for calculation of the Gini Index, or more accurately *coefficient*, is a bit complicated, but it yields a number between 0 and 100 in which 0 represents perfect equality (good), and 100 represents perfect inequality (bad). Below are some of the countries of the world with the highest Gini Index. This method of measure was developed in 1912 by a statistician in Italy by the name of Corrado Geni (hence the name), and it is now widely used by the World Bank and the United Nations.

Listed below are the countries where the unevenness of distribution of wealth is the greatest and the least. Remember, a high number represents a greater unevenness in the distribution of wealth.

Table 5.1. Adapted from *World Development Report 2007, Development and the Next Generation*. (New York: Oxford University Press, 2006).

Gini Indexes
Highest & Lowest

Sweden	25.0
Norway	25.8
Finland	26.9
Germany	28.3
Austria	29.1
Bolivia	60.1
Swaziland	60.9
Central African Republic	61.3
Sierra Leone	62.9
Botswana	63.0
Lesotho	63.2
Namibia	74.3

Look at the top of the list, and then look at the bottom of the list. How do you think of the countries on the top of the list compared to those on the bottom? If one were to generalize, one might conclude that the Geni Index does something beyond just indicate uneven distribution of wealth. Those countries at the bottom are teeming with poverty, oppression, civil strife, and a whole array of problems that the poor and the oppressed of this world tend to face.

Yet, the goal for us who glimpse the poor and the oppressed from our nice and comfortable side of the world ought not to be to merely witness the achievement a low Geni Index for countries like Namibia, Lesotho, Botswana, Sierra Leone, and the like—such would not automatically eliminate the plagues of poverty faced by them. Nor would it create absolute justice for the masses of people in those environments who desperately need more justice in their lives. It wouldn't even solve the glaring uneven distribution of wealth within their soci-ety. So, one might well ask, what is the point of even discussing something like the Gini Index? After all, even the United States doesn't have a super low Gini Index, and this shouldn't be a shock as we all know that there are huge inequi-ties in the distribution of wealth in America.

I can only speak of my own experience. Perhaps yours will be totally differ-ent, and that would be fine. But when I read about the concept of the Gini Index, it ignited a spark of wonderment for me. It somehow elicited in me a sense of the disparity of it all. Why am I in the comfortable setting in which I find my-self. Why am I not a citizen of Namibia? And if I were a citizen of Namibia, would I be one of the few very wealthy and face the same dilemmas I face here in America? Well, these are of course rhetorical questions, and they are far too theological for me to answer. But that's the impact the Gini Index had on me. It raised some questions that may perhaps be worthwhile to contemplate. As I said, it may have no such impact on you, and you have been very bored by this little nugget of world economics called the Gini Index. However, if you are ever in serious discussion with someone about issues of justice, the topic of conversa-tion will almost inevitably get around to distributive justice. When that happens, won't you be glad that you've been introduced to the Gini Index?

Globalization: The Good, the Bad, and the Ugly

Globalization is a hot topic these days. I teach a course entitled *Cultural Anthro-pology*, and you would not believe the amount of space given to the theme of globalization in many of the standard, introductory textbooks for students of anthropology. For instance, in the textbook I currently use for that class, one finds the following blurb in the instructor's edition.

> By weaving the theme of globalization throughout the text, Peoples and Bailey show that, directly or indirectly, globalization is producing social, cultural, po-litical, and economic consequences that are remolding the lives of all the world's peoples. Expanding on this major theme of the book, more examples and issues regarding globalization are integrated throughout the Seventh Edi-tion. . . . *Globalization* sections reemphasize the text's global theme and place select issues under the anthropological lens. This allows students to delve into more detail regarding some of today's most vital discussions in cultural anthro-pology. [16]

Of course, in addition to some of those features and sections, noted above, the textbook has an entire chapter that focuses upon globalization. Thus, for a term that really did not come into commonplace use until the 1980s, *globaliza-tion* is widely used, and, perhaps, poorly understood. It is a multi-faceted con-cept, and, indeed, there is the good, the bad, and the ugly when one considers the out-workings of globalization across the world today.

Whereas one might intuitively think that the process may be of general economic benefit to the poor of the world, that is not necessarily the case. To the contrary, it has been suggested that it actually may increase the poverty level of the poor by further marginalizing them.[17] On the other hand, the argument has been made that globalization has helped the poor, especially by providing new opportunities for them to participate in new export markets.[18] It is a double-edged sword. "While globalization generally produces economic growth, it also has negative consequences. Capitalism tends to concentrate wealth and to widen the gap between the rich and the poor."[19] How big is that gap, that inequality between the rich and the poor? Consider this.

> The distribution of the world's wealth has become so skewed that the total assets of the three richest individuals in the world exceed the annual income of the poorest 600 million, while the richest 200 individuals in the world have wealth that exceeds the annual income of the poorest 2.4 billion people.[20]

Just in case you read that last sentence too fast, I want to draw your attention to it again. That's 2.4 *billion*, not million. Scandalous as that is, it is also depressing because the trend is that the gap is quickly increasing, and there does not seem to be a way to reverse the trend towards greater and greater inequity in the world.

Growth at the Expense of the Poor

Joseph Stiglitz won the Nobel Prize in economics in 2002. In an essay entitled "Poverty, globalization and growth: perspective on some of the statistical links,"[21] he discusses the non-intuitive idea that growth within a given economy doesn't necessarily help the poor. In fact, to the contrary, he points out how in some cases economic growth has worked to the detriment of the poor. As he observes, "By some measures poverty increased in Latin America in the 1990s, even in many countries where there was growth. It was not just that well-off people gained disproportionately from growth: some of the gains may even have been at the expense of poor people."[22] He notes that trickle-down economics simply doesn't seem to work, at least for the poor. Politics aside (you Reagan fans and staunch Christians/Republicans must try to be objective here), the economics of the trickle-down notion doesn't work well for those in poverty. Stiglitz is also critical of the economics of globalization so popular among certain nations. He writes, "studies cannot address the most fundamental criticisms of globalization as it has been practiced: that it is unfair and that its benefits have disproportionately gone to rich people."[23]

It seems trickle-down economics and certain econometric aspects of globalization actually facilitate a scenario in which the rich get richer. Naturally, the rich like that sort of scenario. You probably like a scenario in which you gain; you become richer. But the cost, which may not cross our mind, is the impact upon those in poverty. Take it from a Nobel Laureate, what is best for the rich is usually not what is best for the poor.

How About the Case of Mali?

Do you know anybody from Mali? In all likelihood, you don't. Do you know where Mali is located? I asked ten college students to locate Mali on a blank map of the world. Five got it on the correct continent. Three correctly identified it as being in the region of West Africa, however, nobody correctly identified the exact location of it. "What does that prove?" one might ask in a slightly exasperated tone. My answer would be that it proves nothing, but it might suggestion some things.

But what do you think about this? Mali happens to be a landlocked country. In 2003 the World Bank reckoned Mali's per capita income at $240. That actually converts to $800[24] using a formula known as PPP (purchasing power parity) which is employed to standardize incomes worldwide.[25] Yet, remember that per capita incomes represent averages, and while $800 represents $2.19 per day, a good percentage of the population would actually be earning less than that.

This makes Mali a country in which there is little interest on behalf of foreign investment. Its GNP is only about that of a large city in a moderately rich country.[26] As the *Human Development Report* says, "Facing very high transport costs, and with almost no interest from international firms to invest in production for small domestic markets, such countries are bypassed by globalization."[27]

How Many Street Vendors Are There?

There is something that most American Christians don't readily recognize, namely, the poor just happen to be great entrepreneurs, and as one looks at the millions and millions of poor in developing countries throughout the world, one sees this entrepreneurial spirit. You can see it in the farmers, street vendors, and any number of other occupations in which the poor people of this world engage. They usually operate within what is called the *informal economy*, a sector which accounts for more than one half of all of the economic activity in most developing nations.[28] Unfortunately, businesses which operate within this informal economy are bombarded with the same sorts of problems which others, outside of that sector encounter—namely, corruption, insecure property rights, organized crime, limited access to finance and public services, etc.[29]

Now That's Inflation!

What you know and how you feel about inflation probably depends on your age. American Baby Boomers remember years of high inflation rates. In 1974 the U.S. inflation rate was 12.3%. In 1979 it was 13.3%. However, Gen Xers and Millennials don't have such memories. The current inflation rate (November,

2006) is 1.31%, a far cry from the double-digit inflation that many Americans in the past found to be almost unbearable. Yet, America's plight with inflation pales in comparison to the rates experienced by others around the world. For instance, in the country of Georgia, people faced inflation rates of 100 to 300 percent *every month* in 1993. The amount that would buy an automobile, after a few months of that hyperinflation, would buy only four loaves of bread.[30] Another good example of hyperinflation comes from Bolivia where in one year "between July 1984 and July 1985, prices had risen by more than 3,000 percent (thirty times."[31] Perhaps the mother of all hyperinflation examples is that of Yugoslavia.

> In October of 1993 the government created a new currency unit. One new dinar was worth one million of the old dinars. In effect, the government simply removed six zeroes from the paper money. This of course did not stop the inflation and between October 1, 1993 and January 24, 1995 prices increased by 5 quadrillion percent. This number is a 5 with 15 zeroes after it.[32]

Indeed, five quadrillion percent inflation is about as bad as one could ever imagine. What is astounding about hyperinflation is the fact that it is not exactly rare. There are actually many cases of inflation run wild in a range of countries. For instance in recent history, besides those cases already cited of Bolivia and Yugoslavia, the following countries have all dealt with the problem of hyperinflation: Germany in the 1920's, Greece during the German occupation (1941-44), Hungary at the end of World War II, Mexico (1982-88), Peru (1988-90), Ukaine (early 1990s), and, in the latest case, Zimbabwe. Right now, hyperinflation is having its way in Zimbabwe, and along with the rule of strong-man dictator Robert Mugabe, the poor and oppressed in that country are suffering greatly. At one point, the Zimbabwean government claimed an inflation rate of 66,212 percent.[33] Indeed, the actual rate may, however, be much higher as the "International Monetary Fund believes the rate is closer to 150,000 percent."[34]

What's the latest? In January of 2009, Zimbabwe decided to print a $100 trillion banknote. As it was reported,

> Zimbabwe"s central bank says it will soon introduce a 100 trillion dollar note as the once prosperous country battles to keep pace with hyperinflation that has caused many to abandon the country's currency. The Reserve Bank of Zimbabwe said the new notes that includes 50 trillion, 20 trillion and 10 trillion would be released for the "convenience of the public," according to statement released Thursday.[35]

In the extreme case of Yugoslavia mentioned above, prices were actually doubling every 16 hours! Today, in Zimbabwe the people have to spend any money as soon as they get it, or it's virtually worthless. Notice that no one is exempt as hyperinflation travels the globe. In all fairness, however, it is impossible for Americans to fully comprehend the tragic impact of hyperinflation upon the masses, and as one might expect, it is generally the poor and the oppressed who are hit the hardest by such a thing.

Rich Countries Need to Change

The poorest countries in the world face huge constraints that can only be eased if the richest countries in the world initiate policy changes with regard, particularly, to international trade, debt reduction, and the generosity with which they give toward global development.

Back in 1969, The Prime Minister of Canada, Lester Pearson, had a great idea. He suggested that rich countries designate 0.7% of their GNP for global development, allocating it to the poorest countries. That notion was championed by the UN and passed by the General Assembly the next year. Indeed, it was a noble idea, and that figure was once again endorsed by 22 of the world's richest counties at the 1992 Earth Summit in Rio de Janeiro. Yet, as the plan played out from 1990-2001 the amount of Official Development Assistance (ODA) the donor countries' actually delivered on fell from 0.33% to 0.22%. That is, as a whole, the group of rich countries had been meeting about half the goal, but that figure dropped over the ten year period after 1990 to less than one-third the goal. The drop mostly occurred in the mid-1990's but since then the trend has changed and by 2002 the amount of ODA increased 5%. Yet . . . there is bad news in that, "of the 49 least developed countries, 31 receive less aid today (8.5% of their average GDP) than in 1990 (12.4%).

Oh yes, by the way . . . the United States has never met its goal of 0.7%. In fact, in 2004, the U.S. ranked 21st of the 22 richest countries by allocating a meager 0.16% for global development aid to the poorest people in the world. While Americans generally perceive their country to be the most generous country in the world, the fact of the matter is, we are far from it.[36]

Social Capital: It's a Street That Runs Two Ways

You enjoy a certain amount of social capital, and you are now, perhaps, muttering to yourself, "What is social capital?" It is generally thought of as those benefits that accrue to an individual for being a member of some sort of community or social network. That is, those networks, whether one is in a rich country or in a poor country, provide resources to individuals. One's social connections can impart capital in a variety of ways, and the poor find this social capital to be particularly useful in that it can oftentimes help them to meet needs that they, by themselves, would not have been able to meet.

When crises hit, this capital is available to access. When a flood hits, neighbors or family may take you in. When a health emergency hits, friends or family may help take care of the children for a period of time. When a financial crisis hits, family members or professional associates may provide you with desperately needed capital. Since poor people throughout the world generally don't have insurance to protect themselves against such crises, they are often found spending their social capital. While, indeed, this social capital may be found in neighbors, professional associates, or friends, the interviews and surveys which comprise many of the World Bank's PPA reports make it clear that from the frame of reference of the poor, themselves, they see extended family as the primary source of their social capital. In Costa Rica about 50% of interviewees indicated they had spent social capital from family members.[37] "In Guatemala the family's response to crises is to approach relatives and friends with whom they enjoy a reciprocal relationship. Those individuals give very small loans to cover the cost of medicines, doctors' fees, and transport to medical facilities, or to provide small amounts of foodstuffs in instances of dire necessity."[38]

This is were social capital becomes a "two-way street." It is a two-way street because of the reciprocal relationships that exist in social networks. For while you may well spend some of your social capital by having your in-laws loan you some money during a temporary financial crisis you face, the shoe can be on the other foot, and you may need to loan your in-laws some money if they were to experience an economic shortfall. That is, claims may be made on your resources, for as many in Mali have reported, "accumulating assets at the individual or household level is difficult or impossible because of the claims that family members make on those assets."[39] How many children a couple decides to have may even be impacted by these aspects of social capital because if a couple chooses to have fewer children in hopes of not depleting the resources of the family, it may end up that they will be called upon to care for children of relatives within the network anyway. Such reciprocity, while it may provide a safety net for you in your crisis, it may also mean that you are called upon to be the net for others in their time of crisis.

The 20-Hour Work Day

One of my vivid memories of Ethiopia is driving up to a high vantage point that overlooked the city of Addis Ababa. It was billed as a great place to get a somewhat picturesque view of the city. I remember the horrific road as our vehicle struggled to miss gigantic potholes. As we coiled up towards the peak, we passed scores of women, all of them walking down the almost road with huge bundles of sticks balancing on their heads. They were returning from a day of walking far outside the city to spot where they could harvest firewood, load it up into these immense bundles, and then carry them down, back into the city where they would sell the sticks as fuel for a few pennies.

This type of work is not all that uncommon. Gathering fuel wood is more than a full-time occupation for many people in areas of entrenched poverty. Mostly it's women who perform this task, and they may spend huge portions of the day completing the chore. For instance, a study of 29 villages in the Bolangir district of India found that many women worked "20 hours a day at gathering fuel wood to sell in nearby towns."[40]

Fortunately, the resourcefulness of the poor sometimes comes into play, and cycles of poverty and the oppression of things like a 20 hour workday can be broken.

> In Ethiopia, Etenesh Ayele, thirty-eight, spent twelve years carrying firewood into Addis Ababa. Now she is trying to help women and girls like Amaretch. She runs the Association of Former Women Fuelwood Carriers, whose members teach girls so those girls can stay out of the firewood brigade. Etenesh Ayele and her colleagues also teach women alternative skills, such as weaving, and give them small loans for start-up capital. . . . This association is no panacea—it still has not reached Amaretch—but it shows the kind of homegrown effort that foreign donors could support much more.[41]

Isn't that an uplifting story to hear? Wouldn't you like to invest in that sort of association? That is one of the things American Christians, those of us glimpsing the poor from the rich side of the world, are perfectly capable of doing. Now, we must actually do it; we must redirect some of our resources toward better ends. It's so easy to remain in the mode of the status quo, but might the Holy Spirit be ever so gently nudging you at this very moment to take the initiative to investigate with an aim toward investing? That is, why don't you study and consider some possible enterprises, like that of Former Women Fuelwood Carriers, in which you could invest a little capital. It doesn't take much, but it does take an effort to move in a new direction, to break that status quo of inaction, of inertia, of being oblivious to the needs of others.

What do the Poor See as the Best Way Out of Poverty?

When asked their opinion, people in poverty agree pretty uniformly across the globe in what they see as the best avenue out of their poverty.[42] They see employment or owning a business as the best option out there for them to lift themselves out of their plight. And in this, the private sector would seem to be the on-ramp for potential. One study has found that in developing countries, over 90% of jobs are to be found in that private sector.[43] The poor are quite astute in understanding their dilemma. This might be a clear indication that, perhaps, targeting the creation of jobs and business through the private sector in developing countries would be good strategy for attacking entrenched poverty.

This there any good reason why you should not channel, even if only a modest amount, some of your capital into the private sector to aid people in poverty? That is a burning question. My hunch is that inertia is what keeps many people, especially those with good hearts who really would like to help the poor and the oppressed, from taking the simple step of funneling some of their resources to people who really need it. As means of assisting people elevate themselves out of poverty, such investment would be one of the best things you could do.

Widening Gaps and Disparities: China

China is a mixed bag. China is a mystery. China, undoubtedly, has realized tremendous economic growth in the last two decades. As *the Human Development Report* from 2003 reports, "China is among the few countries performing well overall on the indicators for the Millennium Development Goals."[44] However, even such a glowing report can have a dark side. The *Report* goes on to state, "Yet in recent decades China has shown large disparities in economic and social outcomes between coastal and inland regions—a trend that also reflects cleavages between urban and rural areas. Coastal areas have consistently experienced the fastest economic growth: between 1978 and 1998 per capita incomes increased by an astonishing 11% a year. Ignoring inflation, that means that $100 in 1978 would have jumped to $800 just 20 years later.

In 1999 China's three richest metropolises—Shangai, Beijing and Tianjin—stood at the top of the human development index (HDI) ranking. Those at the bottom were all Western provinces. Moreover, the poorest provinces have the highest inequality. Tibet had the lowest values for education attainment and life expectancy. In income, education and health only some parts of China will achieve the Millennium Development Goals, leaving behind the vast inland areas—particularly the Western provinces."[45]

Widening Gaps and Disparities: Brazil

Brazil is one of those places that has a long tradition of huge disparities between the haves and the have-nots. This is a global phenomenon, but Brazil is a good example. If one considers the wealthiest 10% within that country, they would represent 70 times the income level of the poorest 10% of the population. Yet, income is not the only disparity. The illiteracy rates between rich and poor are increasing at an accelerating rate. [46]

NOTES

1. Ravallion, Martin, Shaohua Chen, and Prem Sangraula, "Dollar a Day Revisted," *World Bank Policy Research Working Paper 4620* (Washington, D.C.: World Bank, 2008).

2. United Nations Development Programme, *Human Development Report 2003*, 41.

3. Ibid., 41-42.

4. Anup Shah, "Poverty Around the World."

5. United Nations Development Programme, *Human Development Report 2003*, 40-41.

6. Ronald J. Sider, *Rich Christians in an Age of Hunger* (Dallas: Word Publishing, 1997, 1-2 who is quoting from Robert L. Heilbroner, *The Great Ascent: The Struggle for Economic Development in Our Time* (New York: Harper & Row, 1963), 33-36.

7. Milburn J. Thompson, *Justice & Peace* (Maryknoll, NY: Orbis Books, 2003), 41.

8. Richard Adams, "Economic Growth, Inequality, and Poverty: Findings from a New Data Set." *World Bank Policy Research Working Paper 2972* (Washington, D. C.: World Bank, 2003), 1.

9. Dollar and Kray, "Growth is Good for the Poor." *World Bank Policy Research Working Paper 2587* (Washington, D. C.: World Bank, 2001), 32.

10. Adams, "Economic Growth," 1.

11. Justin Forsyth, "Letter to the Editor," *The Economist*, 20 (2000), 6.

12. Irma Adelman and Cynthia T. Morris, eds. *African Refugees: Development Aid and Repatriation* (Boulder, CO: Westview Press, 1 1973), 189-93.

13. Adams, "Economic Growth," 5.

14. Ibid., 15.

15. United Nations Development Programme, *Human Development Report 2003*, 155.

16. James Peoples and Garrick Bailey, *Humanity: An Introduction to Cultural Anthropology* (Belmont, CA: Thomson Wadsworth, 2006), 347.

17. S. M. Murshed, *Globalization, Marginalization and Development* (London: Routeldge, 2002).

18. A. Harrison, ed., *Globalization and Poverty* National Bureau of Economic Research Conference Report (Chicago: University of Chicago Press, 2006).

19. Thompson, *Justice & Peace*, 36.

20. Peoples and Bailey, *Humanity*, 2.

21. United Nations Development Programme, *Human Development Report 2003*, 80.

22. Ibid., 80-81

23. Ibid., 81.

24. United Nations Development Programme, *Human Development Report 2003*, 16-17.

25. "The PPP (purchasing power parity) A rate of exchange that accounts for price differences across countries, allowing international comparisons of real output and incomes." *Human Development Report 2003*, 356.

26. The GNP in 2003 was measured at 2.4 billion, which the World Bank equates roughly to a city of about 85,000 people who are making about $30,000 per year. See the *Human Development Report 2003*, 17.

27. United Nations Development Programme, *Human Development Report 2003*, 17.

28. World Bank, *World Development Report 2005, A Better Investment Climate for Everyone* (New York: Oxford University Press, 2004), 3.

29. Ibid., 3-4.

30. Narayan, Patel, Schafft, Rademacher, and Koch-Schulte, *Voices of the Poor*, 72.

31. Sachs, *The End of Poverty*, 93.

32. James Lyon, "Yugoslavia's Hyperinflation, 1993-1994: A Social History," *East European Politics and Societies* 10 (1996): 293-327.

33. Michael Gerson, "Hyperinflation ruining Zimbabwe." *Minneapolis Star Tribune*, February 22, 2008, A15.

34. Ibid., A16.

35. See http://www.cnn.com/2009/WORLD/africa/01/16/zimbawe.currency/.

36. United Nations Development Programme, *Human Development Report 2003*, 146.

37. World Bank, "Identifying the Social Needs of the Poor: An Update." (Washington, D.C.: World Bank, 1997).

38. Narayan, Patel, Schafft, Rademacher, and Koch-Schulte, *Voices of the Poor*, 56.

39. Ibid., 57.

40. PRAXIS, "Partcipatory Poverty Profile Study: Bolangir District, Orissa," U.K. Department for International Development (New Delhi: World Bank, 1998).

41. Easterly, *White Man's Burden*, 27.

42. World Bank (2004), p. 3.

43. OECD, *Highlights of Public Sector Pay and Employment: 2002 Update* (Paris: Organization for Economic Co-operation and Development, 2002).

44. United Nations Development Programme, *Human Development Report 2003*, 62.

45. Ibid., 63.

46. United Nations Development Programme, *Human Development Report 2003*, 62-63.

CHAPTER 6

Issues of Education and Gender

The Parents' Education Makes a Big Difference

It has been argued that the two greatest challenges to public health are the problems of famine and warfare in which civilian populations are targeted.[1] Many places in Africa have been racked by one or the other or both and have suffered a devastating impact as a result. For almost twenty years (1973-1991) Ethiopia suffered from both famine and civilian-targeted warfare simultaneously. The result was that certain regions of the country were ravaged. As one might expect the population group which is normally affected the most by famine and warfare, and in this case the deadly combination of both at the same time, is children, especially those under five years of age.[2]

In an interesting study that focused upon the Tigrai region of northern Ethiopia, researchers investigated the impact of the parents' education upon the children caught up this environment of famine and warfare. The region, itself, is a place where about 85% of the total population is engaged in agriculture.[3] Yet, the area of Tigrai is steeped in a history of draughts, famines, and conflicts.[4] For example, at least 18 different famines have been documented to have occurred in the region since 1800.[5] In addition, the literacy rate within the region is very low as only 20% per cent of people over age 10 are able to read or write.[6] Beyond that, there are huge water and sanitation issues that further exasperate the situation.

> The water situation is characterized by extreme scarcity, poor sanitation, and inaccessibility (along with a very rugged terrain). Only 23% of the population receive clean water while the remaining segment is forced to use unprotected and contaminate water; in most places animals and humans use the same water source. Availability of sanitary facilities is almost negligible.[7]

In this region so troubled by war and famine, the education of the parents actually makes a difference to a child's well being. A high child mortality rate, like that within the Tigrai region, is reduced with the education level of the parents. This is true not only in Tigrai, but across the entire Sub-Saharan panorama.[8] It has been argued[9] that "educated mothers are more likely to shift from a 'fatalistic' acceptance of health outcomes toward the implementation of simple health-promoting practices."[10] It seems that the impact of parental education upon child mortality rates is even greater in times of extreme crisis as educated parents are

> able to protect their children from military conflict, famine, and disruptions of the social and physical environment. Educated parents are more likely to have food reserves for their children during famine period and fathers with higher education are expected to have better coping strategies and better economic resources.[11]

Clearly, it is encouraging to know that educated parents may have a positive impact on high child mortality rates. However, by "educated" in the context of Tigrai, please realize that we are not talking about anything near what we mean by "educated" in the West. We are talking literate parents with somewhat more than a primary level education who can read and write. Of course, now one must take into account the nasty little statistic already mentioned; namely that only 20% of the population is literate. Thus, in famine-ridden, war-torn Tigrai, only 1 out of 5 people are able to positively impact their child's likelihood of dying early because of their education. While the armed conflict in that region has subsided, the awful obstacles of famine, draught, illiteracy, shortages of water and sanitation surround loving families, and children continue to suffer from an extraordinarily high mortality rate.

Could we please join together in a prayer for the parents in Tigrai right now? Father in Heaven—We recognize the mystery of prayer. We realize that our awkward, muttered, seemingly futile words are, in fact, heard by You, and You act upon them. So it is that we can pray, right now, with a confidence that You will act as we are faithful to intercede. Lord, in some unfathomable way, minister to the parents in Tigrai who tonight love their children, but are facing desperate hurdles in caring for them. In a context of shortages of food and water, make a way for them to protect and nurture their youngsters. Encourage aid workers in that region. Place it in the hearts and minds of Christians throughout the world to accelerate health care development in Tigrai through giving. Convict local and regional governmental leaders to attack those barriers of acute poverty faced by the common people. Hear our simple prayer, Lord, and act on behalf of those poor and forlorn parents in Tigrai. Amen.

How Can You Keep Your Kid in School?

People steeped in poverty recognize that literacy is a key to helping themselves have some control over their lives, and they will sacrifice in order to enable their children to attend school. A PPA from Kenya reports that parents will do just about anything to keep their kid(s) in school. "They would sell their possessions, beg, steal, brew and sell beer, pray, go to church, hawk produce, join self-help groups, cajole teachers into letting the children stay in schools, pay in installments, put their children to work, and sometimes become destitute trying to keep their children in school."[12]

On the other hand, in some cases, schooling is not seen as worth the extraordinary effort it takes. The poor of Mali, while they see education as important, are frustrated at the poor quality of the schools. They don't see their kids going to school as translating into actual paying jobs. They don't see their kids getting even a basic level of education at these failing schools. Burkina Faso is another example where the quality of the schools is seen to be so poor that the "investment in fees and loss of field labor are perceived as something of a shot in the dark in terms of realistically securing a raise in an individual's or a family's living standards."[13]

They're Not Going to School

Top Priority Countries, those targeted by the World Bank for special consideration and attention, do not necessarily benefit from that attention. As of 2003, 11 of those "top priority" countries have had a huge problem in making any progress in trying to meet the goal of universal enrollment in primary school. In fact, at least 25% of children in those countries do not attend primary school.[14]

Two Strikes Against Women

The idiom is well known and widely used. Drawn from baseball, the phrase, "two strikes against you," relates the notion of being at a disadvantage. In talking about gender equity one may well want to employ the language of disadvantage, and another idiom which might relate well the dilemma of inequity which women across the world face is, "the deck is stacked against them." In many different types of measures, women face disadvantages. For example, if one looks at developing countries throughout the world, the rate of literacy for boys, ages 15-24, is 80%. However, for girls in the same age group the literacy rate is a mere 60%. Women suffer a higher rate of HIV/AIDS then men. In the developing world, women clearly are fighting huge gender inequities in employment or participation in political life. All in all, women are down in the count in gender equity, however one wants to measure it, particularly in the developing world.[15]

It's a Different Kind of Life for an Educated Girl

For a girl growing up in poverty, an education generally creates a different kind of life for her. The data show that educated girls and women will not only have fewer children, but these educated women will be much better at getting medical attention sooner for themselves and for their children. Beyond that, they will secure better nutrition for their children. Everything seems to be connected, and an education for a young girl will qualitatively enhance a multitude of factors in her life. In fact, "the benefits of girls' education accrue from generation to generation."[16]

Particular Difficulties for Women

Something very interesting is going on in Sub-Saharan Africa and also in Asia. Women actually produce most of the food in those regions. Yet, you can almost assuredly predict the bad news. While they produce most of the food, the women rarely control the land on which they work. When it comes to actually owning land, less than 1 in 10 females who farm in India, Nepal or Thailand own their own land. Thus, they don't have the sort of collateral necessary to invest in resources to improve productivity. Women tend to get the short end of the stick all the way around for in many cultures women simply do not have any claim within their own house to the food that they have produced; the men of the household control what the woman has produced. The problem is even greater for women who need more calories because they are pregnant or nursing.[17]

It Seems That There are Millions of Missing Women

"One clear indicator of the gender crises is the gap in mortality rates between men and women. Despite women's biological advantage, they have higher mortality rates in a number of countries mainly in South and East Asia. The 'missing women' phenomenon refers to females estimated to have died due to discrimination in access to health and nutrition."[18]

The notion of the "missing women" was initially discussed by Jean Drèze and Amartya Sen.[19] They have since provided a nice and concise explanation of this phenomenon in the introduction of their *The Political Economy of Hunger*. Consider their assessment.

> There are, in fact, very asymmetrical survival patterns of men and women in different parts of the world. There is fairly strong evidence that if women and men receive similar nutritional and medical attention, women tend to live significantly longer than men. Women seem to be more resistant to disease and more able to deal with hardship, and the survival advantages are particularly significant for advanced age and also at the other end, especially in neo-natal (and even *in utero*). It is, therefore, not surprising that, in Europe and North America, women have a much higher life expectancy at birth than men, and

that—because of the greater survival rates of women—the female-male ratio in the total population is around 1.05 or so on the average.

However, the female-male ratio is significantly lower than unity in many parts of the world. The ratio is around 0.93 or 0.94 in South Asia, West Asia, and China. It is also lower than unity—though not by much—in Latin America, and quite a bit less in North Africa. Given the natural, i.e. biological advantages of women *vis-à vis* men (when they receive the same nutritional and medical attention), this shortfall of women would tend to indicate a really sharp difference in social treatment (i.e. in the division of necessities of life such as food and medical attention). The shortfalls amount to millions of 'missing women' in Asia and North Africa compared with what would be expected on the basis of the European or North American female-male ratio, and the even on the basis of the ratio for sub-Saharan Africa (around 1.02), then—given the number of Indian males—there would have been 37 million more women in India in the mid-1980s. The number of 'missing women' in China, similarly calculated, is 44 million. There is need for an explanation as to why women's survival pattern has been so adverse in these countries.[20]

When the Poor Speak Up We Should Learn Something

The poor and the oppressed don't have much of a voice in this world. When we do hear their voices, there's the possibility of a very teachable moment if we would only listen to what they are saying. Listen to what Bhawati has to say. She lives in a sprawling slum settlement within the city of Mumbai, India. There are about one million people who live in her particular slum settlement; yes, that's correct—one MILLION people in her *settlement*. Think of it as a big suburb of Mumbai, except it's not a suburb, and it's not pretty. This is what Bhawati said when asked about her life in the slum of Dharavi.

> I have been here for the past 18 years. Right here. Eighteen years ago we had to go to the Ganesh temple for water. We used to go at four in the morning and stand in line until six and get two *handaas* of water. We had to leave the children at home. Five years ago, we got a water connection. But when they drilled a bore well, they broke the pipe. Now, the water we get is dirty and we can only use it for washing. We have to go looking for water.
>
> The toilets are near the road crossing. Every time we use the toilet, we have to pay one rupee. It is a problem. In the morning, I have to send the children to school and husband to the office. I have to cook. There is very little time and there is a long queue at the toilet. Even if you go at 5:30 in the morning, there are at least four people ahead of you. Once you get in, the people in the queue start shouting at you to hurry up.[21]

Did reading the previous two paragraphs give Bhawati a teachable moment to instruct you? That is, did Bhawati's story give you any insight into the life of the poor? Did you listen to what she was saying? Here's an assignment . . . compose a paragraph in which you describe what you learned from Bhawati about what it is like to be poor. Of course, you could just blow off this assignment and never do it. However, I dare you. I double-dog dare you! Don't make me triple-dog dare you. Take a break right now. Put down this book. Stand up and find a pencil and paper, or flip on the computer. Do it; write down what you learned from Bhawati about what life is like being poor. Don't just describe what she literally says, but also try to read between the lines. What message is she trying to communicate?

Who Does Progress Bypass?

Progress, both economic and social, oftentimes bypasses ethnic and racial minorities. Yet even majorities, especially girls and women, will get passed by. Girls and women suffer from less access to schools, jobs, property ownership and service in the public sector. [22]

We know that, generally speaking, economic development tends to help pull women more even with men in a number of human development variables. [23] However, it has also been demonstrated that attitudes toward gender within a culture are especially influenced by whether it is agricultural, industrial or postindustrial. [24] Of course, this exacerbates the problem in that many of the world's poor are in an agriculturally based system.

Women Don't Have it so Good in Russia

The scale of change Russia has undergone since the move to a market economy is huge. Some of the change is good, but some of the change is very bad. Two big surprises emerged in Russia during the 1990's. First, the fast rise of HIV/AIDS, particularly among the 15-29 year old age group was an unexpected development. The second big surprise in Russia during the 90's was the rise in poverty. Once again, as in so many other places in the world, it is women who are especially impacted with regards to poverty. As the *Human Development Report* put it, "The growth of poverty has hit elderly women and female headed households particularly hard, illustrating a worrisome 'feminization' of poverty in Russia. A driving force behind this trend is job instability and, even more, wage discrimination against women." [25]

No Problem

"The achievement of social justice, as a general purpose, is no 'problem' to self-centered persons who care nothing about the well-being of others and about the quality of life in the community. . . . Similarly, racism is no problem to racists, but it is a very serious problem to those suffering from racial oppression." [26]

The previous sentence caught my attention when I first read it. "Racism is no problem to racists," now that's a rather interesting statement. In a like manner, hunger is not a problem to someone who is not hungry. Yet, that is an illusion. Racism *is* a problem to racists, and hunger *is* a problem to well-fed individuals like you and me.

A Day in a Gypsy Church

I've been fortunate in that I have made a number of trips to Bulgaria—seven trips in all. Most of those times I was teaching a short, two-week course at a Bible School in Sofia, the capital city. I happen to be friends with an American couple (North Central University Alumni) who have been in Sofia and connected with the Bible School there for a number of years. Kevin and Wendy Beery have been very kind to have me come, off and on, to teach at this wonderful school in which Bulgarian students are preparing for ministry. Of course, one of the perks of being a university professor is having the subsequent opportunity to drop in on old students wherever they happen to be in the world, and so my travels to this Eastern European country have been a great highlight.

On one particular visit to Sofia, Vlado, a Bulgarian who was on staff at the Bible School at the time, invited me to go with him to a Gypsy church in which he was going to preach the next Sunday. The church was not too far out of Sofia, and so I hitched a ride with him to experience what he said might be an interesting thing to see. Indeed, it was a great experience; the church building was one of the most humble of structures I had ever seen for a church gathering. It was small and quaint with a dirt floor and very rickety benches. I would never have thought that you could jam as many people into that room as they did. Yet, the joy and Christian love that flowed there was stunning. While I understood very little of what was said, words weren't really needed that day. At the end of the service a number of very little, old Gypsy ladies came and hugged my neck. It was one of those surreal experiences in which human connection via the Spirit was realized.

At the time, I really didn't know all that much about Gypsies. Oh, of course, I knew that they were one of the most down-trodden ethnic groups in the world with a long history of being driven from place to place by ruling regimes. I knew they were part of the Hitler genocide program with huge numbers of them being wiped out by the Nazis, and I had, naturally, seen them portrayed in Hollywood films as being the ostracized, wandering nomads of Eastern Europe. My day in a Gypsy church certainly opened me up to an entire people group, that for all practical purposes, could be argued is a quintessential example the biblical poor and oppressed.

Gypsies, or more technically the Roma or Romani people, may forthrightly be said to constitute a truly forgotten and despised community in Europe. Spread throughout Eastern, Central, and Western Europe, the Roma today number perhaps 8-12 million, and they are almost universally perceived and treated as third class citizens. Since that day I dropped in on the Gypsy church in Bulgaria, I have had a growing interest in this unusual and fascinating group of people.

One of the things we do in the Department of Intercultural Studies & Languages at North Central University is to begin each class with prayer, and we use *Operation World* as a springboard in praying for the nations. If you are not familiar with *Operation World*, I urge you to secure a copy and use it to help you systematically pray for the nations and unreached people groups throughout the world. The book is organized by date and nation, i.e. political units. However, there is an emphasis throughout its pages on different ethnic groups and the many needs faced by people who are oftentimes oppressed and neglected. March 13 is the day designated for prayer on behalf of Bulgaria. While Bulgaria does not actually have the largest Gypsy/Roma population among the nations, it is the country and situation with which I am most familiar. As such, I want you to read what is said about the Roma in Bulgaria. In actuality, this quote could easily describe the Gypsies' situation in just about any of the European nations.

> The Roma (Gypsies) are generally despised and at the bottom of the social order with widespread illiteracy. About 60% are Orthodox and 40% Muslim, but most are still deeply involved in the occult, crime and gambling. Between 10,000 and 20,000 have turned to the Lord, mainly through the outreach of the Pentecostal and Baptists in the Bulgarian language. Others are linked to the indigenous Turkish-speaking movement. Pray for specific outreach to them. A Third of all Roma use Romani as their first language. There is now a Romani New Testament.[27]

There are two major ethnic minorities in Bulgaria. One is the Turks, and other is the Roma. While Turks comprise about 9.3 percent of the population, the Roma makeup only about 4.6 percent of the people in Bulgaria. The Roma are a very disadvantaged group within Bulgarian society, and this can be seen in that unemployment among the Roma is particularly high. In certain Roma enclaves within the country, unemployment can be "80 percent among men and 100 percent among women."[28]

The Roma of Bulgaria also face another factor which spirals them continuously downward into poverty—lack of an education. The difference in poverty rates between non-Roma and Roma households in Bulgaria is striking. This is also paralleled in Hungary and Romania where the largest Roma populations in Europe exist. About 3.5 million Roma combined live in Bulgaria, Romania and Hungary, and this accounts for about 40-50% of the total Roma population throughout Europe.[29] What is it that explains the radically differing rates of poverty between the Roma population and the non-Roma in a given country? Well-known correlates of poverty are, of course, factors such as unemployment rates, household size, and perhaps most critical, educational achievement.

The table below demonstrates very vividly the differences between the Roma and the non-Roma populations with regards to how educational achievement impacts the level of poverty. Notice that the trends do not vary much from country to country. When only 7 percent of Roma youth in Bulgaria attend secondary school,[30] it's easy to understand why the cycle of poverty is so difficult to break.

Table 6.1. Education as a Poverty Correlate (Poverty Rate in %). Adapted from A. Revenga, et al., *Poverty and Ethnicity: A Cross-Country Study of Roma Poverty in Central Europe*. World Bank Technical Paper No. 531. (Washington, D.C.: The World Bank, 2002).

	Bulgaria		Hungary		Romania	
	Roma	Non-Roma	Roma	Non-Roma	Roma	Non-Roma
No School	31.24	na	39.63	4.24	84.25	16.52
Primary	39.81	5.25	27.24	5.07	42.56	16.04
Secondary	31.33	2.85	6.24	1.47	31.81	7.47
Higher	0	0.81	0	0	0	0.63

The Roma people have been described in official United Nations reports as living "in the 'most squalid and derelict housing estates' with sanitary facilities that were either extremely poor or non-existent."[31] This is true throughout all of Europe. In any given country, the plight of the Roma is essentially the same. They are found all over the place: Spain, France, Albania, Romania, etc., and in every place the story is the same. They are oftentimes literally ghettoized— forced to live in "makeshift housing located on land no one else wants: contaminated industrial properties or garbage sites isolated from the majority population without public utilities such as clean drinking water, electricity or waste collection."[32]

They face all manner of discrimination, and they are regularly targeted for abuse. As one participant in the Bulgarian city of Dimitovgrad who participated in a World Bank research project said, "They don't pay any attention to us at the hospital. Once they see we're Gypsies they throw us out like dogs."[33] As another Roma man from Dimitrovgrad remarked, "We're worse than a nobody."[34]

Doesn't it seem to you that taking a moment right now to pray for this oppressed peoples group would be very appropriate? Put this book down, move to some isolated area, and begin to intercede for the Gypsies throughout the world. As a down-trodden group, they need our prayer support. This, for most of us, probably falls into the category of not-knowing how to pray for something as immense and overwhelming as the plight of this entire ethnic group. How does one intercede in the face of this flood of poverty, abuse, and hopelessness? Here's where the Spirit works in a mysterious way. Your compassion for a group of people who have no hope such as the Roma will incite the Spirit to empower you to pray. When you pray, something will happen. Beyond that, let me tell you that my day in a Gypsy church gives me hope that it's not a hopeless situation.

NOTES

1. Gebre-Egziabher Kiros and Dennis P. Hogan Hogan, "War, famine and excess child mortality in Africa: the role of parental education," *International Journal of Epidemiology* 30 (2001): 447-455.

2. Studies which support this contention include: Curlin and Hussain (1976); Toole and Ronald (1993); Toole and Waldman (1988); Toole and Waldman (1990); Caldwell and Caldwell (1992).

3. Kiros and Hogan, "War, famine," 447-455.

4. T. Hailu, T. Wolde-Georgis, and P. Van Arsdale, "Resource Depletion, Famine and Refugees in Tigrai." in *African Refugees: Development Aid and Repatriation* (eds. H. Adelman and J. Sorenson: Boulder, CO: Westview Press, 1994), 233-43.

5. M. Rahmato, "Neither Feast Nor Famine: Prospects for Food Security." in *Ethiopia in Change* (eds. A Zegeye and S. Pausewang: London: British Academic Press 1994).

6. Kiros and Hogan, War, famine," 447.

7. Ibid., 448.

8. J. Caldwell, "How is Greater Maternal Education Translated into Lower Child Mortality?" *Health Transition Review* 4 (1994): 224-29.

9. J. Caldwell, "Education as a Factor in Mortality Decline: An Examination of Nigerian Data," *Population Studies* 33 (1979): 395-419.

10. Kiros and Hogan, "War, famine," 448.

11. Idem.

12. Narayan, Patel, Schafft, Rademacher, and Koch-Schulte, *Voices of the Poor,* 54.

13. World Bank, "Visual Participatory Poverty Assessment." (Washington, D.C.: World Bank, 1994).

14. United Nations Development Programme, *Human Development Report 2003,* 44.

15. Ibid., 86.

16. Ibid., 85.

17. Ibid., 90.

18. Ibid., 50.

19. See Jean Drèze and Amartya Sen. *Hunger and Public Action* (Oxford: Oxford University Press, 1989), especially chapter 4.

20. Jean Drèze, Amartya Sen, and Athar Hussain eds. *The Political Economy of Hunger* (Oxford: Oxford University Press, 1995), 23-24.

21. Meera Bapat and Indu Agarwal, "Our Needs, Our Priorities; Women and Men from the Slums in Mumbai and Pune Talk About Their Needs for Water and Sanitation," *Environment & Urbanization* 15 (2003): 71-86.

22. United Nations Development Programme, *Human Development Report 2003,* 16.

23. R. Doyle, "Leveling the Playing Field," *Scientific American* 32 (2005): 68-72.

24. See Ronald Inglehart and Pippa Norris, *Rising Tide: Gender Equality and Cultural Change Around the World* (Cambridge: Cambridge University Press, 2003). They developed a Gender Equality Scale that they used to interpret data from the World Values Survey.

25. United Nations Development Programme, *Human Development Report 2003,* 65.

26. Wogaman, "Towards a Method," 77.

27. Patrick Johnstone and Jason Mandryk, *Operation World* (Waynesboro, GA: Authentic Media, 2001), 130.

28. P. Kabakchieva, I. Illiev, and Y. Konstantinov, "Reeling from Change," in *Voices of the Poor: From Many Land* (eds. Deepa Narayan and Patti Petesch: New York: Oxford University Press, 2002), 251.

29. A. Revenga, D. Ringold, and W. M. Tracy, *Poverty and Ethnicity: A Cross-Country Study of Roma Poverty in Central Europe* World Bank Technical Paper No. 531 (Washington, D.C.: The World Bank, 2002).

30. Kabakchieva, Illiev, and Konstantinov, "Reeling from Change," 253.

31. United Nations Human Settlements Programme, *State of the World's Cities 2006/7.* (Nairobi: UN-HABITAT, 2006), 66.

32. Idem.

33. Kabakchieva, Illiev, and Konstantinov (2002), p. 253.

34. Ibid., 252.

CHAPTER 7

Kids as the Poor and Oppressed

A Street Kid in Khartoum

Street children are found all over the world, and stories similar to Aken's are common. Aken was ten years old when he was interviewed. He was a child living on the streets in Khartoum, Sudan. Khartoum is a very fast growing urban center as the city has realized a huge influx "of people who have moved from the areas affected by war, drought, hunger, and poor rural areas. On moving to the city, and without productive skills, they are exposed to the risk of a transition from relative poverty to absolute poverty."[1] Street children are often the sons and daughters of parents who find themselves mired within such circumstances.

Different governments have different policies of how they deal with street children. The Sudanese government actually captures children from the streets and relocates them into camps without any effort to report this to the child's family or to even bother to find out if the child even has a family.[2] Once in such a camp, the child is given a strict Islamic education that reflects the government's ideals. "The Islamic teacher in the camp (the Imam), teaches children about many Islamic concepts like the holy war (Jihad). He also spiritually charges them to participate in the 'Jihad' to defeat the 'enemies' of Islam. Street children absorb his concept in different ways that reveal their political attitudes toward the civil war in the country."[3] Listen to Aken's story.

> I came from Delling with my friends. We heard that we could find good thing in Khartoum. We only found the policemen who are good at chasing us from one place to the other. I am usually very careful to escape them. One morning I overslept and had no money to buy myself 'sillision' [the glue that street children sniff]. The police kicked me and brought me to 'this prison' [the camps]. I was a Christian like people in my family. But since I came here to Khartoum I became a Muslim. My friends and the Inman advised me to covert to Islam.

The Imam said: if one dies in the war he will be a *Shaheed* [martyr]. Allah will praise those who go to Jihad and send them to Heaven.[4]

What do you see as Aken's future? What do you think *he* sees for his own future?

Sleeping Rough in Port-au-Prince

The phrase, *sleeping rough*, is slang in British colloquial use for homelessness. The strong connotation of the phrase is that it places an "emphasis on the callousness of exposure rather than the lack of a home."[5] *Sleeping Rough in Port-au-Prince* is the title of book that examines the life of street kids in Haiti. In the book we get a sobering look at the everyday struggles faced by the children who make the streets their home. Some of them are four years old; some of them are eighteen years old. However, all of them face an extreme callousness that is a part of sleeping rough.

One of the everyday struggles faced by the street kids is simply that of sleeping. While we who view the poor and the oppressed from the rich side of the world pretty much take for granted the place where we are going to sleep for the evening, the kids of Port-au-Prince don't have that luxury. At evening they will migrate back to what may be called their home bases. Yet, sleeping in safety and security is not a sure thing. "Most children opt for communal seclusion, sleeping in clusters of two or three amid larger, allied cohorts of several dozen youth in a broader radius of space."[6] As one group is described,

> A pattern to their sleeping arrangements is apparent. Younger boys tend to doze off in the larger still-socializing group, to be roused when the teenage boys of the group move singly or in small clusters to separate sleeping spots against the walls of the cemetery. The younger boys usually follow their counterparts, sleeping in clusters of three or four close to (but never up against) the older children for protection.[7]

They employ such sleeping strategies because of what is known as the *lagè domi*, or "sleeping wars." The sleeping wars emerge through the inevitable conflicts and rivalries that arise from living on the streets, even among children. The so-called sleeping war "is rarely if ever employed for the settlement of territorial disputes. Rather it is considered by street youth to be a final solution to long-festering animosities that repeatedly emerge in the form of verbal insults and antagonisms and street scuffles."[8] In the dead of the night, one of the combatants sneaks into the home base of the antagonist and commits a final, violent, surprise attack designed to end forever the conflict. Usually the result is permanent maiming or death to the one who is caught sleeping unaware and unprotected.

For example, there is the case of Nadès, who after a series of confrontations with another boy, was drawn into the sleeping wars.

as Nadès slept against the wall of the National Cemetery, the other boy crept up on him and slashed the bottom of his right foot with a razor and ran. Nadès showed me the healed, four-inch scar that now runs along the side of the bottom of his foot and a quarter of the way around the right outer sole of his heel. It is straight and has healed cleanly, but retains that slightly raised appearance characteristic of a deep and painful would. With the slashing of his foot, Nadès was drawn into the *lagè domi*.

After several days of watching his enemy, ascertaining where he slept and with whom, Nadès was poised for his retribution. This time it was he who crept up on the other boy as he dozed in his sleeping place behind a parked car on a quite side street. . . .Heating the mouth of a plastic juice bottle to melting, Nadès shoved the hot plastic into the sole f the foot of his enemy.[9]

So, when you recline tonight upon your soft mattress, blissfully close your eyes, but instead of anticipating a calm and restful sleep, contemplate what it would be like to be outside, curled up on sidewalk. Consider that you need to be wary of someone you had offended sneaking up to you with a razor in hand. How well would you sleep? Sleeping rough is the norm, night after night after night for the street kids of Port-au-Prince.

What prayer could you utter, right now, for the streets kids? What action could one even conceivably consider on behalf of the children in Port-au-Prince? Remember that in prayer, even the futile situation is susceptible to action by God. Remember that any action, even if it were just a drop in the ocean, is noble within the Kingdom of God.

Postscript

Of course, since the earthquake on January 12, 2010, just about everybody is sleeping rough in Port-au-Prince these days.

Contested Space: Street Kids, Dogs, and Rats

The streets of Port-au-Prince in Haiti constitute what may be called a "contested space." That is to say, there is keen competition for limited space on the city's streets. In his stunning ethnography of the street kids in Port-au-Prince, we learn from Kovats-Bernat, that Port-au-Prince is a nasty, dangerous world inhabited by thousands of kids who face horrible struggles every day.[10] Luckily, we who view things from the rich side of the world don't have to see this. In fact, we are generally blissfully unaware of the plight of the street kids in Haiti. Yet, the following description of the contested streets is riveting to the point of being debilitating to the reader whose hearty is touched.

There simply isn't enough room on the Port-au-Prince streets for the thousands of children who have elbowed their way onto it following their displacement from the home. Densely overpopulated, virtually every square foot of living or marketing space is claimed by someone or something. Where there are not people or produce or structures, there are other things occupying space: rats, roaches, biting ants, stinging centipedes, stray dogs and cats, pigs, goats, roosters, rubble, broken glass, defecation, puddles of filth, piles of garbage, coils of razor wire, taxis, *tap-taps*, other street children.[11]

The risks to the children in such an environment are quite varied. For instance, while rabies is fairly rare in our comfortable world, kids on the street in Haiti face a very real threat from animal attacks, especially from stray dogs and rats. Thousands of dogs and millions of rats roam the streets. Consequently, the rate of rabies infections is shockingly high in Haiti. It's the street kids who are contesting for space on street with such vermin, and as you might surmise, they are the most common victims. "At night, roaches, rates, dogs, cats, mosquitoes, centipedes, and other parasitic or scavenger species vie for limited sheltered space amid boys and girls sleeping in huddles of twos and three in dark crevices as security against rapes, gunfire and the beatings of the police and other street children."[12]

By the way, dying from rabies is inevitable without immunization shortly after contacting the virus. Not only that—it's a horrible way to die. The rabies virus "attacks the brain, causing agitation, terror and convulsions. Victims suffer painful throat spasms when they try to drink or eat. Paralysis follows, yet people infected with rabies are intermittently alert until near death and can communicate their fear and suffering to family and caregivers."[13] Of course, the street kids of Port-au-Prince are not going to get any immunization if they are bit, nor is it likely that there would be any family or caregivers to comfort them in their final hours. It's not a pretty picture, yet it's a vividly realistic and compelling mural of life for the street kids of Haiti.

Who are those street kids, and what do they have to do with you or me? They are like Ti Amos who was one of the street kids who served as an informant for the ethnographic study done by Kovats-Bernat.[14] Ti is featured in the opening chapter of the ethnography as a means of introducing us to the kids.

He wears a filthy, ripped, red T-shirt and a torn pair of dirty, oversized shorts that he has to continuously hitch up when he isn't sitting. His name is Ti Amos and he looks to be not one day over five years old. He wears no shoes, and when I ask him if he finds it difficult to walk about the city in his bare feet, he tells me that he used to have a pair of sandals but they were stolen from him by older street boys as he slept and he never bought a new pair. . . .

Ti Amos keeps a plastic juice bottle full of *siment*-a vaporous cobbler's glue to which he is thoroughly addicted—tucked into the neck of his shirt and he sniffs from it every few minutes. He does this all day, every day. Though his eyes are red and bloodshot and his breath is heavy with the vapor of the glue, he is an exception to the general rule about the sniffer-*zombie*. He is thoughtful and lucid, and at times almost philosophical.[15]

A number of surprising and shocking aspects about the lives of the streets kids in Port-au-Prince surface in the study. First of all, very few of the street kids there are orphans. Most of them have family, and they oftentimes maintain some semblance of contact with them.[16] Indeed, it has been estimated that, worldwide, "well over three-quarters and as many as 90% of the children on the streets . . . work on the streets but live at home and are working to earn money for their families."[17] Of course, not all of them have a desirable situation at home. For instance, Ti Amos left his home because his father beat him, and he was forced to "live a life of misery."[18] Yet, when young Ti became quite sick with a fever, he returned to his parents' home for a few days. However, once he was feeling better, "they asked him to leave because there was not enough food for him."[19]

The street kids also surprise you. It seems they turn out to be about the hardest working residents of the city. From very early in the morning until late at night the great majority of them are usually working service jobs such as shining shoes or washing cars.[20] Still, many of them end up trying to supplement their meager incomes through illicit activities such as "selling drugs or sex or committing petty thefts."[21] While one might think that they would spend a great deal of time begging, that simply isn't the case. Indeed, while virtually all of them engage in begging at some point, that is clearly not the preferred method of the kids to get money. When it comes to begging, it's the younger kids who

> profit more from their begging, because of the same inverse relationship between youth and sympathy observed by other anthropologists who have worked with street children. Older children are increasingly regarded with suspicion as they mature and so are proportionately disadvantaged in their begging efforts.[22]

Another surprising element is the generosity with which the street kids share their money and food with closest friends on the street. They demonstrate a close social tie and camaraderie with their peers through the sharing of food. That is, they have an "integrated system of redistributive exchange. At the end of the each day, street children convene . . . to pool their money and their food so as to ensure that everyone has something to eat in the evening."[23] Wouldn't it be interesting if we were as generous in the sharing of our resources as they are?

Excluded and Invisible

Millions of children around the world are excluded and invisible. In fact, that's the title of a 2006 report by the United Nations Children's Fund concerning the state of the world's children—*Excluded and Invisible*.[24] While the United Nations' MDGs, if reached, will dramatically change the lives of literally millions of excluded and invisible kids, the fact of the matter is that we are not currently on track to reach many of the goals. For instance, MDG number 4 is to reduce by two thirds the mortality rate among children under five by 2015. Sad to say, that isn't going to happen. "At the current rate of progress the goal will be reached 30 years late," in 2045.[25]

> At current rates of progress, for example, 8.7 million children under five will still die in 2015, whereas if the target were met, 3.8 million of those lives would be saved in that year alone.[26]

Why don't you read that little quotation just above once more? Only this time, read it out loud.

That means, if the MDG goal were to be met, only 4.9 million kids under age five would die in 2015. Yet, as it is now projected, the goal will not be met for many years to come, and therefore a staggering 8.7 million of the world's most excluded and invisible children will die in 2015.

Clearly, there are huge hurdles to overcome in order to meet the MDG of slicing by two-thirds the child mortality rate. What are the major causes of large scale, macro-level exclusion to kids that will lead to such high numbers of deaths for children under the age of five? It's pretty basic: armed conflicts, poverty, HIV/AIDS. These present the greatest hurdles.[27]

If you are reading this, you undoubtedly have a birth certificate, and it probably would not be much of a problem for you to get your hands on a copy of your birth certificate if you needed. But what would *your life* be like if *your* birth were unregistered? From the very start of life exclusion began for an estimated "48 million children in 2003—36 per cent of total births that year—whose birth went unregistered."[28] There is actually a wide range in the levels of birth registration around the world. In 2004 the Democratic People's Republic of Korea had, for all practical purposes, 100 per cent of their births registered, while less than 7 per cent of births in the countries of Afghanistan, Uganda, Tanzania, and Bangladesh were registered.[29]

Naturally, the primary responsibility for care of a child resides with the parents, the family. However, for a variety of reasons, many kids throughout the world do not have any kind of family environment. What happens to them? In theory, the child's wellbeing falls to the state according to Articles 20 and 22 of the United Nations' Convention on the Rights of the Child. This is an international convention that sets out the civil, political, economic, social and cultural rights of children. Monitored by the United Nations' Committee on the Rights of the Child (UNCRC), the convention is composed of members from countries around the world. To date, 193 countries have signed and ratified the UNCRC. I'll wager you can't guess the two countries that have not ratified it!

Somalia has not signed nor ratified it. That's not a huge surprise, and it may have been one of your guesses since you know that Somalia hasn't had a functioning national government since 1991. Primary school attendance rates are important indicators of child welfare in general, and more specifically, a low attendance rate in primary school is a good indicator of children being excluded and invisible. Which country has the lowest net primary school attendance ratio in the world? Yes indeed, Somalia. In the horrible environment, racked by years and years of civil and tribal warfare only 12 per cent of boys and 10 per cent of girls get a primary education in Somalia.[30]

What's the other country that hasn't ratified the UNCRC? Surprise, surprise; it's the United States. On top of that bit of news you may be interested to know that Christians are quite divided between support for and opposition against the UNCRC. Some religious conservatives object in that they perceive the UNCRC to be simply one more element of an elitist institution, and they totally distrust the U.N. to properly handle sensitive decisions regarding family issues."[31] On the other hand many Christians along with respected organizations such as World Vision strongly advocate the ratification of the UNCRC. As Smolin puts it,

> Given the traditional Christian emphasis on providing protection and assistance to the vulnerable, poor, needy, and oppressed, the CRC, along with human rights language generally, expresses a positive call and commitment to action. On a worldwide basis, those who seek to minister in the name of Christ among the tragic circumstances of human life apparently find more inspiration than fear in the words of the CRC.[32]

So here we are quibbling while the excluded and invisible of the world are quickly perishing in numbers too large and overwhelming to, evidently, be able to do much about. Shame on us once again.

Yet, while in theory, the state is caring for children without a family, the sad case is that oftentimes the theory does not actually play out into reality. For example, in Dimitrovgrad, Bulgaria there's a state institution for children with mental retardation. However, of the 68 child residents, about one-third are orphans with no hint of any mental retardation. Orphans sent to an institution for the mentally ill—not hardly what the U.N. or anybody else has in mind.

> The children say that in the institution they have decent meals, clothing, and student grants, but that once they leave, they are stigmatized because of where they came from and their lives get much worse. The girls say they have few prospects besides prostitution, and the boys end up in severely underpaid jobs.[33]

It's Not Mr. Rogers' Neighborhood

"It's a beautiful day in the neighborhood, a beautiful day in the neighborhood. Won't you be my neighbor?" So sang Mr. Rogers as he sauntered in and carefully removed his button-down sweater as he invited children to join him in a half hour of learning within a safe environment. For many years Fred Rogers hosted the popular T.V. show, *Mr. Rogers' Neighborhood*. It won accolades for its wonderful presentations to kids. I remember my daughter watching and learning. I rather got into the show a few times myself. It's a scene to which only those of us in the rich side of the world could relate. Most of the urban poor children of the world could not even imagine such a neighborhood. All they know is their neighborhood; and it's not anything like Mr. Rogers' neighborhood—not anything.

Unsafe living conditions characterize most of the urban neighborhoods in which hundreds of millions of children live throughout the developing world.[34] On a daily basis their health and their life is threatened by any number of factors within their very neighborhood, be it crime, foul water, contaminated sites, or a thousand other factors one could cite when talking about urban environments in poverty-ridden countries.

Tragically, the conditions of urban poverty in the developing world are such that even the best parents are not able to insulate their children from innumerable threats against them. Oftentimes it is not the fault of the parents who are faced with no-win scenarios. "Caregivers are repeatedly faced with unforgiving choices. Should young children drink contaminated water or should they go thirsty? Should they play beside streets with heavy traffic or be kept indoors where there is little space and an open fire to contend with?"[35] It's funny, but I don't recall Mr. Rogers ever talking about such no-win scenarios.

It's Both Theatre and War Zone

After observing the lives of street kids for more than ten years, one researcher remarked that the streets which thousands upon thousands of children call home have "increasingly become both theatre and war zone."[36] That notion reflects the paradox of trying to assess the nature of what it really means to have kids living on the streets. First of all, there is a wide range of reaction from the public toward the masses of street urchins who inhabit most large urban centers throughout the world. It doesn't matter where one looks; from city to city, from country to country, from culture to culture, the spectrum of public perception is broad.

> Some people see the children as being worthy of the valor given to heroic survivors, while other afford them the pity due the neglected and abused. Sadly, the most common public response is scorn and hostility. Although I can imagine why they are scorned—their being dirty, uncontrolled by authority, and involved in mischief are enough to explain this—I find it difficult to understand the degree of violence they receive.[37]

While the way in which people perceive these kids is diverse, the reference to violence perpetrated upon the children of the streets is a sobering, if little recognized, fact of the horrific treatment foisted upon street kids, no matter the locale one is considering—that is, violence is a universal aspect of living on the streets. Cases of capital punishment of street kids for petty crimes is not unknown, and even governmental programs to remove kids from the streets and place them into what might well be called indebted servitude has been documented.[38]

Tightly defining who is actually a street kid is a bit more complex of an enterprise than one might expect, and a universally accepted definition does not exist. However, a number of researchers have advocated an array of categories,[39] and the United Nations has developed its own definition.

> any girl or boy . . . for whom the street in the widest sense of the world (including unoccupied dwellings, wasteland, etc.) has become his or her habitual abode and/or source of livelihood, and who is inadequately protected, supervised, or directed by responsible adults.[40]

Still, however one defines or categorizes the street kids, the reality is that large numbers of kids live their life, one way or the other, by being incredibly vulnerable on the streets. Investigating the conditions of the kids, to be sure, is a formidable task. One might suppose that simply asking kids is the best way to get information about them or their way of life. Yet, it is not that easy. "Getting accurate information from the children is quite difficult. They have developed an extraordinary capacity to tell stories. Lying about their ages, family background, the reasons for being on the streets, and their current circumstances is included in their well-rehearsed scripts."[41]

Kids Dying Young

Child mortality rates actually rose in 14 countries during the decade of the 90s. The Child Morality Rate is oftentimes defined in the literature as the "Under Five Morality Rate," and it reflects "the probability that a newborn baby will die before reaching age five. . . . The probability is express as a rate per 1,000.[42] In order to fight this trend of rising rates the World Bank has identified what are known as Top and High Priority countries, and these are earmarked as especially important targets for rapid improvement. Surprisingly, when one examines a number of development variables in these countries, one discovers that 32 Top Priority countries are losing ground rather than improving. In a number of these countries about one in three children do not live to see the age of five.[43] Given that Millennium Development Goal 4 is to cut the child mortality rate around the world by two-thirds by 2015, it should be a sobering wakeup call to us that the trend is not in that direction.

While the goal of cutting the child mortality rate by two-thirds around the globe is still theoretically achievable, there must be a concerted effort to address the horrible situation among the most vulnerable children, namely, those kids who live in rural areas and those who live in urban slums. Naturally, it's in the developing world that high mortality rates are most acute. "Child mortality rates in developing countries are 10 times higher than those in the developed world."[44] Beyond that, it's no secret because the data clearly show it, "Where child mortality rates are high, the proportion of slum households is typical also high."[45] That means the urban poor, those kids living in urban slums are particularly susceptible to dying young. There are five man culprits that account for over half of all childhood deaths: <u>pneumonia, diarrhea, malaria, measles, and HIV/AIDS</u>.[46] Diarrhea—you wouldn't think that would be such a huge factor in child mortality levels, yet it is.

> Infection agents enter the body through four main pathways: air, food, water and fingers; skin, soil, and inanimate objects; insect vectors; and mother-to-child transmission. Children living in slums are likely to come into contact with contaminated air, food, water and soil, and to be exposed to conditions in which parasite-carrying breed. Two conditions—pneumonia and diarrhoea—are prevalent among children in slums and are responsible for a large proportion of child each killing more than 2 million children in developing countries each year.[47]

There is no doubt about it; urban slums are very efficient killing environments. "The ratio of child death in slum areas to child deaths in non-slum areas is consistently high in all developing countries, even in countries that have made progress toward reducing child mortality overall."[48]

The rate at which children die before reaching age five—it's a haunting topic. For those of us on the rich side of the world, it's not a commonplace issue. Our child mortality rate is low; kids on the rich side of the globe live longer. They tend to live much longer, growing into adulthood and experiencing many things during their lifetime. In the particularly gripping quotation below, Amartya Sen, a Nobel winning economist and advocate for the poor, reflects on a short-lived life, so common around the world.

> We try to pack in a few worthwhile things between birth and death, and quite often succeed. It is however, hard to achieve anything significant if, as in sub-Saharan Africa, the median age at death is less than five years. . . . Having made it beyond those early years, it may be difficult for us to imagine how restricted a life so many of our fellow human beings lead, what little living they manage to do. There is, of course, the wonder of birth (impossible to recollect), some mother's milk (sometimes not), the affection of relatives (often thoroughly disrupted), perhaps some schooling (mostly not), a bit of play (amid pestilence and panic), and then things end (with or without a rumble) The world goes on as if nothing much has happened.[49]

How is the Church supposed to respond to something like that quotation? How are you, how am I supposed to respond? One of the objectives of this book is to prod you and me, to prod the Church to respond—to prod us to behavioral changes, to prod us to action instead of contentment with the status quo. A proper response to Sen's quote above might be crying. It might be praying. It might be giving of financial resources to organizations that actually do some good in fighting against high child mortality rates. It might be praying. It might be refocusing your lifetime ambitions—after all, you are one whose lifetime has already been considerable longer than one of the little ones who has died before age five. Think of it, if you are even only twenty-five years old, you've already lived at least five times longer than the majority of people born in Sub-Saharan Africa. A proper response might be . . . well, you fill it in, for there is a multitude of proper responses. The point is to have a response. Do anything, but please, do something.

Kids in Conflict: If You Go to School in the Morning, You May Find Yourself in the Army by the Afternoon

The Army of Liberia in West Africa was pretty aggressive in its recruiting of soldiers during a period of armed conflict from 2000-2003. Who did they recruit for war? They enlisted mere children to do some fighting for them. Most of the kids were taken by force and some voluntarily signed up. As reported by Human Rights Watch, recruiting was so vigorous "that parents stopped sending their children to school fearing they would be recruited."[50] Children as young as nine years old were routinely hijacked from schools and put into the army without their parents ever knowing what happened to them.

They Carry Water and Gather Wood

In countries entrenched in poverty, the plight of the children is oftentimes a gruesome life. It is typical for children who live in farming families to spend a considerable amount of time walking many kilometers every day for the purpose of getting firewood and/or water. Have you ever carried water very far? It's not fun, and it is definitely not easy. Water is heavy. Want an interesting challenge? Try carrying two gallons of water for even just one kilometer—just over one half of a mile. I guarantee that you will not enjoy the experience, but that's alright—now you may better be able to identify with the plight of children of poverty as you imagine an eight-year old girl doing the task, only she probably needs to walk about four to eight times farther than you did in your little experiment.

How does that little girl manage to get the wood and water necessary for her family's subsistence that day and then still be able to go to school? Even if there were a school available for her to attend, and that is not often the case for those engulfed in rural poverty, she will have neither the time nor the energy to attend. In addition to that, worm parasites and malaria reign unchecked as such children have no primary health care for prevention or treatment. It's not a fun life for children of extreme poverty.[51]

A Trend Toward More Child Labor in Azerbaijan

People who responded to a World Bank PPA in Azerbaijan made some interesting observations. They recognized that there seemed to be an ever-increasing number of young kids on the street who were selling things and working at a variety of jobs.[52] Azerbaijan is a member of the International Labor Organisation (ILO) and has ratified a number of ILO conventions such as the one aimed at the prohibition and immediate action for the elimination of the worst forms of child labour."[53] However, the trend remains that more and more kids are working in the streets and being exploited.

Cattle Rustlers in Swaziland

While it sounds like something out of the Wild West, here's an example that drives home a very important aspect of poverty that most of us don't immediately grasp—namely, vulnerability. While we may grasp that the poor don't have resources, I don't think we easily grasp how incredibly susceptible the poor are to all sorts of forces around them. Take the case of some poor farmers in Swaziland. It seems that cattle rustlers have been keeping kids out of school in that African nation.[54] The way in which this happens demonstrates the nasty lack of control the poor have over any number of factors, even something like cattle rustlers. In Swaziland, oxen are crucial to the well being of the poor in a variety of ways. As a respondent in one PPA study relates,

> A lot of people were sending their children to school by using the cattle. Come plowing time, the oxen could be used. Come planting time they would sell the cattle to buy seed and fertilizer. Come drought, a few cattle would be sold to tide the family over till the next harvest. Now with so many kraals [corrals] empty [due to theft], the kids will drop out of school, people will have a problem with farm inputs, and we will be more vulnerable to hunger during the draught.[55]

It has been "observed that poverty alleviation policies have tended to neglect the issue of vulnerability of the poor."[56] It's actually not surprising that we miss elements of poverty along the way—after all poverty is a very complex structure. Remember, poverty is fractal in nature (see Chapter 1). However, the aspect of vulnerability is an interesting one. "Vulnerability is perhaps best understood as a lack of key sets of assets, exposing individuals, households, and communities to increased or disproportionate risk of impoverishment."[57] In the case of the Swaziland farmers, the whims of the rustlers actually dictated that children would ultimately be deprived of education. Thus, one of the few asset-building potentials for the farmers in that region was inhibited, if not eliminated

NOTES

1. Salwa Saad Awad, "The Invisible Citizens Roaming the City Streets." *Educational Review* 54 (2002): 106.

2. Human Rights Watch/AFRICA, *Children in Sudan: Slaves, Street Children and Child Soldiers* (Washington, D.C.: Human Rights Watch, 1995).

3. Awad, "Invisible Citizens," 106.

4. Ibid., 106-07.

5. Christopher Kovats-Bernatm *Sleeping Rough in Port-Au-Prince: An Ethnography of Street Children and Violence in Haiti* (Gainsville: University Press of Florida, 2006), 11.

6. Ibid., 128.

7. Idem.

8. Ibid., 130.

9. Ibid., 131-132.

10. Kovats-Bernatm, *Sleeping Rough.*

11. Ibid., 35.

12. Idem.

13. RodneyWilloughby, "A Cure for Rabies?" *American* April (2007): 89.

14. Christopher Kovats-Bernat is an Assistant Professor of Anthropology at Muhlenberg College whose research focus is upon street children, voodoo, and political violence in Haiti. The actual names of the child informants have been changed within the study for their protection.

15. Kovats-Bernatm, *Sleeping Rough,* 19.

16. Ibid., 108.

17. J. Boyden, *Children of the Cities* (Atlantic Highlands, NJ: Zed Books, 1991) and W. Myers "Urban Working Children: A comparison of four surveys from South Africa, " *International Labor* 188 (1989): 321-335.

18. Kovats-Bernatm, *Sleeping Rough,* 19.

19. Ibid., 19-20.

20. Ibid., 111.

21. Idem.

22. Ibid., 114.

23. Ibid., 119.

24. UNICEF, *State of the World's Children, 2006* (New York: UNICEFF House, 2006).

25. Ibid., 5.

26. Idem.

27. Ibid., 12.

28. Ibid., 36.

29. Ibid., 37.

30. Ibid., 15.

31. David Smolin, "Overcoming Religious Objections to the Convention on the Rights of the Child," *Emory International Law Review* 20 (2006): 81-110.

32. Ibid., 109.

33. Narayan and Petesch, *Voices,* 249.

34. Sheridan Bartlett, "Children's experience of the physical environment in poor urban settlements and the implications for policy, planning and practice." *Environment & Urbanization* 11 (1999): 63-73..

35. Ibid., 64.

36. Lewis Aptekar, "Street Children in the Developing World: A Review of Their Condition." *Cross-Cultural Research* 28 (1994): 195.

37. Ibid., 198.

38. Boyden, *Children.*

39. See, for example, Lusk, Street Children; Cosgrove, "Working Definition," Visano, "Socialization," and Patel, *Overview*.

40. International Catholic Children's Bureau, *Forum on Street Children and Youth* (Grand Bassam, Ivory Coast: International Catholic Children's Bureau, 1985).

41. Aptekar, *Street Children*, 199.

42. World Bank, *World Development Indicators* (New York: Oxford University Press, 2006), 27.

43. United Nations Development Programme, *Human Development Report 2003*, 44.

44. United Nations Human Settlements Programme, *State of the World's Cities 2006/7* (Nairobi: UN-HABITAT, 2006), 108.

45. Idem.

46. Idem.

47. Ibid., 111.

48. Ibid., 109.

49. Paul Farmer *Pathologies of Power: Health, human Rights, and the New War on the Poor* (Berkeley: University of California Press, 2005) .xi.

50. UNICF, *The Impact of Conflict on Women and Girls in West and Central Africa and the UNICEF Response* (New York: UNICEF, 2005), 16.

51. United Nations Development Programme, *Human Development Report 2003*, 75.

52. Narayan, Patel, Schafft, Rademacher, and Koch-Schulte, *Voices*, 76.

53. Idem.

54. Ministry of Economic Planning and Development of the Kingdom of Swaziland and the World Bank, "Swaziland: Poverty Assessment by the Poor," (Washington, D.C.: World Bank, 1997).

55. Narayan, Patel, Schafft, Rademacher, and Koch-Schulte, *Voices*, 61.

56. Idem.

57. Idem.

CHAPTER 8

Housing:
Where the Poor and the Oppressed Live

A Lot of People Live in Slums. So, What's a Slum?

A lot of people live in slums; more than you can imagine. Because we view things from the rich side of the world, we don't often get a nice, close-up view of any slums. Anyway, we tend to cross the street in order to avoid slums. In addition to that, most of the slums are not in America, they are in other places, safely removed from us. Our lives are pretty isolated from slums. What about the people who spend their entire life in a slum? You realize, of course, that most slum dwellers never get out—never. The numbers are crushing; one out of every three people who live in a city lives in slum conditions.[1]

I suppose it could be argued that one person's slum is another person's dream home. Thus, some sort of agreement on what constitutes a slum is needed. So, how does one define a slum? In fact, UN-HABITAT has developed a working definition of a *slum* as, "a settlement in an urban area in which more than half of the inhabitants live in inadequate housing and lack basic services."[2] Naturally, that definition raises the need for quantifiable indicators to define *inadequate* and *basic services*. Since a slum might be a cluster of units or an individual unit geographically removed from other units, UN-HABITAT chose to use "the household as the basic unit of analysis."[3] With that in mind, below is the technical definition of a slum.

> A slum household is a group of individuals living under the same roof in an urban area who lack one or more of the following five conditions:
> Durable housing: A house is considered "durable" if it is built on a nonhazardous location and has a structure permanent and adequate enough to protect its inhabitants from the extremes of climatic conditions, such as rain, heat, cold and humidity.

Sufficient living area: A house is considered to provide a sufficient living area for the household members if not more than three people share the same room.

Access to improved water: A household is considered to have access to improved water supply if it has a sufficient amount of water for family use, at an affordable price, available to household members without being subject of extreme effort, especially on the part of women and children.

Access to sanitation: A household is considered to have adequate access to sanitation if an excreta disposal system, either in the form of a private toilet or a public toilet shared with a reasonable number of people, is available to household members.

Secure tenure: Secure tenure is the right of all individuals and groups to effective protection against forced evictions. People have secure tenure when there is evidence of documentation that can be used as proof of secure tenure status or when there is either *de facto* or perceived protection against forced evictions.[4]

Where are all these slums? Over half of the world's slum population is in Asia. Next comes sub-Saharan Africa, closely followed by Latin America and the Caribbean.[5] While there certainly are slums in the U.S. and in Western Europe, the fact of the matter is that the overwhelming number of people residing in slums is not in the richest countries. Thus, we who are viewing things from the rich side of the world really do need to cross the street in order to more than glimpse the teeming slums of the world.

Ever Been to Victoria Falls?

Victoria Falls is a big tourist attraction. While one generally doesn't think of Zimbabwe when considering a spot to vacation, over one million tourists a year come to Victoria Falls. What's the attraction at Victoria Falls? Of course, what people come to see is the spectacular waterfall, one of the most marvelous sights in the world. They certainly aren't coming to see the nearby Chinotimba area slum that is teeming with shacks and squatter settlements. Isn't it interesting how a thing of such natural beauty as the waterfall is juxtaposed to the horrendous sights and reality of life that the slums provide?

What is so special about the Chinotimba slums? Actually, they are not special; they are not so unusual for slums in the developing world. Here's a quick snapshot of conditions in the Chinotimba slums of Victoria Falls, Zimbabwe:

- 3,000 families live in shacks and squatter settlements
- On average, there is one toilet for every 507 shack dwellers
- One water tap serves 1,350 people
-

Landlords collect, on average, Z$ 4 million per annum in rentals to have people live in these conditions[6]

If You're Not Up To Your Ankles in Water, Your House is Catching on Fire

Fire and water can be real hazards for those living in acute poverty. Those who live in urban areas are especially susceptible to these risks with which most of us on the rich side of the world don't worry about. Of course, even the rich can suffer from flooding, but generally speaking, it's only the poor of this world who live in perennial flood environments. Take the country of Benin for instance. "With scarce affordable housing, poor families often reside on steep hillsides and marshes that are highly susceptible to mudslides and floods."[7] A study focusing on Benin reports that a number of poor must live in areas with "water up to their ankles for three months a year."[8] Naturally, living in that type of an environment means constant struggles with disease, infections, streets that can't be used, and the list could go on and on. How would you like to be up to your ankles in water three months out of the year?

Then there's fire. Urban shacks, those in which many of the poor live throughout the world, tend to be crammed together into crowded settlements that are horribly disposed to fire. Of course, this is nothing new; poverty is not new. Those who perished in Nero's famous urban renewal project of the burning of the slum portions of Rome way back in 68 A.D. were the poor. The nine-day fire gutted the three districts of Rome inhabited by the poor, urban masses. The dangers to over-crowded slums, and tightly packed tenement housing is a timeless problem. A contemporary example is South Africa where large shantytowns are composed of shelters built from cardboard and wood. Add to that the use of paraffin for cooking and for light at night, and you have a tinderbox ready to combust; and they usually do at some point.

Improving the Lives of 100 Million Slum Dwellers—Ya, sure

I'm not very optimistic about reaching Target 11 of Goal 7 of the MDGs. Target 11 is, "Achieve significant improvement in lives of at least 100 million slum dwellers, by 2020." Is it just me, or does the phrasing of that target imply that they are still living in slums after you have improved their lives? Otherwise, shouldn't the target read something like, *relocate 100 million slum dwellers out of the slums into better living conditions*? If they are still living in slums, how much has their life really improved?

Sometime in 2007 the number of people living in slums around the world will surpass the one billion mark. In addition to that, 1 out of every 3 people who live in a city will "live in inadequate housing with no or few basic services."[9] Thus, the target of improving the lives of 100 million slum dwellers seems woefully inadequate, if not "obscene." For it constitutes a

> conscious exclusion of a huge majority of the world's urban and rural poor. In a world of almost one billion slum dwellers, to speak of improving the lives of

less than 10 per cent of the world's poorest citizens and rights-holders under-
scores just how far the Goals [MDGs] stray. . . . Which 100 million slum
dwellers are we actually talking about? Who will choose those whose life will
be improved? Which 900 million or more slum dwellers and homeless citizens
will fall through the cracks?[10]

The outlook is not rosy for making a significant dent in the slums of this
planet. As urban growth accelerates during the next twenty years, 95% of it will
be happening in the developing world, right in the areas least able to deal with it.
By 2030 the overflow of urban growth will reach the point where 80% of the
world's urban population will be in the developing world. Asia and Africa are
destined by 2030 to house the largest urban populations. The sad thing is that
most of this urban growth will be in the form of "slum formation."[11]

A huge factor in the vulnerability of the poor living in urbanized slums is
their susceptibility to natural disasters. The scope of the threat against the poor
in urban areas cannot be overstated as, "the rapidly urbanizing cities and towns
in Africa, Asia and Latin America represent the greatest concentration of vulnerable people there has ever been."[12] The throngs of poor migrants moving into
cities across the globe usually don't know that they are moving into very dangerous places. That is because many of them "live on the worst quality land on
the edges of ravines, on flood-prone embankment, on slopes liable to mudslide
or collapse, in densely packed areas where fires easily start."[13]

Pick any month of any year and you'll be able to find examples of natural
disasters reeking havoc on poor urban dwellers somewhere in the world. For
example, one could cite an earthquake in Turkey in which 17,000 people were
killed, 44,000 injured "and nearly 300,000 homes either damaged or col-
lapsed."[14] Or, there is the case of a couple of cyclones in India that "killed well
over 10,000 people and made 8 million homeless."[15] Of course the sobering fact
is, these are not isolated case studies that are in any sense unusual happenings.
These are the sorts of things the poor and the oppressed throughout the world
deal with all the time. "For millions of poor urban dwellers, managing disaster is
an everyday occurrence, less noticed by outsiders but just as insidious."

Improving the lives of slum dwellers will be a difficult goal to realize if the
people continue to dwell in a poor, urbanized area. The scope of natural disasters in their lives is such an overwhelming factor that, frankly, I'm not terribly
optimistic about actualizing Target 11 of Goal #7 of the MDGs. As Sanderson
concluded in his study of livelihoods of the urban poor and how best to address
disaster mitigation, "If the poor's increasing vulnerability to disasters is not addressed by policy, management or implementation then, simply put, urban living
for them cannot be sustainable."[16]

Property Rights Can Change Things

China has an amazing story to tell which should teach us all a lesson. China's great economic growth in the last number of years is a well-known story. Over the past 20 years the country has realized an average growth rate of about 8 percent a year.[17] That is outstanding growth against any sort of measure. Beyond that, in 1981, 64% of the population in China lived on less than $1 a day. By 2001, less than 17% of the population lived on less than $1 a day.[18] What created such a turn around? While the answer might be more complex than we know, the simple and short answer is that a new "rudimentary system of property rights that created new incentives for a substantial part of its economy"[19] is at the heart of the matter. Peasants were given new opportunities, and they seized those opportunities to improve their lives.

Justice does produce fruit, and a government that works on behalf of its people to initiate change against injustice will reap benefits.

The Feeling of Being Trapped in Rio

Rio de Janeiro, Brazil is usually thought of by most people on the rich side of the world as one of the true glamour spots on the planet. It's a scene of beautiful beaches filled with jet-set tourists. Yet, there is an ugly, underside of Rio—it's the side of the city where the poor live. In one interesting study of the urban poor of Rio, slum residents were interviewed back in 1968-69. More than thirty years later (2001-03), they were interviewed again with the aim of discovering types of longitudinal changes within the slums of the city.[20] One finding that emerged from the study was the perception of the residents that deadly violence within their living environments had greatly escalated over that thirty year period. Whereas in 1968 they were largely afraid of being removed from their homes by the ruling military regime, in the 2001-03 interviews they were most afraid of "dying in crossfire between drug dealers and police or between rival gangs."[21]

The level of violence within the poor areas of the city has skyrocketed.[22] Lethal violence has so increased in the slums of Rio that the poor who live there feel hopelessly "trapped between the drug dealers and the police. In 2003, 81 percent said that neither group helps them and that both elements commit violent acts with impunity. As the gangs are better financed and armed, it is easy to bribe the police. It is not uncommon for police to barge into low-income homes with the excuse of searching for a gang member and then tear the home apart and kill family members at random to demonstrate power and 'instill respect.'"[23]

Hear the voice of Nilton who is 60 years old and speaks of what it is really like to live in the slums of Rio.

> To live here is to live in a place where daily you do not have the liberty to act freely, to come and go, to leave your house whenever you want to, to live as any other person who is not in jail. It is imprisoning to think: 'Can I leave now

or is it too dangerous?' Why do I have to call someone and say that they shouldn't come here today? It is terrible; it is oppressive. Nobody wants to live like this.[24]

Indeed, nobody *wants* to live like that, but that is the reality of life for the slum dwellers of Rio de Janeiro. They are trapped within the beautiful city. The only thing is, their portion of the city is not so beautiful.

The Slums of Sub-Saharan Africa

If you were asked what regions of the world are particularly susceptible to having slums, I suspect that that your first answer would not include sub-Saharan Africa. While the popular image of that region may be deserts and desolate locations, the fact of the matter is, sub-Saharan Africa "has the highest prevalence of slums in the world—71.8 percent of its urban population lives in slums."[25] Compare that rate to some of the other regions of the world, and it is clear that sub-Saharan Africa far outstrips the rest. For example, the region with the next highest percentage of urban dwellers living in slums is Southern Asia with 57.4 %. Eastern Asia is fourth with 34.8%, and Latin American/Caribbean is at 30.8%.

On top of that, because of the huge growth rate of the slums in sub-Saharan Africa, the population of slum dwellers within that region is expected to nearly double by 2020 (from 199 million in 2005 to about 400 million).[26] The picture is nothing but bad and getting worse for sub-Saharan Africa.

What Does Mumbai Have To Do With Norway & Sweden?

Have you ever heard of the city of Mumbai? Can you find Mumbai on a map? Here's a hint; you probably know Mumbai, but you likely know it by its former name. Here's another hint—it's in India. What's so special about Mumbai? It's soon to become a *metacity*. Never heard that term before? Get ready—you're going to be hearing it a lot in the coming years as more and more cities become one. Perhaps you've heard of its smaller cousin, the *megacity*. Megacities are small comparatively speaking; they are only half the size of their bigger cousin the *metacity*. While a megacity has a population of over 10 million people, a *metacity* has a population of twice that, 20 million people![27] Can you just imagine living in a city of 20 million people? What sorts of problems would be inherent in such an environment? The first *metacity* was Tokyo, but there is a list of megacities experiencing a growth rate that will push them over the 20 million mark in the next few years. That list of soon to be *metacities* includes Mumbai, Delhi, Mexico City, Sān Paulo, New York, Dhaka, Jakarta, and Lagos. These cities are almost unimaginably large—as big as entire countries, not in size of course. What does Mumbai have to do with Norway and Sweden? Not much except that Mumbai already has a larger population than those two countries combined![28] Oh, by the way, Mumbai is what used to be called Bombay.

What is Life Like in Kibera?

The short answer to the above question is this—life is nasty in Kibera. "On a typical day in Kibera, the smell of chips, *mandazi* (a local doughnut), and roast meat mingle with the odor of raw sewage. Plastic bags, some used as 'flying toilets' (bags that people defecate in and throw on the rooftops or just in the streets), litter the lanes that separate each shack."[29] Doesn't sound too great, does it?

The poor and the oppressed live in Kibera. It's a slum settlement within the city of Nairobi, the capital of Kenya. It's the densest and most populous slum settlement in the city with a population that nobody can really count—but it's estimated to be between 400,000 and 600,000.[30] While it certainly wouldn't be anybody's first choice to live there, many of residents "cited affordability as the most critical determinant of whether they would stay."[31] They simply are not able to afford even a low end one-bedroom apartment in another section of the city. Such a place would cost about $100 a month whereas most of the residents of Kibera earn less than $70 per month.

Patrick Obwaya lives in Kibera. He has lived there for more than 20 years in a one-room shack with no running water or toilet. He shares that small area with his three teenage sons. "On his walls, next to newspaper cutouts of Mother Teresa and Jomo Kenyatta, Kenya's first president, is a photo of him and his wife at their wedding."[32] He has not been able to afford to live with his wife for more than twenty years. Life is pretty nasty in Kibera.

Problems Faced by the Poor in Getting Around

The poor people of Karachi have horrible problems when trying to get from point A to point B within their own city. Yet, the urban poor of Karachi are not alone in their struggles with transport; it is a problem common to most urban poor throughout the developing world. The relationships between transportation and urban poverty are very complex and little studied.[33] However, Karachi was the focus of a study that graphically brings to our attention the types of difficulties the poor masses within an urban setting face daily.

First of all, are you able to locate Karachi on a map? It is, after all, a fair size city with a population of probably about 13 million people. I say "probably" because the last official government census in 1998 listed the city as having 9.8 million residents. However, the best guess estimate now is considerably higher. Satellite images from 1987 suggested that 37% of city's residents live in squatter settlements and another 34% live in semi-permanent, high-density dwellings.[34] Within that mass of settlements and humanity, a sewage system reaches only

40% of the city's population. It is a place where the average monthly income for households within the poor urban settlements is about US $25-42.[35]

> What is the experience of the urban poor with regard to transport? Interviews were conducted with 108 transport users living in eight low-income settlements of Karachi . . . the focus of the interviews was on bus, coach and minibus journeys.
>
> There is often intense competition, with drivers speeding and driving dangerously to get an edge over others. While the buses follow a specific route, stops are neither regular nor predetermined. They are free to pick up or drop off passengers anywhere along their route, sometimes stopping in the centre of the road, far from the curb.
>
> The bus drivers follow their own time schedules. They either speed dangerously to meet deadlines or stop in places for as long as 30 minutes waiting for the bus to fill up. . . . Often, at their own convenience, drivers choose to leave their trip unfinished and turn back midway, causing further problems for commuters.[36]

Can you imagine such things? Most of us on the rich side of the world will never have to put up with that sort of thing. But the above samples only scratch the surface of the multitude of problems faced by the urban poor in using public transport. For instance, they also face the burden of paying high fares. It is not unusual for the poor to spend 10% of their income on fares. Beyond that, the poor are not treated well. "The behaviour of the conductors and drivers is extremely rough and rude, they often do not return the change due after payment of the fare."[37] Other problems cited by interviewees include the lengthy duration of travel, limited hours of operation, absence of schedules, overcrowding, lack of safety, horrible pollution, and sexual harassment.

While Pakistan has a whole set of gender issues, the plight of poor women is epitomized by the fact that 48 different types of problems were cited by women who were interviewed. "The comments recorded varied widely and include the shortage of seats; seating on top of the hot engine cover; women not using empty seats in men's section; and harassment from male fellow-passengers (such as the rubbing of body parts, leers from drivers through mirrors and vulgar music) and conductors rudeness and unnecessary touching."[38] As Ayesha Hanif said in her interview, "The drivers make the college girls sit beside them on top of the engine compartment and then, with the excuse of needing to change gear, tries to touch them again and again."[39]

While I've never been in Karachi, I do have some vivid memories related to public transportation in Nairobi, Kenya. I remember being instructed by my host never to use public transportation—never! Now, I'm actually the type of guy who really prefers to take public transportation when visiting somewhere. I like riding the trams in Sofia, and I like riding buses in China. However, after seeing the *matatoos* of Nairobi, nobody had to tell me a second time not to travel by such a means. A *matatoo* is a kind of bus in which you jam about 600% over capacity on board while the driver wildly, and without any regard for your personal safety, transverses the streets at a quite unreasonable rate of speed. There is a kind of lore around Nairobi about *matatoo* drivers and the horrible accidents that are a common, daily experience within the city. I remember thinking, "Those people are all going to be killed," the first time I saw a *matatoo* weaving down the street. The fact is, for many of the poor in the crowded urban centers of the world, simple transportation is a daily struggle with frustration and danger.

Which Road Should We Take?

Being isolated and located far from good roads is oftentimes the situation with the poorest of the poor communities throughout the world. "In India many of the poorest villages are located 15-20 kilometers from the nearest infrastructure; during the rainy season villagers find themselves completely isolated from the more developed areas."[40] Such a state of affairs marginalizes those villagers in a variety of ways. They don't have access to health care or educational institutions beyond the primary level. Nor do the residents of villages with no easy access to roads have any real hope of effective inter-village or rural-urban trade.[41]

Can you imagine what your life would be like if you had to walk over three miles to the nearest road? Think about walking everywhere. I mean *everywhere*. Even if you walk the 15-20 kilometers to a road, your problems are not solved at that point, for it is very likely that it's a poor road that may be quite impassable much of the year. And even if the condition of the road is good, it may be a dangerous road that is frequented by bandits. In Kenya, government officials tend to avoid villages where the only access is by poor or dangerous roads. Of course, those officials are then unable to see, first-hand, the problems faced by the people in those remote areas, and the government doesn't initiate the type of changes necessary to correct the many dilemmas faced by the isolated villagers.[42]

World Bank sponsored fieldwork in seven rural villages in Ghana also revealed that poor roads were perceived by the local people as creating huge problems for the community, and the conditions of the roads were even seen by some as a "significant cause of poverty."[43] A group of men in the study spoke of how their road, the only connection to the market, was impassable during the long rainy season.[44] Consequently, "truck drivers charge very high fees to transport farmers' crops because of the rough road. As a result, the men say, a large share of their harvest remains on the farms, crating post-harvest losses and deterring farmers from improving yields."[45]

I live in Minnesota, and Minnesota roads have a notorious reputation among the people living there due to the pothole phenomenon. Because of the seasonal temperature extremes of Minnesota, especially the brutally cold winters followed by the spring thaw, the roads tend to develop numerous craters. These craters, known as potholes, can vary considerably in size, scope, and potential damage to your car. Of course, then there's the melting going on at the same time, so the potholes oftentimes fill with water. This creates a tricky hazard as one literally has to dodge every single pothole, for the one hole you fail to avoid typically will be very deep, but filled with water—it doesn't appear to the novice to present any great peril. I've learned; it's a big mistake if you don't assume that every pothole filled with water is a foot and a half deep. Of course, only about 3% of them are that deep, however if you've ever hit one of those at 35 MPH, you've learned your lesson. All of this to say, I have some experience with what we on the rich side of the world would call bad roads. However, I've also been on roads in Ethiopia and China that were more horrible than anything I've ever imagined. Many people in remote, rural regions of the world face nightmarish roads and the multitude of problems those create. Being poor might well mean walking 15 kilometers to the nearest road, or it may mean being stranded and isolated because the road is totally impassable. When I think of that, all of a sudden, potholes are not such a problem.

NOTES

1. United Nations Human Settlements Programme, *State of the World's Cities 2006/7.* (Nairobi: UN-HABITAT, 2006), x.

2. Ibid., 19.

3. Idem.

4. Idem.

5. Ibid., viii.

6. Beth Chitekwe and Diana Mitlin, "The Urban Poor Under Threat and in Struggle: Option for Urban Development in Zimbabwe, 1995-2000" *Environment & Urbanization* 13 (2001): 91.

7. Narayan, Patel, Schafft, Rademacher, and Koch-Schulte, *Voices*, 59.

8. World Bank, *Visual Participatory Poverty Assessment* (Washington, D.C.: World Bank, 1994).

9. United Nations Human Settlements Programme, *State of the World's Cities 2006/7*, viii.

10. Ibid., 36.

11. Ibid., viii.

12. David Sanderson, "Cities, disasters and livelihoods," *Environment & Urbanization* 12 (2000): 93.

13. Ibid., 93-94.

14. Idem.

15. Idem.

16. Ibid., 101.

17. World Bank, *World Development Report 2004*, 7.

18. Idem.

19. Idem.

20. Janice Perlman, "The Chronic Poor in Rio de Janeiro: What has Changed in 30 Years?" in *Managing Urban Futures: Sustainability and Urban Growth in Developing Countries* (eds. Marco Keiner *et. al.*; Burlington, VT: Ashgate, 2005).

21. Jancie Perlman and Molly O'Meara Sheehan, "Fighting Poverty and Environmental Injustice in Cities." in *State of the World 2007: Our Urban Future* (ed. Linda Starke; New York: W.W. Norton & Company, 2007), 175.

22. Luke Dowdney, *Children of the Drug Trade* (Rio de Janeiero: Viveiros de Castro Editoria, 2003).

23. Perlman and Sheehan, "Fighting Poverty," 175.

24. Idem.

25. United Nations Human Settlements Programme, *State of the World's Cities 2006/7*, 11.

26. Idem.

27. United Nations Human Settlements Programme, *State of the World's Cities 2006/7*, 6.

28. Idem.

29. Rasna Warah, "Life in Kibera," in *State of the World 2007: Our Urban Future* (ed. Linda Starke; New York: W.W. Norton & Company, 2007), 148.

30. Idem.

31. Idem.

32. Ibid., 149.

33. Urban Resource Center, "Urban Poverty and Transport: A Case Study From Karachi," *Environment & Urbanization* 13 (2001): 223-33.

34. Arif Hasan, *Understanding Karachi* (Karachi: City Press, 1999).

35. Urban Resource Center, "Urban Poverty," 224.

36. Ibid., 226.

37. Idem.

38. Ibid., 229.

39. Idem.

40. Narayan, Patel, Schafft, Rademacher, and Koch-Schulte, *Voices*, 46.

41. Centre for Community Economics and Development Consultants Society, *Report on Social Assessment for the District Poverty Initiatives Project: Baran District* (Jaipur, India: Institute of Development Studies, 1997); Jesko Hentschel, William Waters, and Anna Kathryn Vandever Webb, "Rural Poverty in Ecuador—A Qualitative Assessment," (Washington, D.C.: World Bank, 1996).

42. Deepa Narayan, and David Nyamwaya, "Learning from the Poor: A participatory Poverty Assessment in Kenya," (Washington, D.C.: World Bank, 1996).

43. Ernest Kunfaa and Tony Dogbe, "Empty Pockets," in *Voices of the Poor: From Many Lands* (eds. Deepa Narayan and Patti Petesch; New York: Oxford University Press, 2002), 24.

44. Idem.

45. Idem.

CHAPTER 9

Toilets of the Poor:
Issues of Water and Sanitation

Toilets Aren't Funny If You Don't Have One

My wife, Pat, has had an interesting project underway for a few years. She collects pictures of toilets and bathrooms from around the world—from places we've traveled or locations to which our friends have gone. On one of our latest trips to China with a group of students, she gave them the assignment to take some pictures of interesting toilets for her. She's good at getting others involved in the project. Our bathroom wall displays a montage of shots from around the world. I rather like the one of a powder-blue outhouse in foothills of southern California with the sign, "CAUTION! Watch for Rattlesnakes" posted on the door. Our bathroom gallery is a great conversation piece as just about everyone who visits our house remarks what an interesting bathroom wall we have. Of course, the point is not to make fun of others, it's to display the array of how people live—it's really quite anthropological of my wife to undertake such a project. I find that people are really interested by the range of facilities throughout the world. I know Pat has a book in mind with the bathroom theme portrayed in a photographic essay, and I am anxiously anticipating its appearance.

While there is, within our culture, a certain amount of bathroom humor, it is also certainly true that toilets aren't funny if you don't have one. Unfortunately, there is a huge number of people in the world that don't have access to such a luxury as *any type* of sanitation facility. Without a doubt, basic sanitation is a huge element in assessing one's quality of living. It's one of the basic indicators of determining if one lives in a slum or not.[1] As you might think, access to basic sanitation has huge implications for the health factors within a given population. Yet, as it now stands, over one-quarter of the urban population in the developing world does not have adequate sanitation.[2] China and India, in particular, are noteworthy for the shear number of people living without proper sanitation. In spite of that, those countries have been making good advances as of late in improving access. Thus, while studies show that "South-Eastern Asia and Southern Asia have made significant progress in recent years to improve sanitation coverage in urban areas, access lags far behind in sub-Saharan Africa and Eastern Asia, where 45 per cent and 31 per cent of the urban population still lacks access to improved sanitation respectively."[3]

One place hit particularly hard by this situation is Afghanistan. That country, which has undergone such horrendous heartache yields a statistic which is numbing—if one takes the entire urban population of that country, only 16% of the people have access to adequate sanitation facilities. The ramifications are stark. People die without proper sanitation facilities. The number of people throughout the world who die each year because of poor sanitation and resultant hygiene problems may be as high as 1.6 million—yes, that's MILLION.[4]

What Happens Downstream From Kumasi?

When people don't have access to sanitation, it is oftentimes those who live downstream a bit who suffer from that situation. In Africa, as a whole, only about 60% of the people have decent sanitation facilities. Certain countries, such as Rwanda and Congo are much worse off. In those two countries less 15% of the urban populations have adequate sanitation coverage.[5] Ghana is another country suffering from a very poor sanitation infrastructure. "More than 70 percent of households in three of Ghana's ten administrative regions have no toilet facilities in or near their homes."[6] Naturally, the consequences of such circumstances is most acute in the urban areas that have a high density of population.

A good example of such a place is the city of Kumasi, Ghana which has a population of 1.2 million people. It's a place where only 8% of the people have toilets that are actually connected to a sewage system.[7] About 12% of the population in Kumasi uses what are known as pan latrines. Those of us who view things from the rich side of the world are probably not familiar with the terminology nor with the construction of such a thing. It consists of a pan or a bucket that is placed under a raised platform of sorts within a house. It is emptied manually by workers who come to perform their task, normally about every third day.[8]

Because wastewater in Kumasi is produced from the general population, not industry, huge increases in population in the last few decades combined with lack of governmental investment in sanitation infrastructure have overwhelmed the existing facilities. The result is that large volumes of untreated or partially treated wastewater finds its way to the many streams that flow through the city. Downstream these contaminated waters are used for irrigation. Consequently, high levels of faecal coliform are found, not only in the city, but also on vegetables sold in the markets.

It seems that for the farmers who live downstream from the city, the most common form of irrigation is simply to use watering cans and pour the contaminated water directly onto the crops. This raises, considerably, the likelihood of crop contamination. Yet, it seems that the poor farmers are so concerned about their income from selling their vegetables that they don't see anything wrong in using the contaminated water on their crops. After all, their very livelihood depends on the water they use to irrigate their crops. Everyone knows the water is contaminated water—both the farmers and the people who buy the vegetables know it. "Among the interviewed consumers, eight out of ten know that some farmers used polluted water, and almost all of them knew that this could have health implications. . . . Only 10 per cent suggested stopping the farm use of polluted water. Despite this knowledge, there was very little demand and incentive for safer food production."[9]

Think about using a pan latrine in your house that is only emptied every third day. Think about eating a piece of fruit you just bought from the local stand, knowing full-well that, in all likelihood, it had contaminated water poured directly into it. Think about what it would be like to be poor and be living in Kumasi. Think about the fact that there are over a million people sleeping there tonight. I hope that they have sweet dreams, but I suspect that is a rarity.

Access to Water and Toilets in India

Listen to the voice of Jayashree Gautam Waghmare, a slum dweller who was interviewed by researchers Meera Bapat and Indu Agarwal as they conducted research among the inhabitants of some of the slum areas of the cities of Mumbai and Pune in India.

> We had to cross two railway tracks to fetch water. We paid 100 rupees for water every month and could collect as much water as we wanted. But there was such a crowd that sometimes we could not get any water. The tap was only five minutes walk away, but because we had to cross the railway tracks it used to worry us. As we balanced *handaas* full of water on our heads, it used to be difficult to know which side the train was coming from. Even when we were warned about the approaching train, we did not know which way to run. We used to go to fetch water at four in the morning. Even my parents-in-law used to fetch water. There were seven of us in the house, so we needed lots of water. We used to stand in the queue, fill our *handaas* and take them home, and then queue again for a second round. Each tap had at least 25 people queuing.
> . . . we used the railway tracks as toilets. We used to go between midnight and four in the morning because at other times there were people around. Men would go in the daytime also, but women could not do that. We sat between the railway tracks, and, if a train came, we used to jump onto the other track. There were frequent accidents and, every week or so, someone used to get hit by a train and got killed on the tracks. So, many times, we used to find pieces of flesh outside our doors.[10]

What do you hear in that voice? Try to think of at least three words which describe the feelings or emotions that Jayashree Gautam Waghmare is communicating to us through this portion of her interview. Write those words in the margin of this book, right next to the tale. I penciled in "frustrated," "humiliated," and "exhausted." I felt the *frustration* of constant battle to get water. I felt *humiliation* at having to use the railway tracks as toilets. I felt *exhaustion* in having to go to the toilet (or tracks) between midnight and four, and then getting water at four.

Just in case you were wondering, Jayashree's experience is not unique nor exaggerated—there are many very similar stories by the people of that region. Listen to Mangal Sadashiv Kamble's description of her situation concerning access to water and toilets.

> There used to be many people who came to fill the water and they came from far. I used to drop my children at school and then go to fetch water around one o'clock in the afternoon. I used to finish filling water by five in the evening. To fill one *handaa*, I needed to stand in the queue for one hour. I would take it home, empty it and go back and stand in the queue again. . . . If I was not well, my husband used to fetch the water in the evening after he returned from work.
>
> For toilets, we had to use the railway tracks. There were public toilets, but they were some distance away—about half an hour walk. They used to be so dirty that we did not feel like using them. And there were such long queues! Instead of using those filthy toilets, we used to go on the tracks after ten at night or early in the morning at four or five o'clock.[11]

The slums of India are a nasty place to live. The picture which emerges from interviews with the residents is that one spends a considerable portion of one's day walking to where there is water, waiting in line for the water, transporting the water home, returning for more water, waiting in line again for water, transporting more water home, and staying up late or arising very early to go to the railroad tracks or some other open place to defecate. What is it like to be among the poor and the oppressed? While we on the rich side of the world normally catch just a glimpse of them, these voices of the poor in India give us a rather vivid window of insight into their lives, don't you think?

The Life of Jyoti Bhende

You don't know Jyoti Bhende. He lives in one of the slum settlements of the city of Pune in India. I've never been there, but it sounds like an interesting place. Of its population of 2.8 million, about a million people live in slums scattered around the city. Like many slum settlements throughout the world, there is a problem with easy access to clean water. Listen in as Jyoti tells a little bit about his life as a poor slum-dweller to researchers studying water and sanitation in the area.

I live in Jaibhavani Nagar on Parvanti Hill. It is part of a very large slum area. My shack is near the top of the hill. Until seven years ago, there was no piped water supply anywhere in the settlement. There were just three water taps near the toilets.

I used to get up in the morning and first bring two *handaas* of water from the taps near the toilets. Sometimes, the toilets would get blocked and nobody did anything to get them repaired. Filthy water used to collect near the urinals. And we had to fill the water in all that mess. There used to be flies and insects flying all around. They would fall in the water. There are neither paved pathways in our settlement nor are there properly laid out drains. People have made trenches to carry off the wastewater. When my children were small, they used to follow me when I went to fetch the water. Sometimes, they would fall into the trenches. So, half my attention was on my children. In addition to this worry was the anxiety to get to work on time.[12]

As one might well expect, water and sanitation are inexorably linked. Jyoti's health, and the lives of his children are in peril because of the conditions he describes as his everyday way of life. Of course, these conditions are not unique only to Pune, or to India. Worldwide, those who live in slums always face the hazard of water contamination because of inadequate sanitation facilities. In the late 1990s there was a series of cholera outbreaks in East Africa which began "in slums, where rainwater washed accumulated human waste into boreholes and other water sources and spread quickly throughout Kenya, Tanzania and Uganda."[13] Yet, much more common than cholera is the threat of diarrhea. While that may not sound as bad, or as serious to your ear, the fact of the matter is that diarrhea is a huge killer of children.

Latrines Are Scary Places

For a small child the world can be full of scary places. I have a very faint memory of being afraid the first time I was in some sort of a scary funhouse at the state fair. You know those things they call a *funhouse*; they have a winding corridor that leads you through all sorts of rooms with creepy things jumping out at you here and there. I was probably about six years old, and I vaguely recall being in a darkened area and not being able to find my way out. I think a split second before I was about to let out a blood-curdling scream my sister pulled me to safety.

A public latrine is a place you may not have thought of as a particularly scary place, but in fact, it can be a very frightening spot for many young kids in the developing world. Think about it, they are dark and dank with an unforgiving smell. Not only that, there is almost always an open pit. "The fear of falling in is not unreasonable—it happens. Reports from both Malawi and Nepal point out that children rarely use latrines until the are five to seven years old because of their fear of falling into the pit."[14]

While you may think this is just an irrational fear of a child too young to know any better, it does happen. Kids *do* fall into latrine pits. In fact, I have a first-hand account for you. No, I didn't fall into a latrine pit, but the four-year-old daughter of some very good friends of mine fell into a sewage culvert. I wasn't an eyewitness, but my dear friends e-mailed me the account of their harrowing experience of nearly losing their daughter. It happened recently in the Yunnan Province of Southwest China.

They were in a restaurant for a wedding celebration in the town in which they work. It was a festive night, and the kids were running around and playing. When it was time to go home they started to gather the family, but their youngest daughter was nowhere to be found. Frantic, they, along with all the other wedding guests, searched high and low. Desperate, crying, and in a panic they finally ended up at the local police station as some of the Chinese nationals took them there in the hope of getting the police involved in the search. There, to everyone's surprise, was their daughter—covered from head to toe in sewage and sobbing uncontrollably.

The story actually takes an even more dramatic turn. After unraveling what happened, it became very clear that it was a miracle that their daughter actually survived her fall into the scary pit. After taking a tumble into the sewage line coming from a latrine, she was swept into an underground culvert and carried for several blocks in complete blackness by flowing water and sewage two to three feet deep. She popped up above ground where the culvert emerges from under a footbridge. There, the water flows in the open for about 20 feet before the flow again submerges underground for a distance of about 20 kilometers where it next surfaces above ground again in the neighboring village. It was there, in that 20-foot span where the water flowed in plain view that the miracle happened. By the grace of God, a villager was standing along the bank, right next to the stream when the little child popped up like a bobber. He reached into the water and yanked her out in the knick of time. Had he not been there, she would have been carried underground by the swiftly moving current until her little body would have come out in the next village over six miles away.

The whole town now recognizes her as a "miracle child," and the peasant who saved her life is the town hero who my friends recognized by throwing a huge banquet in his honor. My friends sent me a couple of photos, one was the pit in the restaurant she fell into and one was that portion of the culvert where little Mia popped up and was pulled safely to shore. While this story has a very happy ending, one might wonder how many kids across the world have the same story, but with no town hero there on the spot to rescue them.

Indeed, children have a good reason to see a latrine pit as a scary place. Of course, the child's fear of the latrine inevitably leads to other problems. The child, in fear of falling into the pit, simply chooses to squat outside, and

their caregivers can be excused for allowing them to do so. It does not require many small children taking this option for an area to become completely fouled. Considering the number of young children in any poor urban settlement, it is no wonder that community latrines fail in most cases to be an adequate solution.[15]

The sad fact is, throughout the world, huge health problems exist, in part, because of something as fixable as inadequate sanitation facilities. Naturally, we who are on the rich side of the world generally don't have to hassle with such problems—that is, unless we travel to the poor side of the world.

Postscript—after writing this little piece, I visited our friends in China, and they took me to the very spot of the miracle. It was sobering, and yet inspiring. There's no way she should have lived as she was sucked underground in water over her head. I stood right at the spot where the old Chinese guy reached in a pulled her out of the water. Again, as I stood there, I wondered how many little kids around the world don't get pulled out.

Access to Safe Water

In developing countries, one person out of every five individuals does not have access to safe drinking water; that is more than one billion people. Another 2.4 billion people lack access to improved sanitation. Since diarrhea is known to be a killer of young children, this is literally a life and death situation. In the decade of the 1990s this lack of access to safe water killed more children than the sum total of everyone killed in wars since World War II. Naturally, those hit the hardest were poor people in rural and slum areas.[16]

Now, what flashes through your mind when you walk to the kitchen faucet and turn on the water? How many times have you filled your glass with clean, safe water and gulped it down? I do it all the time; after all, aren't they telling us that we should be drinking eight glasses of water a day? In much of the world, drinking eight glasses a day of readily available, safe water is simply not a possibility.

Kick the Can & Carry the Can

I have very fond memories of playing a game called *Kick the Can* when I was a youngster of about eight or nine years. I liked the game, as I remember, because I was pretty good at it. I remember summer evenings about dusk, and the usual contingent of neighborhood kids would gather in somebody's back yard to play a rousing game of *Kick the Can*. Like many childhood games, rules can vary a bit from location to location, but the gist of the game is this. One person is *it*. That person sets a can, upside-down, in an open area. All the other players go hide themselves as the person who is *it* counts to 100 or whatever. The object is then for the ones who are hiding to run "home" and kick the can before they are tagged by the player who is *it*. The player who is *it* tries to find those who are hiding, but doesn't want to stray too far from the can which she/he is trying to keep from being kicked.

Of course I grew up on the rich side of the world. I played *Kick the Can* in a nice, safe backyard. Many kids in the undeveloped world, the world of poverty, play a different kind of game every single day. Let's call their game *Carry the Can*. The rules of that game are pretty set. The goal of the game is to survive. In order to reach the goal, you have to carry water from point A to point B. In the urban slums of Bangladesh, the average trip to collect water is thirty minutes, and you have to make at least two trips per day.[17] Two trips are needed because "the quantity of water available to a household is considered even more important than the water quality in ensuring the conditions necessary for children's health and survival."[18] Just as one might expect, it's the kids who are oftentimes the water carriers in poor-urban settings. Now, here's the not-so-fun part of *Carry the Can*. Water is heavy, and carrying the needed load of water twice a day can be physically debilitating for the child. Many will suffer from neck, spine and head injuries for the rest of their life.[19] I know I don't like to carry water; it's very heavy. But then, I never had to play *Carry the Can* when I was a youngster. Did you?

No Running Water

What is a fairly foolproof method for being able to tell the difference between the poor and the non-poor? The answer is *water security*, that is, easy access to safe water. In rural regions of the Kyrgyz Republic, less than half the houses (45%) have access to running water.[20]

It's No Bed of Roses

Living on top of a garbage dump is no bed of roses. Someone from the rich side of the world might well ask, "Why would *anyone* live on a garbage dump?" That's actually not a bad question from someone with our perspective—a perspective from the rich side of the world. The answer comes to us from the urban poor of this world who do, in fact, live atop garbage dumps and eek out a living amid almost indescribable conditions. An interesting case study of a garbage dump that served as a village for some of the urban poor in Seoul, South Korea is the slum of Nanjido. Judged as "one of the worst dwelling areas for the urban poor in Seoul . . . most of the residents . . . live by collecting and selling garbage."[21] From 1978 until 1992 all the garbage in Seoul was dumped in Nanjido. Since then, dumping has ceased there, and Nanjido is no longer functioning as a dump or as a living village with all the residents who lived there when the study was made. A new dumping area has been opened "in Kumpo which is 14.7 kilometres from the city. All the garbage pickers in Nanjido have left and there is no data on where they have gone."[22] However, that does not diminish the relevancy of the case of Nanjido—it serves as a vivid example. After all, there are still plenty of garbage villages across the world, and they all pretty much mirror the dynamics of what life was like for the residents of Nanjido.

A day on the top of the garbage dump is difficult to describe with words; one really needs to be there in order to fully appreciate any written description of the odor. Essentially, the residents employ basic survival strategies while living in deep poverty that help them increase their income as much as it is possible within that setting. There are two groups of pickers. "The first-picking group collects the recyclable materials immediately after the trucks dump the garbage, and their goods are more valuable than those of the second-picking group. To be first-pickers, they have to pay for the right to collect the garbage. But the second-picking group are free to collect the garbage without any payment."[23] Since garbage-picking is heavy work, it is possible for second-pickers who are who are healthier and heartier to make more money than some of the first-pickers.[24]

One of the best of the survival strategies employed by those living in poverty is to increase their labor as much a possible since that is usually the only available avenue they have to increase their income. That is, they try to make more by working more. "Another option is to bring other family members into the labour market."[25] Hence, small children are part of the family practice of picking and sorting through the dump. Also, it's typically a long day of toil on the mound as "65 per cent of residents work for more than 11 hours a day."[26] The pickers earn money based on a system that is commonly known as piece-work or piece-rate work whereby one is paid by the number of hours one works and the efficiency or intensity of work.

Another survival strategy employed by the poor is that of minimizing expenditures. At the Nanjido dump consumption by the residents was very low due, of course, to the low level of income. Nevertheless, they minimized their expenditure of housing and travel by living right on the dump. Expenditures are further reduced by reduced use of medicines. Yet, "because of the poor housing environment and because of the strenuous work, the probability of contracting diseases or injuries is very high. . . . Accident rates are very high because the garbage has to be collected quickly whilst the garbage trucks and bulldozers are still moving."[27] Working under such conditions, the garbage pickers "usually drink two or three bottles of hard liquor every day. The vicious circle of overdrinking and overwork accelerates the deterioration of their productivity."[28]

Given the disastrous environment of the dump, it is truly amazing that 84% of those residents who were interviewed indicated that they moved to the Nanjido dump to live through a recommendation of a friend or relative. It's difficult for us who view things from the rich side of the world to fathom, but for some of the world's urban poor, moving to a garbage heap is a step up. It presents them with opportunities to employ survival strategies they might, otherwise, not be able to implement. When one is looking merely to survive the day, even a garbage dump may seem like the best option out there.

NOTES

1. United Nations Human Settlements Programme, *State of the World's Cities 2006/7*, 19.

2. Ibid., xi.

3. Idem.

4. Idem.

5. Keraita, Drechsel and Amoah, "Urban Wastewater," 171.

6. Ibid., 172.

7. Ibid., 173.

8. Idem.

9. Ibid., 177.

10. Bapat and Agarwal, "Our Needs, Our Priorities," 76-77.

11. Ibid., 77.

12. Bapat and Agarwal, "Our Needs, Our Priorities," 83.

13. United Nations Human Settlements Programme, *State of the World's Cities 2006/7*, 131.

14. Bartlett, "Children's experience," 66-67.

15. Ibid., 67.

16. United Nations Development Programme, *Human Development Report 2003*, 9.

17. R. Afsar, "Rural-Urban Dichotomy and Convergence: Emerging Realities in Bangladesh." *Environment and Urbanization* 11 (1999): 235-247.

18. Bartlett, "Children's experience," 65.

19. A. Nicol, *Carrying the Can: Children and their Water Environments* (London: Save the Children UK, 1998).

20. Narayan, Patel, Schafft, Rademacher, and Koch-Schulte, *Voices*, 47.

21. Ik Ki Kim, "Differentiation among the urban poor and the reproduction of poverty: the case of Nanjido," *Environment and Urbanization* 7 (1995): 185.

22. Ibid., 186.

23. Ibid., 188.

24. Idem.

25. Ibid., 189.

26. Idem.

27. Ibid., 191-92.

28. Ibid., 193.

CHAPTER 10

Governments, Corruption and Armed Conflict

Even Before the Conflict Begins, Things go Bad

It seems like there has been a non-stop series of armed conflicts in West and Central Africa over the past decade. Indeed, in places like Liberia, Côte d'Ivoire, the Democratic Republic of the Congo, and Sierra Leone armed conflict has ruled the day for a long time. Yet, even before armed conflict broke out in any of those places, bad things started to happen. That is to say, it is typical in a pre-conflict period for there to be a deterioration in certain key services in a country or region. Naturally, as one might predict, the collapse of services most dramatically will impact those people who are in most need of the services, that is, the very poor. What types of services usually face a breakdown in an immediate pre-conflict period? Certainly things like health care and education suffer.

Young women are especially susceptible to the sorts of health care problems that typically arise right before the outbreak of armed conflict. For example, they face an increased "vulnerability to physical abuse and sexually transmitted infections, particularly HIV/AIDS, increases during conflicts due to the high mobility of troops and internally displaced persons, and the use of sexual violence as a strategic and tactical weapon of war."[1] It has been reported that under such conditions, the great majority of women and girls who were injured by sexual assaults "are either unable to access appropriate medical treatment or are deterred from seeking assistance for fear of being stigmatized."[2]

In the case of the fighting in Liberia from 2002-2003 there was a huge increase in the maternal mortality rate because of the lack of obstetric care. During the war, less than half of the clinics in the country were operating.[3] The Democratic Republic of the Congo yielded the same dramatic rise in maternal mortality rate during its most recent foray into armed conflict as pregnant women were two to three times more likely to die of violent causes than other women.[4] Thus, even before the war begins and certainly while it rages, there are plenty of victims, and those victims will almost inevitably be predominately women and young girls.

Life After A Civil War

Life is very messy after a civil war. Indeed, the fact of the matter is, "civil wars continue to kill people indirectly, well after the shooting stops."[5] In that sense, the human misery that is a result of a civil war persists for extended periods of time after the fighting has ceased, and the consequential suffering is the bulk of the iceberg with the actual civil war, itself, accurately characterized as only the tip—a small, visible portion of the massive entity.[6] Make no mistake about it, there is definitely not a shortage of wars, the majority of which could be defined as civil war. There's plenty to go around. For instance, in a just a six year period (1989-1995) there were anywhere from 31 to 54 recorded conflicts in EACH of those years. At any one time, 15 major wars were occurring.[7]

The faces of those who are killed as a result of war is quickly changing. More and it is the civilian population that suffers the brunt of the casualties. For instance,

> In the American Civil War (1861-65) and World War I (1914-18) is estimated that 95 per cent of the casualties were soldiers. In World War II, civilian and combatant casualties were roughly equal. In Bosnia, Rwanda and Somalia it has been estimated that perhaps as many as 95 per cent of casualties were civilians.[8]

It is thought that that as many as 90% of all war deaths in the late 20th century, *i.e.* since WWII, have been civilian.[9] Yet, it is the aftermath of the actual fighting that produces, in large measure, long-range and intense human suffering. While studies of the long-term impact of civil war upon health care systems and public health are growing in number, it is still a relatively new arena of investigation. Examples of such studies include: the impact of infectious disease and the breakdown of health care over a period of one year after conflicts,[10] an analysis of tuberculosis in the Guinea-Bissau conflict,[11] and a stunning report that deaths from disease as the result of the civil war was six times more frequent than deaths from the actual fighting in the Congo.[12]

A wide variety of conditions that expose civilian populations to increased risks of death, injury, or disease are the natural result of civil war or armed conflicts within a country. One of the problems that always figures in such a situation is that of displaced persons. Civil wars are notorious for producing refuges. For instance, the civil war in Rwanda "generated not only 1.4 million internally displaced persons, but another 1.5 million refugees into neighboring Zaire, Tanzania, and Burundi."[13] Even after the war was over, most of them were not able to return home, but remained in camps, oftentimes for years. In that environment of over-crowding, poor sanitation and bad water, the people were hit by tuberculosis, cholera, typhoid, measles, pneumonia, and dysentery.

In the 1994 genocide of Rwanda about 800,000 people were killed; that is about 10% of the population.[14] Not only was the infrastructure of the country decimated, but HIV/AIDS ran rampant because of the flood of rape and violence. The long-term impact is still being felt as 85,000 households are headed by children.[15]

Child Soldiers

It is estimated that, at any given time, over 300,000 children are exploited as soldiers in various armed conflicts around the world. One of the best-known cases of overt use of children as soldiers comes from Uganda where a movement known as the Lord's Resistance Army (LRA) for years readily forced and recruited kids to fight for them. One study found that the average age of the children who had unwittingly become a part of the rebellion in northern Uganda was just over 12 years.[16] The average time spent as a child-soldier was over two years (744 days), and 39% of the kids who were interviewed said that they had killed someone while they were a part of the Lord's Resistance Army.[17] The LRA's fighting force grew from a meager force of about 200 to an estimated 14,000 soldiers who were predominantly child-soldiers.[18]

Horrific descriptions abound about the brutality and oppression foisted upon people by the child soldiers.[19] All populations within reach of the LRA have suffered incredible evil, and it has gone on for years and years and years. Nobody has done much. The latest move by the UN is a mere warning.

> The Security Council Working Group on Children and Armed Conflict today adopted recommendations regarding children in armed conflict in Uganda and Somalia, was well as examining recent report by the Secretary-General on the situation in Chad and the Democratic Republic of the Congo (DRC).
> The Working Group called on the Lord's Resistance Army in Uganda to unconditionally release children used in their ranks.[20]

Unfortunately, warnings from the UN generally don't carry much force in the world of evil and oppressive regimes. Far beyond that, even if LRA and its ruthless leader Joseph Kony were immediately dismantled, the long-term impact upon the children of Uganda will never be able to be fully measured.

Much of the problem of the LRA abducting children for the purpose of making them soldiers had its origin in 1994. It was then that the government of Sudan greatly increased the sale of arms to the LRA. The result was that they had guns, mortars and landmines than they had people to use the munitions. "It was from this date that the mass abduction of young people began."[21] Of course, once a child is forcefully secured for military service, there is a certain amount of training necessary to transform the child into an efficient soldier.

In the LRA, for example, recruits physical fitness is assessed and then built up by having them run around the camp's perimeters while carrying stones on the their shoulders. Those who spill the stones or collapse are killed. Those who disobey during marksmanship training risk having their fingers cut off.[22]

Tragic as the situation has been in Uganda, it's only one example of a much broader reality. The very sobering fact is that the phenomenon of child soldiers is certainly not unique to Uganda. Nor it is unique to Africa. In fact, it's virtually a worldwide occurrence that kids are active combatants. In the last 15 years alone "child soldiers have fought in Colombia, Ecuador, El Salvador, Guatemala, Mexico (in the Chiapas conflict), Nicaragua, Paraguay, and Peru."[23] Surprised? Would you be surprised that another thirty countries could be added to that list—countries in Europe, Asia, and Africa? Take, for example, the case of Ishmael Beah whose best selling book graphically depicts his life as a child soldier in Sierra Leone. In one of his vivid recollections he recounts the following episode.

My face, my hands, my shirt and gun were covered with blood. I raised my gun and pulled the trigger, and I killed a man. Suddenly, as if someone was shooting them inside my brain, all the massacres I had seen since the day I was touched by war began flashing in my head. Every time I stopped shooting to change magazines and saw my two young lifeless friends, I angrily pointed my gun into the swamp and killed more people. I shot everything that moved, until we were ordered to retreat because we needed another strategy.[24]

The reality of child soldiers is numbing. How must they view life? How have we enabled such atrocities to have been and continue to be placed upon minds and bodies of children—simply because they are in a poor, war-torn country? Perhaps we can consider that in the face of such a frightful evil, prayer penetrates the mind and heart of God.

Father, forgive us. How can we allow such a thing? Is it not, in any way, our responsibility to do something? We perceive ourselves as not being able, as an individual, to do anything against this horrific evil. Yet prayer is the great enabler. Might we not be able to intercede for child soldiers? We don't know their names, but that shouldn't inhibit our prayers for them. Many are missing fingers or legs. We don't know their particular situation. We know only that they are in crisis. However, we are able to pray for them—aren't we? What power does an intercessory prayer have? I'm not sure we can fully comprehend that. However, Lord, I do believe that feeble words drawn from a compassionate heart are able to move and incite You to action on behalf of the children in warfare. Hear our prayer Lord. Redeem captive children. Make ways for them to escape. Reunite them with parents. Deliver them from very real and powerful evil. Heal their minds, their consciousness, from the nightmares of their recollections of war. Sustain them and heal them in the name of Jesus. Amen.

The Toll of Violent Conflict

During the decade of the 1990's nearly 60 countries were involved, on some level, in violent conflict. The obvious toll of tribal, ethnic, or national violence is that people die. Yet, the impact is incredibly far reaching beyond the obvious. For instance, "conflict can undermine economies, destabilize governments, damage infrastructure, disrupt social service delivery and provoke mass movements of people. More than 14 million people face hunger due to present or recent conflicts."[25]

One of the outcroppings of conflict is the rapid spread of infectious disease. HIV/AIDS is a prime example as it is not unusual for Sub-Saharan militias to have more than half of the soldiers be HIV positive. Yet, when one looks at infant mortality in areas of conflict, the data can be a little confusing. First, one sees the expected. Much higher infant mortality rates resulted from conflict in places like Ethiopia, Uganda, and Liberia. However, quite unexpectantly, infant mortality dropped in Guatemala, El Salvador, and Mozambique during sustained period of violent conflict.[26]

Young Girls in Conflict—The Case of Sierra Leone

In most of the armed conflicts around the world, it's oftentimes the civilians who suffer the most, and among them it's usually the poor and vulnerable who are picked on most of the time. Most soldiers in armed conflicts are usually pretty good at intimidating the weakest elements of society. They are purposeful in what they do as "violence against civilians is used as a military tactic, and is not just a by-product of the normal course of war."[27] That was certainly the case in the civil war that raged in Sierra Leone for over a decade. While the war was officially declared over in January 2002, the ramifications of that conflict will continue in the lives of thousands upon thousands of people for years to come. During the course of the war, over "100,000 people were mutilated, and over one quarter of a million women were raped."[28]

Conflicts in West and Central Africa have been decimating, especially to women. In Liberia, Côte d'Ivoire, the Democratic Republic of the Congo, and Sierra Leone "the epidemic proportions of gross sexual violence have resulted in such extreme psychological and physical damage that many, if not most, will never fully recover."[29] In 2000 field research was conducted in Sierra Leone which revealed that of "733 randomly selected women who were interviewed, 383 (52 per cent) said they had been subjected to sexual violence."[30] The impact of such abuse is acute and as the examples below demonstrate.

> Victims of sexual violence become social pariahs. They are rejected by their husbands, families and communities, and face impoverishment and humiliation. One woman interviewed had been forced to relocate to Bukavu [Democratic Republic of the Congo], where she sold avocados and struggled to support

herself and her six children. Another woman who had been raped by several combatants became pregnant and was forced to flee to Goma, where she lived in the ruins of destroyed houses and eked out a living by transporting heavy loads.[31]

Everyone agrees that vulnerable people who are caught in the middle of a conflict must be protected by the international community, especially the U.N., both during and after the fighting. The sad fact of the matter is, however, that doesn't often happen.

Safi was 17 Years Old

Some of the most horrible things I read as I did research for this book were the stories of how armed conflicts around the world have impacted people, particularly the poor and the oppressed. There is definitely no shortage of armed conflicts—they're all over the place. One particular study focuses upon recent conflicts in Western and Central Africa where Côte d'Ivoire, the Democratic Republic of the Congo, Liberia and Sierra Leone have all experienced intense periods of warfare.[32] The scope of suffering produced by these conflicts is impossible to measure; even collecting statistics and interviewing survivors does not suffice. However, the statistics and the interviews are telling.

The following portions of a first person account give you a peak through a horribly disturbing window. It is a narrative that will stay with you and will, perhaps, even haunt you. One cannot read Safi's story and not feel the pain from what war has done to her.

> My name if Safi. I come from Uvira, Democratic Republic of the Congo, near the Burundi border. I am 17 years old. It was April 2002 when they came to our house. It was six armed men. They pushed their way into our home with their guns. We were all there—my mother, my father, my older brother, and my four younger brothers and sisters. They told my father, 'You papa, You must have sex with your daughter in front of us. Now!' They pushed me to the centre of the room My father pleaded with them that he could not do that, that it was wrong and that I was just a child. The men laughed at him. Then, they shot him dead in front of all of us.
>
> The men then grabbed my older brother and me by the arm and forced us out of the house. We walked a little way and then they pushed me into the forest. The forced me to have sex with them many times. I felt like I was watching from the outside. Like I was watching a bad film. Then I don't remember anything. For the next three months I was held as their prisoner at their military camp. During that whole time, I felt I was going crazy. I was like a person unconscious. I was alive but not living. Every day they raped me. I stayed there for a long time—more than one year. I was like a dead person.[33]

Safi's story actually goes on, with at least, a glimmer of hope. After arriving at a hospital, she received help from female counselors who persuaded her that she had done nothing wrong. Whereas she initially wanted to kill herself, she gradually came to see a future ahead.

> In my mind I could not forgive those men for what they did and I couldn't love their baby. But I have talked with the counselors a lot and now I believe that I must forgive them so that I can free myself, and I know that my baby is innocent and has done nothing wrong and will need me when it is born. I still cry a lot, but I feel a bit better and I don't want to be sad—it's not good for my baby. I need to be strong. This is how our life is. . . . Before this all happened, I was in school and I wanted to become a journalist. My father told me it was a good job because you can learn lots of things and you can tell people things that help them. I still want to be a journalist when I am through all of this.[34]

There are literally thousands of stories similar to Safi's narrative. However, unlike the case of Safi's tale, most of them don't end with any sense of hope; most of them end in death.

Corruption and the Poor

The poor and the oppressed are harassed by corruption. Aid doesn't reach them because of corruption. Their rights in the courts are trampled upon because of corruption. The rich and powerful are even better able to take advantage of them because of corruption. The details of corruption can take many forms, but we know full-well the basic susceptibility of people to engage in it. "Corruption is a crime of calculation, not passion. True, there are saints who resist all temptations, and honest officials who resist most. But when the size of the bribe is large, the chance of being caught small, and the penalty if caught meager, many officials will succumb."[35]

Oftentimes the poor and oppressed are harangued because of bad and corrupt governments, and it has been noted that, "poor countries have bad governments."[36] Add to that the fact that corrupt "politicians will promote hatred when it helps achieve other unrelated political goals,"[37] and one finds that corruption can run rough-shod over the poor with them having little, if any, means of removing themselves from those influences.

When Doctors Take Bribes

The next time you go to the doctor for a physical or a shot or some sort of care, be sure to bring a pound bag of coffee with you in order to pad her or his payment. If you don't you may not even be seen by the doctor. How does that strike you? How would Americans react if all of sudden it took a little bribe of coffee or some such thing in order to get in and see a health-care worker? Fortunately, the bribe system is not a part of the American cultural system, and you won't have to give the doctor a little extra something in order to get some care. However, such is not the case all over, and in some areas of the world, bribes are an entrenched part of the health-care system.

When such corruption exists in a health-care system, it is the poor who have no option but to submit and pay more if they want any sort of care. Macedonia is a good example of a place that faces the burden of entrenched corruption within the country's health-care system. The capital city of Macedonia is Skopje, and it seems fair to say that you don't want a hospital room there. A 1998 study[38] found widespread evidence of corruption within the health-care system as is exemplified by the following case studies.

- One woman with . . . gangrene of the foot tried for seven years to get a disability pension. Three doctors composing the commission deciding on the issue of disability, after they learned she had a brother in Germany, determined a bribe in the amount of 3,000 German marks.
- One person interviewed had to repair the doctor's car as compensation for a kidney operation.
- One man who needed a kidney operation had to pay a bribe to get a referral to Skopje.
- According to one of the interviewed, patients at the Oncology Department at the clinical center in Skopje have to pay up to 1,000 to 2,000 German marks for good accommodations and good services.
- Doctors openly told one man from Debar whose wife needed an ulcer operation, 'If you have a thick envelope it is all right, if not, scram.' In general the opinion prevails that in Skopje hospitals a patient has to pay about 2,000 to 3,000 German marks for one operation.[39]

Be assured, Macedonia isn't unique in facing the problem of corruption in the health-care system. Rather, such examples are plentiful throughout the developing world.

When Professors Take Bribes

As a person who has spent a fair amount of time in academia, I have heard the standard jokes offered by students many times as they have said things to me like, "How much would it cost me for an A on this paper?" or "Do you take bribes?" But, of course, both parties then laugh together knowing that neither is serious in any way about actually engaging in bribery, by either offering or accepting. Then I read about what is happening in Moldova. It was heartbreaking. The professors were asking for bribes, and those who couldn't or wouldn't pay were refused admission to the university. For instance, a frustrated mother in Moldova reported that her son failed the entrance exam when she was unable to pay the 2,000 *lei* bribe being asked of her.[40] The poor are oftentimes the ones most impacted by corruption in the form of bribery. What do you think such an episode does to the psyche of the mother, or the son, in the example just sited? The section of Scripture known as the Covenant Code in the book of Exodus addresses bribery, and it admonishes, "Do not take a bribe, for a bribe will actually blind those who see, and it will distort the words of the righteous" (23:8).

After Genocide: Hotel Rwanda Some Years Later

1994 was a very nasty year in Rwanda. Genocide swept through the country as about one million Tutsis and moderate Hutu sympathizers were slaughtered by the Hutu military and other militias know as the *Interahamwe*.[41] The well-known historical drama, *Hotel Rwanda* (2004), portrayed events during that genocide, and the film won wide acclaim. Yet, it's a disturbing film to watch as it captures quite well the terror created by the militias as they randomly and chaotically roamed through the countryside killing Tutsis in a helter-skelter fashion. The stories one hears of those days is sickening. Narratives and testimonies of some of those who survived can impact you like a quick, unexpected punch to the stomach.

> No one who heard the tall, shy Rwandan woman testify that day in 1997—the day when the past finally caught up with indicted war criminal Jean-Paul Akayesu—has ever quite forgotten it.
>
> It was mesmerizing. The woman spoke as if in a trance, her large, luminous dark eyes focused somewhere in the distance, on a world only she could see, Words flowed from her in a steady, strong current that swept those sitting in the courtroom of the International Criminal Tribunal for Rwanda along with her as she spoke. She told of her rape by militiamen in the dirt of the sorghum field. Of her rape in the darkness of the forest. Then of her rape inside the grounds of the Bureau Communale of Taba, where Akayesu had been mayor. There were so many rapes over so many days by so many men she could no longer count them.[42]

About a year later the Rwanda Tribunal found Akayesu guilty of genocide. One might be surprised to find that he "became the first man in history to be found guilty of genocide by an international tribunal."[43] While "genocides" have clearly long been a part of human history, the term, itself, wasn't coined until quite recently—that is, recently in the long historical scheme of things. One would look in vain for any reference of *genocide* before the later years of the Nazi slaughter of Jews because the term was only first coined in 1944 by a Polish Jewish lawyer by the name of Raphael Lemkin.[44] He combined the Greek root for race, tribe, or family (*genos*) with the Latin root for killing (*cide*), and *presto*—a new word with which we are now all too familiar. As a young man, Lemkin had been deeply impacted by the Simele massacre of 1933 in which thousands of Assyrian Christians were horribly slaughtered in Iraq. As a result, in that same year he presented a paper entitled, "Acts of Barbarism and Vandalism under the Law of Nations" at a conference on international criminal law in Madrid.[45] In that paper he proposed to the Legal Council of the League of Nations that acts of barbarism be outlawed. Six years later he personally experienced the very horrors he had been decrying as the Nazis invaded his homeland of Poland. In a story worthy of Hollywood, he was shot in the hip, eluded capture, lost 49 relatives in the Holocaust and later his writings ultimately became the basis of legal rulings at the Nuremburg Trials.[46]

Alas, Lemkin's dream of ending acts of barbarism hasn't caught on. The last half of the 20th century landscape, just like the first half, was filled with genocide. The 21st century hasn't diminished the pace of mass killings as the horrors of Darfur are widely known. It's just that nobody is really doing anything about it. That has a familiar ring to it.

Even the gruesomeness of it doesn't seem to matter. The debacle in Rwanda was just like the others. The genocide was characterized by crimes of extraordinary brutality as described in a Human Rights Watch report:

> Some killers tortured victims, both male and female, physically or psychologically, before finally killing them or leaving them to die. An elderly Tutsi woman in Kibirira commune had her legs cut off and was left to bleed to death. A Hutu man in Cyangugu, known to oppose the MRND-CDR, was killed by having parts of his body cut off, beginning with his extremities. A Tutsi baby was thrown alive into a latrine in Nyamirambo, Kigali, to die of suffocation or hunger. Survivors bear scars of wounds that testify better than words to the brutality with which they were attacked. Assailants tortured Tutsi by demanding that they kill their own children and tormented Hutu married to Tutsi partners by insisting that they kill their spouses. Victims generally regarded being shot as the least painful way to die and, if given the choice and possessing the means, they willingly paid to die that way.[47]

In a compelling work in which the Rwandan killers are interviewed, the brutality is stark. As one killer named Adalbert recalled,

> There were some who brutalized a lot because they killed overmuch. Their killings were delicious to them. . . .they felt frustrated when they simply struck down a Tutsi. They wanted seething excitement. They felt cheated when a Tutsi died without a word. Which is why they no longer struck at the mortal parts, wishing to savor the blows and relish the screams.[48]

What happens after genocide? Naturally, the answer varies from historical situation to historical situation. No two genocides are the same. But as one might well imagine, recovery is usually slow and traumatic. In the case of Rwanda, consider simply the impact of the number of children who are now running the household because of parents lost in the genocide. Ten years after the event, a UNICEF report stated:

> There are an estimated 101,000 children that are heading approximately 42,000 households. These children have lost parents for various reasons – many were murdered during the genocide, some have died from AIDS and others are in prison for genocide-related crimes.[49]

How does one begin to measure the impact of that upon the children? What will become of that generation of kids who survived the mass killings only to be thrust into the position of caring for younger siblings because everybody else in the family was dead? What is their life like?

Yet, the United Nations has reported that, in fact, "Rwanda has experienced a remarkable recovery since the 1994 genocide that devastated the country's human and physical capital, as well as its social and institutional fabric."[50] That's a pretty rosy picture, and I'm not sure it includes a true sense of the long-term psychological scarring that genocide produces. While the U.N. report speaks of the "country's human capital," I wonder if the souls of those people are, perhaps, not a part of its equation.

Speaking of Genocide

Sadly, genocide didn't end with the 1994 Rwandan debacle. In fact, the very next year, in the summer of 1995, 8,000 Bosnian Muslim men and boys were slaughtered by a paramilitary force of Serbians known as the Scorpions.[51] It seems the so-called ethnic cleansing[52] had blurred into genocide as a definition offered a year before the event spoke of using "all possible means" to eliminate a group from a territory.[53]

> It is the present writer's view that ethnic cleansing is a well-defined policy of a particular group of persons to systematically eliminate another group from a given territory on the basis of religious, ethnic or national origin. Such a policy involves violence and is very often connected with military operations. It is to be achieved by all possible means, from discrimination to extermination, and entails violations of human rights and international humanitarian law.[54]

Yet, as the 20th century came to a close, it might be fair to say that many believed that perhaps things could be different in the coming new millennium. It seems that there is always a popular, natural optimism that emerges at the turn of a century and particularly at brink of a new millennium. Maybe our long history of genocides had come to an end. After all, hadn't the millions of genocidal deaths through that horrible 20th century taught us to avert such human travesty?

However, it wasn't long into the 21st century until a new genocide appeared. In Darfur—a region of Sudan not many people had ever heard of before, something was happening; scattered news reports appeared indicating something very bad was going on there. Even though the *New York Times* first used the word "genocide" in a story about Darfur on March 31, 2004, there was violence going back several years. In the summer of 2003 things seemingly grew to a new level.

New patterns of repression emerged. First aircraft would come over a village, as if smelling the target, and then return to release their bombs. The raids were carried out by Russian-built four-engine Antonov An-12s, which are not bombers but transports. They have no bomb bays or aiming mechanism, and the 'bombs' they dropped were old oil drums stuffed with a mixture of explosives and metallic debris. . . . The result was primitive free-falling cluster bombs, which were completely useless from a military point of view since they could not be aimed but had a deadly efficiency against fixed civilian targets.[55]

Large-scale killing was at hand in Darfur. Of course, the big question is, how many have been killed so far? The answer is murky; there have been a number of estimates that vary considerably, but in 2005, the U.S. Department of State set the total at 98,000 to 181,000. If that weren't enough, there is also a gargantuan problem because of the incredible number of people who have been displaced because of the violence. A recent United Nations report puts the total of displaced person at 2.2 million!

In July 2007 the UN Office for the Coordination of Humanitarian Affairs (OCHA) reported that 160,000 people had been newly displaced since January 2007, putting the total number of displaced at 2.2 million and the total number of people receiving relief assistance at 4.2 million, nearly two-thirds of Darfur's population. OCHA reported that many of Darfur's IDP camps can no longer absorb new arrivals.[56]

The plight of the poor and the oppressed who are bearing the brunt of the situation.

'If you go to these villages you will not find any man during the day, only women and children,' he said. 'Even now, during the harvest, you will find no men in the fields, just women working. The men are hiding. They are afraid that they will be killed.' (HRW Interview Kounoungo camp, Chad, November 7, 2006).[57]

An amazing historical aspect of genocide has been our slow reactions in the face of evidence. I us the word "our" because it's not just governments and nation-states bear a responsibility to confront evil. Followers of Jesus, just as much (if not more), must be voices in the silence that oftentimes has engulfed genocide. Perhaps the best-written presentation of genocide that I have seen comes from Samantha Power. In her book, *A Problem From Hell*, she has noted with regards to the Rwandan horror in which Hutus slaughter 8,000 Tutsi people a day for 100 days without any foreign interference that,

Genocide occurred *after* the Cold War; *after* the growth of human rights groups; *after* the advent of technology that allowed for instant communication; *after* the erection of the Holocaust Museum on the Mall in Washington, D.C.

   The most common responses, "We didn't know." This is not true. To be sure, the information emanating from countries victimized by genocide was imperfect. . . . But although U.S. officials did not know all there was to know about the nature and scale of violence, they knew a remarkable amount.[58]

It's a thing so horrific that the reality of genocide somehow probably seems unreal to us. Yet, while it may seem unreal to us who are securely living on the rich side of the world, it is all too real to the poor and the oppressed who are, of course, most often the victims of genocidal atrocities. There is, most certainly, a responsibility here. It is a responsibility to be borne by, not only a nation, but also by an individual. The call from Yahweh to enact justice (Micah 6:8) demands that followers of Jesus cry out in loud voices at even the hint of such despicable evil.

A Typical Government Project—One That Doesn't Work

Virtually across the board, poor people seem to have very low opinions of their government's ability to truly help them in their fight against poverty. In fact, almost all government programs are seen by those people who are in desperate need of relief as being ineffective to the point of being a joke. India stands out for having, perhaps, the largest network of public assistance for the low castes, poor, and ethnic minorities in the world.[59] These programs have very lofty goals; they are designed to do things like provide housing, free schooling, health care, food, water, disaster relief, etc. The problem is, when the poor, themselves, evaluate those programs, they find them to be untenable, unresponsive, and broken. For example, there was a government project in one district of India that was designed to provide housing for those in need. They were to build 1,061 houses, but only 350 were actually constructed. Yet, beyond that, "all of the houses were damaged and not one was occupied because the poor found them 'alien to their lifestyle and socio-cultural way of living.'"[60] Unfortunately, this is nearly the norm; it's not an isolated case of government incompetence. Nor is the phenomenon peculiar to India. Rather, it is found over the entire planet, but especially in countries whose populations are engulfed in poverty. The sad news is that, "poor countries have bad governments."[61] Nor is it necessarily due only to incompetence; it's also due to corruption.

The Global Weapons Trade and the Health of Poor People

Many things impact the poor and the oppressed. Their life is usually a complicated and complex web of factors beyond their control bearing on their well-being—or more likely, their lack of well-being. For example, the worldwide trade in weapons dramatically affects the health of the poor.[62]

Blatantly obvious is the fact that weapons kill people, both rich and poor—but mostly poor. Also, you are quite mistaken if you think that it is mostly soldiers who are killed by weapons. As it turns out, noncombatants are the ones who suffer about 90% of the casualties.[63] This figure was based upon conflicts then current in a 1996 study. The percentage is probably even greater today given the situations in Darfur, Iraq, and Afghanistan where civilian populations are suffering greatly at the hands of people who have the weapons.

Landmines are a good example of weapons that are most effective in directly destroying the lives of the poor. Various studies have demonstrated how tens of thousands of people have been killed by landmines in Afghanistan, Angola, Mozambique, Cambodia, and Somalia.[64] Indeed, the very direct and measurable impact of the weapons themselves in killing and maiming bodies is profound. Yet, far beyond that, there is also a devastating indirect impact that the international weapons trade has upon the poor and the oppressed.

The amount of money that is diverted away from basic and essential needs for the poor in order to buy weapons is scandalous. In many countries such critical arenas as health care, education, nutrition, water, sanitation, and a host of others suffered because money was funnel into the arms trade rather than into those services that would aid the needy. For example, in 1992, "Pakistan ordered 40 Mirage 20001 fighter jets from French TNCs [Transnational Corporations] at a cost that could have provided potable water for two years for the 55 million Pakistanis who lack safe water; essential medicine for the 13 million Pakistanis without access to medical care; and basic education for 12 million Pakistani children."[65] Right across the border India was doing the same thing—depriving its citizens who were in deep need in favor of buy some jets. They purchased 20 MiG-29s from Russia. How might those funds have been used? It would have been enough to provide a basic education to all of the 15 million young girls in India who were not able to attend school at the time of the purchase.[66]

It is not only the governments who buy the weapons that are culpable, it's also the governments which sell the weapons that bear responsibility. Unfortunately, the United States is at or near the top of the list in such undertakings. The U.S. has a rich history of selling arms to countries engaged in ethnic or territorial conflicts. Again, it tends to be the poor who are caught up in those conflicts and suffer the exploding furry of American-made arms. Of course, the argument can be made that if the U.S. didn't sell the weapons, somebody else would. Yes, that is correct, but does that make it right? We who view the poor and the oppressed from the rich side of the world tend to like having a robust economy, and the arms trade certainly does feed into a growing economy.

Number Three and Climbing

What are the three largest money making enterprises when it comes to international crime? That is, which transnational criminal activities produce the greatest profits? The United Nations' rankings are: number one—drugs, number two—weapons, and number three—human trafficking.[67] Just in case you haven't noticed, the global slave trade is flourishing. Human trafficking is a huge enterprise in which, for instance, there is estimated to be somewhere between 5,000-

8,000 different Russian crime organizations with their hands in the sex-slave industry with, perhaps, as many as 3 million people involved.[68]

In what has to be a stunning and sobering realization, upon investigation, one finds that the numbers of "women and children trafficked across international borders each year range from 800,000 to four million."[69] The immensity of this scandal is largely buried in secrecy, and the scope of the numbers of people who are trafficked are not widely known. Do you think the people in your church are aware of the vast networks and the sheer, huge numbers of women and children who are trafficked *each year*? Sadly, no nation is exempt from the truly global phenomenon of slavery. It's even pervasive in America as the "United States government estimates that up to fifty thousand women and children are illegally brought into the country and sold each year."[70]

I always find case studies to be rather interesting, and the one below is a graphic, yet typical, example of how the slave industry is alive and flourishing today.

a young woman from Nigeria was brought by a 'recruiter' to Italy. This young woman understood that she would be a prostitute and had consented to being transported and to working as a prostitute. However, on arrival she found that she was required to repay an enormous sum. In addition, following Nigerian traditional 'magical' practice, a sachet of her blood, hair, and nail clippings was assembled that gave traffickers extreme psychological power over her. Italian police report that freed Nigerian women often refuse to give statements until their 'magical' sachets are recovered. While some Nigerian prostitutes are able to purchase their freedom, others fall into enslavement, are paid nothing, and are regularly brutalized.[71]

However, even within the desperate and seemingly hopeless situations of those caught in the huge web of human trafficking, hope does exist. That is the nature of the Kingdom of God—there is hope in a hopeless situation. "Jesus' teaching emphasizes friendship with outcasts and the powerless."[72] Who could be more of an outcast and who could more powerless than the Nigerian prostitute described above? Encouragingly, some have heard the call, á la Mother Teresa, to serve and love the loveless. For example, Beth Grant describes the promising ministry of *Project Rescue* in India which creates "Homes of Hope" that have served, since its founding in 1997, over 1,000 trafficking victims and their children in nine Indian and Nepalese cities.[73]

As Grant relates a common scenario,

A high percentage of women entrapped in sexual slavery in the brothels in Bombay have been trafficked from poverty-stricken villages in Nepal. For those ministered to by Project Rescue who desire to return home to Nepal, the ministry aids in repatriation and provides aftercare at the Home of Hope in Katmandu, Nepal. If the women desire to reconnect with their families, Project Rescue workers facilitate that process. However, since an increasingly high percentage of the women being rescued are HIV+ or already suffering from full-blown AIDS, they are often not welcomed back by their families or communities in Nepal. In such tragic cases, the Home of Hope staff and other rescued women in the program who have become their new family of faith surround their 'sisters' in Christ with love, dignity and support even as they leave this life and go into God's presence.[74]

In desiring to bring awareness and incite action, this book has presented examples of a significant number of injustices against the poor and the oppressed. I pray that, for you, this does not create a defeated spirit, considering such conditions to be insurmountable. This little vignette, while flashing the immensity of the human trafficking industry, also serves notice to you and to me that we can make a difference. Project Rescue had very humble beginnings. You and I can be involved in efforts of humble beginnings. In the face of something like human trafficking which seems to be an evil that is so great and so pervasive that nothing could break its hold on the poor and oppressed, it might be good to remember some words of Mother Teresa.

Everything starts from prayer. Without asking God for love, we cannot possess love and still less are we able to give it to others. Just as people today are speaking so much about the poor but they do not know the poor, we too cannot talk so much about prayer and yet not know how to pray.[75]

If you wish, you could put this book down for a few moments and pray for what appears, from the human perspective, to be the hopeless situation of some young person caught in grips of human trafficking. It's not necessary that you know the individual—I think it's enough for God to take action that you simply know such a person exists, and as a result of your faith, you articulate to the Father a prayer of intercession that He reach down in love to rescue someone you don't even know from a horrible situation. Remember, "Everything starts from prayer."

NOTES

1. UNICF, *The Impact of Conflict on Women and Girls in West and Central Africa and the UNICEF Response* (New York: UNICEF, 2005), 19.

2. Human Rights Watch, *The War Within the War: Sexual violence against women and girls in Eastern Congo* (New York: Human Rights Watch, 2007).

3. UNICF, *Impact of Conflict*, 19.

4. Les Roberts, *et. al. Mortality in Eastern Democratic Republic of the Congo: Results from eleven mortality surveys* (New York: Health Unit/International Rescue Committee, 2001).

5. Hazem Ghobarah, Paul Huth, and Bruce Russett, "Civil Wars Kill and maim People—Long After the Shooting Stops," *American Political Science Review* 97 (2003), 189.

6. Idem.

7. Frances Stewart and Valpy Fitzgerald, "Introduction: Assessing the Economic Costs of War," in *War and Underdevelopment, Vol I: The Economic and Social Consequences of Conflict.* (eds. Frances Stewart, and Valpy Fitzgerald; New York: Oxford University Press, 2001).

8. Eric Greitens, "The Treatment of Children During Conflict." in *War and Underdevelopment, Vol I: The Economic and Social Consequences of Conflict.* (eds. Frances Stewart, and Valpy Fitzgerald; New York: Oxford University Press, 2001), 149.

9. C. Ahlstram, *Casualties of Conflict: Report for the Protection of Victims of War* (Uppsala: Department of Peace and Conflict, Uppsala University, 1991).

10. M. J. Toole, "Complex Emergencies: Refugee and Other Populations." in *War and Public Health.* (eds. Barry S. Levy and Victor W. Sidel; Washington, D.C.: American Public Health Association 1997).

11. Per Gustafson, *et. al.*, "Tuberculosis Mortality during a Civil War in Guinea-Bissau," *Journal of the American Medical Association* 286 (2001), 599-603..

12. Roberts, *et. al.*, *Morality.*

13. Ghobarah, Huth, and Russett, "Civil Wars," 192.

14. Humberto Lopez and Quentin Wodon, "The Economic Impact of Armed Conflict in Rwanda," *Journal of African Economies* 14 (2005), 587.

15. Idem.

16. Ilse Derluyn, Eric Broekaert and Gilberte Schuyten, "Post-traumatic Stress in Former Ugandan Child Soldiers," *The Lancet* 363 (2004), 861-863.

17. Idem.

18. Peter Singer, *Children at War* (Berkeley: University of California Press, 2006), 54.

19. Dr. Nan Muhovich, my colleague at North Central University, is currently working on a book that will incorporate interviews she conducted with Ugandan children in which they reflect upon their life as a child soldier.

20. United Nations Office for the Coordination of Humanitarian Affairs, *Press Release*, July 10, 2007.

21. Andrew Mawson, "Children, Impunity and Justice: Some Dilemmas from Northern Uganda," in *Children and Youth on the Front Line: Ethnography, Armed Conflict and Displacement* (eds J. Boyden and J. de Berry; New York: Berghahn Books 2004), 133.

22. Singer, *Children at War*, 79-80.

23. Ibid., 16.

24. Ishmael Beah, *A Long Way Gone: Memoirs of a Boy Soldier* (Farrar, Straus & Giroux, 2006), 119.

25. United Nations Development Programme, *Human Development Report 2003*, 77.

26. Idem.

27. Jean-Paul Azam and Anke Hoeffler, "Violence Against Civilians in Civil Wars: Looting or Terror?" *Journal of Peace Research* 39 (2002), 462.

28. UNICF, *The Impact of Conflict*, 4.

29. Ibid., 7.

30. Idem.

31. Ibid., 9.

32. UNICF, *The Impact of Conflict*, 4.

33. Ibid., 12.

34. Idem.

35. Robert Klitgaard, "Subverting Corruption," *Finance and Development* 37 (2000), 3.

36. Easterly, *White Man's Burden,* 115.

37. Ibid., 128.

38. Institute for Sociological and Political-Legal Research, "Qualitative Analysis of the Living Standard of the Population of the Republic of Macedonia," (Skopje: Institute for Sociological and Political-Legal Research, 1998).

39. Narayan, Patel, Schafft, Rademacher, and Koch-Schulte, *Voices,* 94.

40. Hermine De Soto and Nora Dudwick (1997).

41. In Kinyarwanda, the chief spoken language of Rwanda, *Interahamwe* means "those who stand, or kill together."

42. Elizabeth Neuffer, *The Key to My Neighbor's House: Seeking Justice in Bosnia and Rwanda* (New York: Picador, 2001), 271.

43. Ibid., 272.

44. Raphael Lemkin, *Axis Rule In Occupied Europe: Laws Of Occupation, Analysis Of Government, Proposals For Redress* (Washington: Carnegie Endowment for International Peace, Division of International Law, 1944).

45. Raphael Lemkin, "Akte der Barbarei und des Vandalismus als *delicta juris gentium,*" (Acts of Barbarism and Vandalism under the Law of Nations), *Anwaltsblatt Internationales* 19 (1933), 117-119.

46. William Korey, "Raphael Lemkin: 'The Unofficial Man'" *Midstream,* June/July (1989): 45-48; J. Martin, "Raphael Lemkin and the Invention of 'Genocide,'" *The Journal of Historical Review,* 2 (1981), 19-34, Samantha Power, *A Problem from Hell: America and the Age of Genocide* (New York: Basic Books, 2002).

47. Human Rights Watch, *Children in Sudan: Children in Sudan: Slaves, Street Children and Child Soldiers* (Washington, D.C.: Human Rights Watch, 1995).

48. Jean Hatzfeld, *Machete Season: The Killers in Rwanda Speak* (New York: Farrar, Straus and Giroux, 2003), 129.

49. UNICEF, *Impact of Conflict.*

50. United Nations Development Programme Rwanda, *Turning Vision 2020 into Reality: From Recovery to Sustainable Human Development* (New York: United Nations Development Programme Rwanda, 2007), 5.

51. Tone Bringa, "Averted Gaze: Genocide in Bosnia-Herzegovina, 1992-1995," in *Annihilating Difference: The Anthropology of Genocide* (ed. Alexander Laban Hinton; Berkeley: University of California Press, 2002); David Rhode, *Endgame: The Betrayal and Fall of Srebrenica: Europe's Worst Massacre since World War II* (New York: Farrar, Strauss and Giroux, 1997); Michael Sells, *The Bridge Betrayed: Religion an Genocide in Bosnia* (Berkeley: University of California Press, 1996).

52. Andrew Bell-Fialkoff, *Ethnic Cleansing* (New York: Palgrave MacMillan, 1999).

53. Drazen Petrovic, "Ethnic Cleansing—An Attempt at Methodology," *European Journal of International Law* 3 (1994), 11.

54. Idem.

55. Gérard Prunier (2007), *The Ambiguous Genocide* (Ithaca: Cornell University Press, 2007) 99-100

56. Human Rights Watch, *The War Within the War.*

57. Ibid., 28.

58. Power, *A Problem from Hell*, 303-305.

59. Narayan, Patel, Schafft, Rademacher, and Koch-Schulte, *Voices*, 86.

60. Ibid., 87.

61. Easterly, *White Man's Burden*, 115.

62. Joyce Millen and Timothy Holtz, "Transnational Corporations and the Health of the Poor." in *Dying for Growth: Global Inequality and the Health of the Poor* (eds Kim, Jim Yong, Joyce V. Millen, Alec Irwin, and John Gershman; Monroe, Maine: Common Courage Press, 2000, 177-223.

63. UNICEF, *State of the World's Children, 1996*.

64. Alberto Ascherio, Robin Bielik, Andy Epstein, *et. al.* "Death and Injuries Caused by Landmines in Mozambique," *Lancet* 346 (1977), 721-724; Eric Stover, A.S. Keller, J.C. Kobey, *et al.* "The Medical and Social Consequences of Landmines in Cambodia," *Journal of the American Medial Association* 272 (1994), 331-336.

65. Millen and Holtz, "Transnational Corporations," 13.

66. Lora Lumpe and Jeff Donarski, *The Arms Trade Revealed: A Guide for Investigators and Activists* (Washington, D.C.: Federation of American Scientists), 1998.

67. Kevin Bales, *Understanding Global Slavery* (Berkeley: University of California Press, 2005), 79.

68. James Finckenauer, "Russian Transnational Organized Crime and Human Trafficking," in *Global Human Smuggling* (eds. David Kyle and Rey Koslowski; Baltimore: Johns Hopkins University Press, 2001).

69. Beth Grant, "Sexual Slavery and the Gospel," in *Java & Justice: Journeys in Pentecostal Missions Education* (eds. B. Brenneman, W. R. Brookman and N. Muhovich, Minneapolis: North Central University Press, 2006), 173.

70. Bales, *Understanding Global Slavery*, 135.

71. Ibid., 131.

72. Stassen and Gushee, *Kingdom Ethics*, 52.

73. Grant, "Sexual Slavery," 181.

74. Ibid., 183.

75. Mother Teresa, *Everything Starts from Prayer* (Ashland, Oregon: White Cloud Press, 2000), 1.

CHAPTER 11

Thinking, Acting, and Praying
Through Global Scenes of Biblical Injustice

Adam Smith and the Respect Owed to the Poor

Most good American capitalists are familiar with the name Adam Smith. In his work, *The Wealth of Nations,* he set forth those economic theories and practices that would lead to the growth of modern capitalism. Published in 1776, his work became the Bible of American economic theory as movers and shakers such as Benjamin Franklin and David Hume literally gushed over his book upon its first printing. Yet, in all of its magisterial economic theory, a little-known sentiment by Smith has gotten lost in the shuffle of supply and demand economics. Thankfully, a Nobel Prize winner by the name of Amartya Sen has made note of something Smith said that seems to have escaped the larger economic landscape that Americans embrace so enthusiastically. Sen reminds us that Smith "insisted that all human beings should have 'the ability to appear in public without shame.'"[1]

Humiliation and shame are fundamental obstacles the poor must overcome, and unfortunately those of us glimpsing the poor from the rich side of the world, don't do a whole lot to empower them to overcome those hurdles. In the post-Soviet CIS this has been a particularly potent aspect of poverty. Several studies have shown that "poverty assessments from the former Soviet bloc underscore the intense shame and humiliation that people feel when confronted by their own poverty. . . ."[2]

Have you ever, even if only in your own mind, ridiculed a poor person? Our view from the rich side of the world actually acts as a catalyst and enhances our natural propensity to do that. I suspect that many of us stereotype the poor as lazy. Consider how that magnifies within us the power to rationalize humiliating thoughts about the poor. Yet the poor are very intuitive; they pick up the humiliating thoughts of the rich and powerful. What would it take on our part to engage those beaten down with humiliation and indignity in such a way that a poor human being could appear in public without shame?

Can Kenosis be a Model for Us?

Because you and I view the poor from the rich side of the world, we are akin to the "rich man" in the parable of Lazarus (Lk. 16:19-31). No matter how much we wiggle to get out of that description, no matter how uncomfortable we are with that label, the fact remains, you and I *are* the rich man. If one is to take Jesus seriously, one needs to reckon a proper response to our position. Clearly, the rich man in the parable failed to reckon a proper response to Lazarus, and just look at what happened as a result of his failure.

Kenosis is the Greek word used in the New Testament (Phil. 2:7) to describe the action of Jesus in "taking on the very nature of a servant." The term carries the sense of making empty, especially with regard to power and/or reputation. The word is often explained as Jesus emptying Himself of His power in order to become a servant. Perhaps here Jesus provides for us a model, a template, in how to respond to this world. Just as He emptied Himself of power and took on the form of a servant, so also, we, the people of the rich side of the world, should voluntarily remove or yield the status of our power or resources, be it economic, political, otherwise, in order to serve. Yet, such a response is only possible if we really do desire to be disciples of Jesus. Because, "Christ's humiliation of himself, his self-emptying (*kenosis*), his abandoning of his status, is absolutely crucial to the understanding of the work of Christ, and is exemplary for disciples."[3]

As renunciation of status was one of the two great values one finds in early Christianity,[4] the words of Jesus to His disciples seem clearly to have hit home. On this particular occasion, Jesus called His disciples together. I think He may have been a bit miffed after they had been arguing about status. If you recall the story (Mt 20:20-24), there had been some maneuvering and jockeying for positions of eminence among some of the disciples. I picture Jesus rather getting in their faces on this issue. I picture a fire in the evening, and all the disciples are sitting around it, and Jesus is leaning over them, invading their personal space, looking into their faces, eyeball to eyeball, and saying,

> You know that the rulers of the Gentiles lord it over them, and their high officials exercise authority over them. Not so with you. Instead, whoever wants to become great among you must be your servant, and whoever wants to be first must be your slave—just as the Son of Man did not come to be served, but to serve, and to give his life as a ransom for many.[5]

The rest of the story is that renunciation of status became one of the basic hallmarks of early Christianity. How do we rich respond to the poor and oppressed? We may easily lord it over them. Or, as a true follower of Jesus, we just might identify with the poor and oppressed *a.k.a.* Lazarus, via a renunciation of our status. That is, we might employ the *kenosis* and identify ourselves with the poor rather than lording it over them.

Invalidating a Charism

There seems to be an interesting relationship between one's embracing the kingdom of God and embracing the poor. Is it really possible to embrace one without the other? Can a true disciple of Jesus embrace the kingdom without enacting the principles of that kingdom towards to the poor?

> The ethic of being a disciple rests on this meeting with Christ in the poor. This is the great theme of Matthew's gospel, where the preaching of Jesus is presented as beginning with the promise of the kingdom to the poor (ch. 5) and ending with entry into it through a specific gesture towards the poor (ch. 25). The kingdom and the poor form an indissoluble unity. . . . The behaviour of the disciple is judged on this basis, and Matthew tells us the criterion for this judgment: 'By their fruits you shall know them' (Matt. 7:20). These fruits, whose absence invalidates the exercise of any charism for the kingdom, (see Matt. 7; 1 Cor. 13), are what the Bible describes with the technical term 'works of mercy' or 'good works'. They are shown to be specific gestures towards the poor: giving food, drink, clothing.[6]

Can you remember doing any works of mercy towards the poor? If you are not able to name something quickly, it probably has been a long time since you did something for the poor—that's not a good indicator as works of mercy are so tightly tied to the behavior of a true disciple.

Letting Die

Peter Unger, in a stunning and compelling work,[7] issues forth a clarion call from a position of moral philosophy which should certainly induce you and me to action. He begins rather abruptly by pointing out that "each year millions of children die from easy to beat disease, from malnutrition, and from bad drinking water." He notes that simple, Oral Rehydration Therapy (ORT) is a cost-efficient and very effective way to save lives, and he then provides the address of UNICEF. He writes, "Now, you can write that address on an envelope well prepared for mailing. And, in it, you can place a $100 check made out to the U.S. Committee for UNICEF along with a note that's easy to write: WHERE IT WILL HELP THE MOST, USE THE ENCLOSED FUNDS FOR ORT."[8]

He calculates that $3 is a "realistic figure" for saving a child's life via ORT, and he notes that, "If you'd contributed $100 to one of UNICEF's most efficient lifesaving programs a couple of months ago, this month there'd be over thirty fewer children who, instead of painfully dying soon, would live reasonable long lives."[9]

Next, he sets up a moral dilemma. After presenting the indisputable data which demonstrates that literally millions of children die every year from very preventable diseases, he gives us the main point: "Through the likes of UNICEF, it's well within your power, in the coming months and years to lessen serious suffering."[10]

Since you now have this information, Unger begs a question. How are you going act as a result of having this information; namely that ORT saves lives, and you have the mailing address to send a donation which will save lives? He notes that "The thought occurs that each of us ought to contribute . . . quite a lot to lessen early deaths; indeed, it's *seriously* wrong not to do that."[11] He points out that while most people agree, in a general way, that it's good to provide aid, almost everyone also says that "it's *not even the least bit wrong* to do *nothing* to help save distant people from painfully dying soon."[12] What in the world is going on?

The remainder of Unger's book is a delightful romp through a series of moral dilemma cases and puzzles that he relates as he builds the case "for the likes of us, a morally decent life is bound to be terribly costly."[13] I love his cases, and a brief sample of two that play a central role throughout his book ought to be shared.

The Shallow Pond
The path from the library at your university to the humanities lecture hall passes a shallow ornamental pond. On your way to give a lecture, you notice that a small child has fallen in and is in danger of drowning. If you wade in and pull the child out, it will mean getting your clothes muddy and either canceling your lecture or delaying it until you can find something clean and dry to wear. If you pass by the child, the, while you'll give your lecture on time, the child will die straightaway. You pass by and, as expected, the child dies.[14]

Everyone agrees this behavior is horrible, if not criminal. It's outrageous, and nobody excuses the lack of a saving act in the case of *The Shallow Pond*. Unger notes that people's intuitive responses to this case are uniform and predictable. Now, compare the above scenario with the following.

The Envelope
In your mailbox, there's something from (the U.S. committee for) UNICEF. After reading it through, you correctly believe that, unless you soon send in a check for $100, then, instead of each living many more years, over thirty more children will die soon. But, you throw the material in your trash basket, including the convenient return envelope provided, you send nothing, and instead of living many years, over thirty more children soon die than would have had you sent in the requested $100.[15]

Unger relates how, in response to *The Envelope*, "almost everyone reacts that your conduct isn't even wrong at all."[16] Why are there such discrete, widely divergent reactions to the two puzzles? He harkens back to a work by Peter Singer, who obviously had a strong impact on Unger.[17] He credits Singer as being the one "who first, seriously and systematically" argued that "it's wrong for us not to lessen distant serious suffering."[18] In fact, the case of *The Shallow Pond* originally comes from Singer, and it figures prominently in the premise that Singer and Unger advocate—"If we can prevent something bad without sacrificing anything of comparable significance, we ought to do it."[19]

Something Old and Something New

Think about this. "That a large segment of humankind lives in extreme poverty is nothing new. What is comparatively new, however, is that another large segment is living in considerable affluence."[20] As we catch a glimpse of the poor, it is important for us to realize that our view is from the rich side of the world. We *are* a member of that rich segment, and consequently, we exist in the midst of considerable affluence. Given that situation, what are some responsibilities you might imagine each of us has as a result of our predicament? I use the word, "predicament", because we on the rich side of the world are in a bit of a bind. That's because we equate with the rich within the gospels, and as we know, the "gospel of Christ is unmistakably tilted in favor of the poor, the hungry, and the oppressed."[21]

Lest One Be Naïve

To be sure, an image has been presented within this book of you and me scanning the panorama of the globe from the rich side of the world and catching brief glimpses of the plight of the poor and the oppressed. That's all well and good, but perhaps you have noticed the geography of this endeavor—focus has been on the poor side of the world. Yet, where exactly is the poor side of the world? The array of vignettes suggests that it's all over the place—Central Europe, South Asia, Latin America, Sub-Saharan Africa, the Caribbean, West Africa, Eastern Europe. That is, it seems that one may go anywhere and find injustices that haunt the poor and the oppressed. Yet, I suspect that you have noticed a glaring absence so far in this book—no vignette has yet talked about anything in America. Lest one be naïve and believe that the plight of the poor and the oppressed is totally missing from the American landscape, this might be a good place to, at least, allude to the notion of poverty within the United States.

This is actually, at least in my mind, somewhat of a difficult, if not delicate, topic. My thinking has evolved a bit on this issue. In the past, I have felt that, in a qualitative and comparative measure, real poverty doesn't exist in America. However, before you completely indict me, let me complicate the issue by pointing out that there are a variety of ways of talking about, and even defining poverty. My position has changed somewhat; as I would now readily admit that there, clearly, is poverty in America.

On the other hand, I've seen extreme poverty, and by comparative standards, extreme poverty in America is qualitatively quite different from extreme poverty in the developing world. On a fully comprehensive, comparative scale, the poor in America face a different reality than the poor of Ethiopia. Yet, hunger is hunger, and there are hungry kids in America. Even a child who lives in a furnished apartment with cable TV and a parent who has a cell phone can be hungry.

Clearly, the bar for poverty is set higher in America than in developing countries. While the World Bank considers an income of $1 to $2 per person per day to be the standard of poverty in the developing world,[22] the U.S. government set $17,170 (for the year 2006) for a family of three to be the poverty line in America. There are, of course, a variety of methods of measuring poverty, and the above poverty threshold line is an example of what is known as an absolute measure. Absolute measures tend to set a "measurable subsistence level of income or consumption below which people should be deemed economically disadvantaged or deprived."[23] There are also relative measures. These measures try to get at a comparative sense of economic well-being, and the existing level of economic development in a given locale is an important key upon which measures are taken.

> Implicit is the assumption that people are social beings who operate within relationships. Those whose resources are significantly below the resources of other, even if they are physically able to survive, may not be able to participate adequately in social organizations and relationships, and are thus incapable of fully participating in society.[24]

And so, there is a bit of a caveat in my little attempt at acknowledging poverty in America. The gist of which is this—in an absolute sense, extreme poverty in America, in no way, compares to extreme poverty in the developing world. However, in a relative sense, many Americans when measured against other Americans can certainly be shown to be poor. Fortunately, my focus of interest is not in the American landscape, because frankly, it's a little dicey to navigate that terrain while keeping an eye on the rest of the world. Suffice it to say, we who glimpse the poor and the oppressed from the rich side of the world may very well find that our literal neighbor, living just down the street, is economically on the other side of the world from us. That fact also presents us with opportunities for greater engagement than might realistically be the case with poor neighbors who are geographically more distant.

Zacchaeus, A Hindu Lady, and Your Basal Ganglia

I read the following account from Mother Teresa's book, *No Greater Love*. Those of us who glimpse the poor and the oppressed from the rich side of the world come from all sorts of places, even India. We also come from many religious frames of reference as evidenced from this story by Mother Teresa.

> Not so long ago a very wealthy Hindu lady came to see me. She sat down and told me, "I would like to share in your work." In India, more and more people like her are offering to help. I said, "That is fine." The poor woman had a weakness that she confessed to me. "I love elegant saris," she said. Indeed, she had on a very expensive sari that probably cost around eight hundred rupees. Mine cost only eight rupees. Hers cost one hundred times more.
>
> Then I asked the Virgin Mary to help me give an adequate answer to her question of how she could share in our work. It occurred to me to say to her, "I would start with the saris. The next time you go to buy one, instead of paying eight hundred rupees, buy one that costs five hundred. Then with the extra three hundred rupees, buy saris for the poor." The good woman now wears 100-rupee saris, and that it is because I have asked her not to buy cheaper ones. She has confessed to me that this has changed her life. She now knows what it means to share. That woman assures me that she has received more than what she has given.[25]

What are we to think when a wealthy Hindu woman has exactly the sort of response to the poor that I think Christ expects from us? In the same vein, what are we to think of Zacchaeus? Remember the short tax collector who we meet at the start of Luke 19? He was wealthy, just like the Hindu woman who spent 800 rupees on a single sari. He also modified his behavior to benefit the poor, just like the Hindu woman. However, Zacchaeus' response was quite drastic and dramatic. He exclaimed, "Look Lord, here and now I give half of my possessions to the poor, and if I have cheated anybody out of anything, I will pay back four times the amount." At that point, Jesus said to him, "Today salvation has come to this house."

Could this extreme behavior of Zacchaeus be some sort of template of action that you and I should embrace? Yikes! Isn't that asking a bit too much? Perhaps we could start out like the wealthy Hindu woman who cut back just a bit on her spending for expensive items she craved—spending the difference, instead, on the poor. Notice in Mother Teresa's story of this Hindu woman that this change of behavior seemed to excite and gratify her so much that she continued down-grading the amount she was spending on herself and diverting more and more to the poor. We see two methods here. Zaccchaeus immediately gave half of what he owned to the poor. The wealthy Hindu woman gradually weaned herself off spending exorbitant amounts on items of dress. Her focus clearly shifted away from what she was wearing, à la Luke 12:23, to caring for the poor instead. My hunch is that the model of the Hindu woman would be a more likely transition for you and for me. Wow, I can't even imagine doing it the Zacchaeus way. That would be too quick, too dramatic and too scary. I don't think it's going to happen that way for most people. Hats off to Zacchaeus, but I suspect the way to get at our problem (yes, we have a problem) might best be to follow the model of the wealthy Hindu woman. This is not meant to discourage those of you who are bent of following the Zacchaeus model, and there probably are people out there who absolutely need the sort of radical transformation experienced by the short tax collector.

What both the Hindu woman and Zacchaeus successfully did was break free from a force of habit. The fact is, much of our everyday behavior is characterized by habitual repetition.[26] Clearly, the American culture is awash with consumerism, and you and I are certainly not exempt from the allure of that aspect of our culture simply because we profess a faith in Christ. We have developed habits of consumerism that seem very natural, and these habits have a powerful pull upon us. However, embracing principles of the kingdom of God requires, oftentimes, that we decry aspects of our very own culture that so often run contrary to the teachings of Jesus.

Having identified conspicuous consumption as a habit we might wish to abandon, or at least diminish, the reality still exists that it is difficult for us to break habits of behavior. As one study notes,

> One explanation for this failure to change behavior is that many aspects of unwanted lifestyle habits are immediately gratifying. That is, habits are maintained by incentives (e.g., the convenience of taking the car), biological factors (e.g., addiction to nicotine in cigarettes, metabolism in obesity), or the psychological needs they serve (e.g., self-esteem boost from shopping).[27]

The wealthy Hindu woman did, in fact, get a "self-esteem boost" when she bought herself an 800 rupee sari. You get the same boost when you buy a (fill in the blank). I get that boost when I buy a new book. Here we might get into intentions as opposed to habits. It's easy to have good intentions, but it's difficult to break behavioral habits. Thus, "when a behavior is new, untried, and unlearned, the behavioral-intention component will be solely responsible for the behavior." However, that changes over time, and intention become less of a factor, and circumstances of environment become a very strong force. This grows to the point that, "as behavior repeatedly takes place, habit increases and becomes a better predictor of behavior than behavioral intentions."[28]

What causes that? It seems that our brains work in such a way that habit formation is a very natural thing. The major mechanism in how we tend to establish habit formation is found in a part of the brain known as the basal ganglia. That's a term I had heard before, but I really did not know anything about it. Thus, I went to Wikipedia.com. Perhaps you should know that I have this love/hate relationship with Wikipedia. While it certainly does have its flaws, it also does sometimes serve as a good starting point when one is trying to find out a little information concerning something about which one knows nothing.

What I discovered, after some investigation, is that when it comes to the basal ganglia, one of the leading hotshots (that's a complement) is Ann M. Graybiel. She is the Walter A. Rosenblith Professor of Neuroscience in the Department of Brain and Cognitive Sciences at MIT. Graybiel is a 2002 recipient of the National Medal of Science, and she has written extensively about this fascinating bundle of nerves that is largely responsible for the neural patterns we know as habits.[29]

You and I both know that there are good habits, and then there are bad habits. While the assumption might be made that habits can't be broken, the fact seems to be that there is a certain plasticity of the brain that allows for changes in habitual behavior.[30] Of course, we all know that's difficult to do. Anyone who has tried to quit smoking, change eating habits, or quit watching TV knows that changing habitual patterns of behavior is a challenge. That's because several factors are at play that favor habit over intent. For instance, given that strong habits are "cued relatively directly by the environment with minimal decision making, the practiced response is likely to be more immediately available than thoughtfully generated alternatives."[31] A second factor is that "habits require minimal regulatory control."[32] That is, a "greater capacity is required to suppress habits than to carry out alternative behaviors that require conscious guidance and deliberation."[33] This is where the basal ganglia comes into play. That wonderful and complex structure of the brain, according to Graybiel's research, is crucial in the circuitry and processing of behavior that becomes habit.

Research demonstrates that habits are very susceptible to environment or circumstances into which we place ourselves.[34] In fact, putting yourself into familiar circumstances, whether that's location, friends, mood, etc., can trigger habitual behavior totally aside from your intentions or decisions; that's your basal ganglia at work.[35] On the other hand, changing a habit is very achievable, and oftentimes it is accomplished through changing one's circumstances.[36] That is to say, habitual gambling can more easily be thwarted by not going to casinos rather than by mere good intentions not to gamble.

Fascinating as this brief exposé into the neuroscience behind much of our human behavior has been, one might be asking, "What's the point of this?" You may be wondering something like this—"I thought we were exploring aspects of poverty; what does the basal ganglia have to do with that?" In seeing the response to the poor by Zacchaeus and the wealthy Hindu woman, one is impressed that what might have been years and years of habitual behavior was, in fact, reversed. That's the point of all of this. We, like Zacchaeus and the Hindu woman, need a behavioral change with regards to our posture toward the poor and the oppressed of this world.

Establishing such new habitual behavior can be very desirable, and the good news is, that's very doable. What would it take to get our basal ganglia to drive us to prayer in the same manner that it drives an addictive gambler to gamble? What would it take for us to reduce conspicuous consumption on ourselves and direct our resources toward the poor? Actually, simple repetition goes a long way to establishing and conditioning the sort of neuro-firing circuitry within the basal ganglia that will make desirable behavior habitual.

Zacchaeus and the wealthy Hindu woman didn't know a lick about the basal ganglia or the neuroscience of habitual behavior. Zacchaeus encountered Jesus, and he gave half of what he owned to the poor. The wealthy Hindu woman started with the good intention of helping to assist the poor, and she responded to Mother Teresa's suggestion to reduce what she spent on herself, and redirect that money to the poor. As a result, a new habitual behavior was established in her life—she became enthralled with the joy of giving to those in need. The challenge for you and for me is to restructure our behaviors toward the poor. If our behavior has been habitually ignoring of the poor (like the rich man ignored Lazarus), we need to initiate the steps to change that destructive behavior (and it would seem to be very destructive given what happened to the rich man—Lk 16:19-31).

Want to change some of your habitual behaviors and attitudes toward the poor and the oppressed? Pray this prayer with me now.

> Lord, Your creation is beyond compare. When one sees how you crafted the human brain, the intricacies of its design and function, one can only respond with awe and reverence for You. While I don't pretend to fully understand the neuroscience behind my thinking and my habitual behaviors, I do know, Father, that I can change in my attitudes and behavior towards the poor. Like Zacchaeus and the wealthy Hindu woman, whose name You know, I also desire to change my destructive habits which, right now, more closely match those of the rich man who ignored Lazarus or those of Zacchaeus before he encountered Jesus. Forgive me Lord for those actions or inactions of the past which inhibited my relationship with the poor and the oppressed around me, and may Your Holy Spirit empower me to create new habitual behaviors which will change me as Zacchaeus and the wealthy Hindu woman were changed. Amen.

Thus, you and I want to actually *do* something rather than merely *intend* to do something. That's the best way to build a new habit—one that favors the poor. Select something in your life and focus upon that as a means to better serve the poor and the oppressed. Be repetitive, and be enthusiastic in your pursuit of change. Pretty soon that change will produce habit—a good habit.

Can There Even be a Concluding Thought?

The sad thing is, it's a never-ending string of vignettes and stories that could comprise a little volume like this. One is never going to exhaust the tales of the plight of the poor and the oppressed in this world. Indeed, Jesus said that we're always going to have the poor with us. Please remember, however, that eradicating poverty is not the end-game. Rather, it's our response to those who are mired in such horrible life-circumstances as those that have been surveyed here that would seem to be the point. Remember the Rich Man and Lazarus. Remember that you and I are representative of the Rich Man in that story. We are the ones who are going through life merely glimpsing the poor and the oppressed.

Yet, congratulations are in order. You have taken a chance and ventured into the ocean, metaphorically speaking. You have had a chance to experience just a little bit of the lives of some of your neighbors who are the poor and the oppressed in our world. You've seen how their lives are overwhelmed by the floods of poverty and injustice that exist. Now, at the conclusion of this book, the options for your response to all of that are somewhat limited. They are limited in the sense that, either you can enact justice as you never have before, or you can maintain a pattern of life that you've established over the years in which you've been very content to sit back and merely glimpse the others.

Jesus' point of not neglecting the poor, driven home in his parable of Lazarus, must shake us. Remember what was said in the introduction. The intent (of this book) is to incite you to act on behalf of the poor and the oppressed. Yet, where on Earth does one begin against the overwhelming onslaught of poverty and injustice that we have seen? At this point, we may wish to remember the sentiment of Mother Teresa that "everything begins with prayer."[37] And so, we end this book by beginning with a simple prayer.

Lord,
    (I'll fill in my words, which are adequate only for me, and you fill in your words which are adequate only for you.)

Amen

NOTES

1. Forrester, *On Human Worth*, 20.
2. Narayan, Patel, Schafft, Rademacher, and Koch-Schulte, *Voices*, 68.
3. Forrester, *On Human Worth*, 94.
4. Gerd Theissen, *A Theory of Primitive Christianity* (London: SCM Press, 1999), 71ff. The other great value held and acted on in the primitive Church was that of loving one's neighbor.
5. Matt 20:25-28.
6. Gustavo Gutiérrez, . "The Violence of a System." in *Christian Ethics and Economics: The North-South Conflict.* (eds. Dietmar Mieth and Jacques Pohierm; New York: Seabury Press, 1980), 97-98.
7. Peter Unger, *Living High & Letting Die* (New York: Oxford University Press, 1996), 3.
8. Idem.
9. Ibid., 4.
10. Ibid., 7.
11. Idem.
12. Idem.
13. Ibid., 148.

14. Ibid., 9.

15. Idem.

16. Idem.

17. Peter Singer, "Famine, Affluence and Morality," *Philosophy and Public Affairs* 1 (1972): 229-43.

18. Unger, *Living High*, 8.

19. First cited in Peter Singer, *Practical Ethics* (New York: Cambridge University Press, 1979), 230.

20. Thomas W. Pogge, "Human Rights and Human Responsibilities," in *Global Justice and Transnational Politics: Essays on the Moral and Political Challenges of Globalization*, (ed. Pablo de Greiff and Ciaran Cronin: Cambridge, MA: MIT Press, 2002), 152.

21. Bruce C. and Larry L. Birch and Rasmussen, *The Predicament of the Prosperous* (Philadelphia: Westminster Press, 197), 48.

22. Martin Ravallion, "Issues in Measuring and Modeling Poverty," *Policy Research Working Paper* no. 1615, (Washington, D.C.: World Bank, 1996).

23. John Iceland, *Poverty in America* (Berkeley: University of California Press, 2006), 21.

24. Ibid., 25.

25. Mother Teresa, *Everything Starts from Prayer* (Ashland, Oregon: White Cloud Press, 2000), 43.

26. Wendy. Wood, "Habits: A Repeat Performance." *Current Directions in Psychological Science* 14 (2006): 198-202.

27. Bas Verplanken and Wendy Wood, "Interventions to Break and Create Consumer Habits." *Journal of Public Policy & Marketing* 25 (2006): 92.

28. H. C. Triandis, *Interpersonal Behavior.* (Monterey CA: Brooks/Cole Publishing, 1977), 205.

29. A. M. Graybiel, "Guide to the anatomy of the brain: the basal ganglia." in *Encyclopedia of Learning and Memory* (ed. J. H. Byrne: New York: MacMillan, 2002); A. M. Graybiel and S. Grillner, eds. *Microcircuits: The Interface Between Neurons and Global Brain Function* (Cambridge, MA: MIT Press, 2006); A. M. Graybiel and E. Saka, "The basal ganglia and the control of action." in *The New Cognitive Neurosciences* (M.S. Gazzaniga, ed: Cambridge, MA: MIT Press, 2003).

30. Graybiel and Grillner. *Microcircuits.*

31. Verplanken and Wood, "Interventions," 93.

32. Ibid., 93.

33. Idem.

34. Ibid., 91.

35. J. A. Ouellette and Wendy Wood, "Habit and Intention in Everyday Life: The Multiple Processes by Which past Behavior Predicts Future Behavior," *Psychological Bulletin*, 124 (1998): 54-74.

36. Wendy Wood, L. Tam, and M. Guerrero Wit, "Changing Circumstances, Disrupting Habits," *Journal of Personality and Social Psychology* 88 (2005): 918-33.

37. Mother Teresa, *Everything Starts from Prayer*, 1.

APPENDIX A

United Nations Millennium Declaration

I. Values and principles

1. We, heads of State and Government, have gathered at United Nations Headquarters in New York from 6 to 8 September 2000, at the dawn of a new millennium, to reaffirm our faith in the Organization and its Charter as indispensable foundations of a more peaceful, prosperous and just world.

2. We recognize that, in addition to our separate responsibilities to our individual societies, we have a collective responsibility to uphold the principles of human dignity, equality and equity at the global level. As leaders we have a duty therefore to all the world's people, especially the most vulnerable and, in particular, the children of the world, to whom the future belongs.

3. We reaffirm our commitment to the purposes and principles of the Charter of the United Nations, which have proved timeless and universal. Indeed, their relevance and capacity to inspire have increased, as nations and peoples have become increasingly interconnected and interdependent.

4. We are determined to establish a just and lasting peace all over the world in accordance with the purposes and principles of the Charter. We rededicate ourselves to support all efforts to uphold the sovereign equality of all States, respect for their territorial integrity and political independence, resolution of disputes by peaceful means and in conformity with the principles of justice and international law, the right to self-determination of peoples which remain under colonial domination and foreign occupation, non-interference in the internal affairs of States, respect for human rights and fundamental freedoms, respect for the equal rights of all without distinction as to race, sex, language or religion and interna-

tional cooperation in solving international problems of an economic, social, cultural or humanitarian character.

5. We believe that the central challenge we face today is to ensure that globalization becomes a positive force for all the world's people. For while globalization offers great opportunities, at present its benefits are very unevenly shared, while its costs are unevenly distributed. We recognize that developing countries and countries with economies in transition face special difficulties in responding to this central challenge. Thus, only through broad and sustained efforts to create a shared future, based upon our common humanity in all its diversity, can globalization be made fully inclusive and equitable. These efforts must include policies and measures, at the global level, which correspond to the needs of developing countries and economies in transition and are formulated and implemented with their effective participation.

6. We consider certain fundamental values to be essential to international relations in the twenty-first century. These include:

• Freedom. Men and women have the right to live their lives and raise their children in dignity, free from hunger and from the fear of violence, oppression or injustice. Democratic and participatory governance based on the will of the people best assures these rights.

• Equality. No individual and no nation must be denied the opportunity to benefit from development. The equal rights and opportunities of women and men must be assured.

• Solidarity. Global challenges must be managed in a way that distributes the costs and burdens fairly in accordance with basic principles of equity and social justice. Those who suffer or who benefit least deserve help from those who benefit most.

• Tolerance. Human beings must respect one other, in all their diversity of belief, culture and language. Differences within and between societies should be neither feared nor repressed, but cherished as a precious asset of humanity. A culture of peace and dialogue among all civilizations should be actively promoted.

• Respect for nature. Prudence must be shown in the management of all living species and natural resources, in accordance with the precepts of sustainable development. Only in this way can the immeasurable riches provided to us by nature be preserved and passed on to our descendants. The current unsustainable patterns of production and consumption must be changed in the interest of our future welfare and that of our descendants.

• Shared responsibility. Responsibility for managing worldwide economic and social development, as well as threats to international peace and security, must be shared among the nations of the world and should be exercised multilaterally. As the most universal and most representative organization in the world, the United Nations must play the central role.

7. In order to translate these shared values into actions, we have identified key objectives to which we assign special significance.

II. Peace, security and disarmament

8. We will spare no effort to free our peoples from the scourge of war, whether within or between States, which has claimed more than 5 million lives in the past decade. We will also seek to eliminate the dangers posed by weapons of mass destruction.

9. We resolve therefore:

• To strengthen respect for the rule of law in international as in national affairs and, in particular, to ensure compliance by Member States with the decisions of the International Court of Justice, in compliance with the Charter of the United Nations, in cases to which they are parties.

• To make the United Nations more effective in maintaining peace and security by giving it the resources and tools it needs for conflict prevention, peaceful resolution of disputes, peacekeeping, post-conflict peace-building and reconstruction. In this context, we take note of the report of the Panel on United Nations Peace Operations and request the General Assembly to consider its recommendations expeditiously.

• To strengthen cooperation between the United Nations and regional organizations, in accordance with the provisions of Chapter VIII of the Charter.

• To ensure the implementation, by States Parties, of treaties in areas such as arms control and disarmament and of international humanitarian law and human rights law, and call upon all States to consider signing and ratifying the Rome Statute of the International Criminal Court.

• To take concerted action against international terrorism, and to accede as soon as possible to all the relevant international conventions.

• To redouble our efforts to implement our commitment to counter the world drug problem.

• To intensify our efforts to fight transnational crime in all its dimensions, including trafficking as well as smuggling in human beings and money laundering.

• To minimize the adverse effects of United Nations economic sanctions on innocent populations, to subject such sanctions regimes to regular reviews and to eliminate the adverse effects of sanctions on third parties.

• To strive for the elimination of weapons of mass destruction, particularly nuclear weapons, and to keep all options open for achieving this aim, including the possibility of convening an international conference to identify ways of eliminating nuclear dangers.

• To take concerted action to end illicit traffic in small arms and light weapons, especially by making arms transfers more transparent and supporting regional disarmament measures, taking account of all the recommendations of the forthcoming United Nations Conference on Illicit Trade in Small Arms and Light Weapons.

• To call on all States to consider acceding to the Convention on the Prohibition of the Use, Stockpiling, Production and Transfer of Anti-personnel Mines and on Their Destruction, as well as the amended mines protocol to the Convention on conventional weapons.

10. We urge Member States to observe the Olympic Truce, individually and collectively, now and in the future, and to support the International Olympic Committee in its efforts to promote peace and human understanding through sport and the Olympic Ideal.

III. Development and poverty eradication

11. We will spare no effort to free our fellow men, women and children from the abject and dehumanizing conditions of extreme poverty, to which more than a billion of them are currently subjected. We are committed to making the right to development a reality for everyone and to freeing the entire human race from want.

12. We resolve therefore to create an environment— at the national and global levels alike—which is conducive to development and to the elimination of poverty.

13. Success in meeting these objectives depends, *inter alia*, on good governance within each country. It also depends on good governance at the international level and on transparency in the financial, monetary and trading systems. We are committed to an open, equitable, rule-based, predictable and non-discriminatory multilateral trading and financial system.

14. We are concerned about the obstacles developing countries face in mobilizing the resources needed to finance their sustained development. We will there-

fore make every effort to ensure the success of the High-level International and Intergovernmental Event on Financing for Development, to be held in 2001.

15. We also undertake to address the special needs of the least developed countries. In this context, we welcome the Third United Nations Conference on the Least Developed Countries to be held in May 2001 and will endeavour to ensure its success. We call on the industrialized countries:

• To adopt, preferably by the time of that Conference, a policy of duty- and quota-free access for essentially all exports from the least developed countries;

• To implement the enhanced programme of debt relief for the heavily indebted poor countries without further delay and to agree to cancel all official bilateral debts of those countries in return for their making demonstrable commitments to poverty reduction; and

• To grant more generous development assistance, especially to countries that are genuinely making an effort to apply their resources to poverty reduction.

16. We are also determined to deal comprehensively and effectively with the debt problems of low- and middle-income developing countries, through various national and international measures designed to make their debt sustainable in the long term.

17. We also resolve to address the special needs of small island developing States, by implementing the Barbados Programme of Action and the outcome of the twenty-second special session of the General Assembly rapidly and in full. We urge the international community to ensure that, in the development of a vulnerability index, the special needs of small island developing States are taken into account.

18. We recognize the special needs and problems of the landlocked developing countries, and urge both bilateral and multilateral donors to increase financial and technical assistance to this group of countries to meet their special development needs and to help them overcome the impediments of geography by improving their transit transport systems.

19. We resolve further:

• To halve, by the year 2015, the proportion of the world's people whose income is less than one dollar a day and the proportion of people who suffer from hunger and, by the same date, to halve the proportion of people who are unable to reach or to afford safe drinking water.

• To ensure that, by the same date, children everywhere, boys and girls alike, will be able to complete a full course of primary schooling and that girls and boys will have equal access to all levels of education.

• By the same date, to have reduced maternal mortality by three quarters, and under-five child mortality by two thirds, of their current rates.

• To have, by then, halted, and begun to reverse, the spread of HIV/AIDS, the scourge of malaria and other major diseases that afflict humanity.

• To provide special assistance to children orphaned by HIV/AIDS.

• By 2020, to have achieved a significant improvement in the lives of at least 100 million slum dwellers as proposed in the "Cities Without Slums" initiative.

20. We also resolve:

• To promote gender equality and the empowerment of women as effective ways to combat poverty, hunger and disease and to stimulate development that is truly sustainable.

• To develop and implement strategies that give young people everywhere a real chance to find decent and productive work.

• To encourage the pharmaceutical industry to make essential drugs more widely available and affordable by all who need them in developing countries.

• To develop strong partnerships with the private sector and with civil society organizations in pursuit of development and poverty eradication.

• To ensure that the benefits of new technologies, especially information and communication technologies, in conformity with recommendations contained in the ECOSOC 2000 Ministerial Declaration, are available to all.

IV. Protecting our common environment

21. We must spare no effort to free all of humanity, and above all our children and grandchildren, from the threat of living on a planet irredeemably spoilt by human activities, and whose resources would no longer be sufficient for their needs.

22. We reaffirm our support for the principles of sustainable development, including those set out in Agenda 21, agreed upon at the United Nations Conference on Environment and Development.

23. We resolve therefore to adopt in all our environmental actions a new ethic of conservation and stewardship and, as first steps, we resolve:

• To make every effort to ensure the entry into force of the Kyoto Protocol, preferably by the tenth anniversary of the United Nations Conference on Environment and Development in 2002, and to embark on the required reduction in emissions of greenhouse gases.

• To intensify our collective efforts for the management, conservation and sustainable development of all types of forests.

• To press for the full implementation of the Convention on Biological Diversity and the Convention to Combat Desertification in those Countries Experiencing Serious Drought and/or Desertification, particularly in Africa.

• To stop the unsustainable exploitation of water resources by developing water management strategies at the regional, national and local levels, which promote both equitable access and adequate supplies.

• To intensify cooperation to reduce the number and effects of natural and man-made disasters.

• To ensure free access to information on the human genome sequence.

V. Human rights, democracy and good governance

24. We will spare no effort to promote democracy and strengthen the rule of law, as well as respect for all internationally recognized human rights and fundamental freedoms, including the right to development.

25. We resolve therefore:

• To respect fully and uphold the Universal Declaration of Human Rights.

• To strive for the full protection and promotion in all our countries of civil, political, economic, social and cultural rights for all.

• To strengthen the capacity of all our countries to implement the principles and practices of democracy and respect for human rights, including minority rights.

• To combat all forms of violence against women and to implement the Convention on the Elimination of All Forms of Discrimination against Women.

• To take measures to ensure respect for and protection of the human rights of migrants, migrant workers and their families, to eliminate the increasing acts of racism and xenophobia in many societies and to promote greater harmony and tolerance in all societies.

• To work collectively for more inclusive political processes, allowing genuine participation by all citizens in all our countries.

• To ensure the freedom of the media to perform their essential role and the right of the public to have access to information.

VI. Protecting the vulnerable

26. We will spare no effort to ensure that children and all civilian populations that suffer disproportionately the consequences of natural disasters, genocide, armed conflicts and other humanitarian emergencies are given every assistance and protection so that they can resume normal life as soon as possible.

We resolve therefore:

• To expand and strengthen the protection of civilians in complex emergencies, in conformity with international humanitarian law.

• To strengthen international cooperation, including burden sharing in, and the coordination of humanitarian assistance to, countries hosting refugees and to help all refugees and displaced persons to return voluntarily to their homes, in safety and dignity and to be smoothly reintegrated into their societies.

• To encourage the ratification and full implementation of the Convention on the Rights of the Child and its optional protocols on the involvement of children in armed conflict and on the sale of children, child prostitution and child pornography.

VII. Meeting the special needs of Africa

27. We will support the consolidation of democracy in Africa and assist Africans in their struggle for lasting peace, poverty eradication and sustainable development, thereby bringing Africa into the mainstream of the world economy.

28. We resolve therefore:

• To give full support to the political and institutional structures of emerging democracies in Africa.

• To encourage and sustain regional and subregional mechanisms for preventing conflict and promoting political stability, and to ensure a reliable flow of resources for peacekeeping operations on the continent.

• To take special measures to address the challenges of poverty eradication and sustainable development in Africa, including debt cancellation, improved market access, enhanced Official Development Assistance and increased flows of Foreign Direct Investment, as well as transfers of technology.

• To help Africa build up its capacity to tackle the spread of the HIV/AIDS pandemic and other infectious diseases.

VIII. Strengthening the United Nations

29. We will spare no effort to make the United Nations a more effective instrument for pursuing all of these priorities: the fight for development for all the peoples of the world, the fight against poverty, ignorance and disease; the fight against injustice; the fight against violence, terror and crime; and the fight against the degradation and destruction of our common home.

30. We resolve therefore:

• To reaffirm the central position of the General Assembly as the chief deliberative, policy-making and representative organ of the United Nations, and to enable it to play that role effectively.

• To intensify our efforts to achieve a comprehensive reform of the Security Council in all its aspects.

• To strengthen further the Economic and Social Council, building on its recent achievements, to help it fulfil the role ascribed to it in the Charter.

• To strengthen the International Court of Justice, in order to ensure justice and the rule of law in international affairs.

• To encourage regular consultations and coordination among the principal organs of the United Nations in pursuit of their functions.

• To ensure that the Organization is provided on a timely and predictable basis with the resources it needs to carry out its mandates.

• To urge the Secretariat to make the best use of those resources, in accordance with clear rules and procedures agreed by the General Assembly, in the interests of all Member States, by adopting the best management practices and technologies available and by concentrating on those tasks that reflect the agreed priorities of Member States.

• To promote adherence to the Convention on the Safety of United Nations and Associated Personnel.

• To ensure greater policy coherence and better cooperation between the United Nations, its agencies, the Bretton Woods Institutions and the World Trade Organization, as well as other multilateral bodies, with a view to achieving a fully coordinated approach to the problems of peace and development.

• To strengthen further cooperation between the United Nations and national parliaments through their world organization, the Inter-Parliamentary Union, in various fields, including peace and security, economic and social development, international law and human rights and democracy and gender issues.

• To give greater opportunities to the private sector, non-governmental organizations and civil society, in general, to contribute to the realization of the Organization's goals and programmes.

31. We request the General Assembly to review on a regular basis the progress made in implementing the provisions of this Declaration, and ask the Secretary-General to issue periodic reports for consideration by the General Assembly and as a basis for further action.

32. We solemnly reaffirm, on this historic occasion, that the United Nations is the indispensable common house of the entire human family, through which we will seek to realize our universal aspirations for peace, cooperation and development. We therefore pledge our unstinting support for these common objectives and our determination to achieve them.

8th plenary meeting
8 September 2000

APPENDIX B

Millennium Development Goals, Targets, and Indicators

GOAL 1   Eradicate extreme poverty and hunger

Target 1: Reduce by half the proportion of people living on less than a dollar a day

1. Proportion of Population Below $1 (PPP) per Day (World Bank)

2. Poverty Gap Ratio, $1 per day (World Bank)

3. Share of Poorest Quintile in National Income or Consumption (World Bank)

Target 2: Reduce by half the proportion of people who suffer from hunger

4. Prevalence of Underweight Children Under Five Years of Age (UNICEF)

5. Proportion of the Population below Minimum Level of Dietary Energy Consumption (FAO)

GOAL 2   Achieve universal primary education

Target 3: Ensure that all boys and girls complete a full course of primary schooling

6. Net Enrolment Ratio in Primary Education (UNESCO)

7. Proportion of Pupils Starting Grade 1 who Reach Grade 5 (UNESCO)

8. Literacy Rate of 15-24 year-olds (UNESCO)

GOAL 3   Promote gender equality and empower women

Target 4: Eliminate gender disparity in primary and secondary education preferably by 2005, and at all levels by 2015

9. Ratio of Girls to Boys in Primary, Secondary, and Tertiary Education (UNESCO)

10. Ratio of Literate Women to Men 15-24 years old (UNESCO)

11. Share of Women in Wage Employment in the Non-Agricultural Sector (ILO)

12. Proportion of Seats Held by Women in National Parliaments (IPU)

GOAL 4   Reduce child mortality

Target 5: Reduce by two thirds the mortality rate among children under five

13. Under-Five Mortality Rate (UNICEF)

14. Infant Mortality Rate (UNICEF)

15. Proportion of 1 year-old Children Immunised Against Measles (UNICEF)

GOAL 5   Improve maternal health

Target 6: Reduce by three quarters the maternal mortality ratio

16. Maternal Mortality Ratio (WHO)

17. Proportion of Births Attended by Skilled Health Personnel (UNICEF)

GOAL 6   Combat HIV/AIDS, malaria and other diseases

Target 7: Halt and begin to reverse the spread of HIV/AIDS

> 18. HIV Prevalence Among 15-24 year-old Pregnant Women (UN-AIDS)

> 19. Condom use rate of the contraceptive prevalence rate and Population aged 15-24 years with comprehensive correct knowledge of HIV/AIDS(UNAIDS, UNICEF, UN Population Division, WHO)

> 20. Ratio of school attendance of orphans to school attendance of non-orphans aged 10-14 years

Target 8: Halt and begin to reverse the incidence of malaria and other major diseases

> 21. Prevalence and Death Rates Associated with Malaria (WHO):

> 22. Proportion of Population in Malaria Risk Areas Using Effective Malaria Prevention and Treatment Measures (UNICEF):

> 23. Prevalence and Death Rates Associated with Tuberculosis (WHO):

> 24. Proportion of Tuberculosis Cases Detected and Cured Under Directly-Observed Treatment Short Courses (WHO)

GOAL 7   Ensure environmental sustainability

Target 9: Integrate the principles of sustainable development into country policies and programmes; reverse loss of environmental resources

> 25. Forested land as percentage of land area (FAO)

> 26. Ratio of Area Protected to Maintain Biological Diversity to Surface Area (UNEP)

> 27. Energy supply (apparent consumption; Kg oil equivalent) per $1,000 (PPP) GDP (World Bank)

> 28. Carbon Dioxide Emissions (per capita) and Consumption of Ozone-Depleting CFCs (ODP tons):

Target 10: Reduce by half the proportion of people without sustainable access to safe drinking water

> 29. Proportion of the Population with Sustainable Access to and Improved Water Source (WHO/UNICEF)

> 30. Proportion of the Population with Access to Improved Sanitation (WHO/UNICEF)

Target 11: Achieve significant improvement in lives of at least 100 million slum dwellers, by 2020

> 31. Slum population as percentage of urban population (secure tenure index) (UN-Habitat)

GOAL 8   Develop a global partnership for development

Target 12. Develop further an open, rule-based, predictable, non-discriminatory trading and financial system Includes a commitment to good governance, development, and poverty reduction — both nationally and internationally

Target 13. Address the special needs of the least developed countries Includes: tariff and quota free access for least developed countries' exports; enhanced programme of debt relief for HIPCs and cancellation of official bilateral debt; and more generous ODA for countries committed to poverty reduction

Target 14. Address the special needs of landlocked countries and small island developing States

Target 15. Deal comprehensively with the debt problems of developing countries through national and international measures in order to make debt sustainable in the long term.

Target 16: In cooperation with developing countries, develop and implement strategies for decent and productive work for youth.

Target 17: In cooperation with pharmaceutical companies, provide access to affordable essential drugs in developing countries

Target 18: In cooperation with the private sector, make available the benefits of new technologies, especially information and communications

Official development assistance

> 32. Net ODA as percentage of OECD/DAC donors' gross national product (targets of 0.7% in total and 0.15% for LDCs)

> 33. Proportion of ODA to basic social services (basic education, primary health care, nutrition, safe water and sanitation)
> 34. Proportion of ODA that is untied

35. Proportion of ODA for environment in small
island developing States 36. Proportion of ODA for transport sector in
landlocked countries

Market access

37. Proportion of exports (by value and excluding arms) admitted free
of duties and quotas

38. Average tariffs and quotas on agricultural products and textiles and
clothing

39. Domestic and export agricultural subsidies in OECD countries

40. Proportion of ODA provided to help build tradecapacity

Debt sustainability

41. Proportion of official bilateral HIPC debt cancelled

42. Total Number of Countries that Have Reached their HIPC Decision
Points and Number that Have Reached their Completion Points (Cumu-
lative) (HIPC) (World Bank-IMF)

43. Debt Service as a Percentage of Exports of Goods and Services
(World Bank)

44. Debt Relief Committed Under HIPC Initiative (HIPC) (World
Bank-IMF)

45. Unemployment of 15-24 year-olds, Each Sex and Total (ILO)

46. Proportion of Population with Access to Affordable, Essential
Drugs on a Sustainable Basis (WHO)

47. Telephone Lines and Cellular Subscribers per 100 Population (ITU)

48. Personal Computers in Use and Internet Users per 100 Population
(ITU)

BIBLIOGRAPHY

Adams, Richard. "Economic Growth, Inequality, and Poverty: Findings from a New Data Set." *World Bank Policy Research Working Paper 2972*. Washington, D. C.: World Bank, 2003.

Adelman H. and J. Sorenson, eds. *African Refugees: Development Aid and Repatriation.* Boulder, CO: Westview Press, 1994.

Adelman, Irma and Cynthia T. Morris. *Economic Growth and Social Equity in Developing Countries.* Stanford: Stanford University Press, 1973.

Afsar, R. "Rural-Urban Dichotomy and Convergence: Emerging Realities in Bangladesh." *Environment and Urbanization* 11:1 (1999): 235-247.

Agarwal, Bina. "Gender Relations and Food Security: Coping with Seasonality, Drought and Famine in South Asia." in Lourdes Benería and Shelley Feldman, eds. *Unequal Burden: Economic Crises, Persistent Poverty, and Women's Work.* Boulder, CO. Westview Press, 1992.

Agence France-Presse, "Military clash with rebels in Central African Republic." www.reliefweb.int/rwr. (April 27, 2007).

Aggarwal, Rimjhim M. "Resource-Poor Farmers in South India." World Institute for Development Economics Research Paper No. 2006/97. Helsinki: UNU-WIDER, 2006.

Ahlstram, C. *Casualties of Conflict: Report for the Protection of Victims of War.* Uppsala: Department of Peace and Conflict, Uppsala University, 1991.

Ahmad, Sultan. 2003. "Purchasing Power Parity for International Comparison of Poverty: Sources and Methods," World Bank, www.worldbank.org/data/ICP.

Ambrose, Saint. "Duties of the Clergy" in *Selected Works and Letters.* Philp Schaff, ed. *Nicene and Post Nicene Fathers.* Series II Volume X. Grand Rapids: Michigan: William B. Eerdmans, 2002.

Amstutz, Mark R. "The Churches and Third World Poverty." in *On Moral Business: Classical and Contemporary Resources for Ethics in Economic Life.* Max L. Stackhouse, Dennis P. McCann, and Shirely J. Roels eds. Grand Rapids, Michigan: William B. Eerdmans Publishing Company, 1995.

Aptekar, Lewis. "Street Children in the Developing World: A Review of Their Condition." *Cross-Cultural Research* 28 (1994): 195-224.

Aptekar, Lewis and Robert Giel. "Walks in Kaliti Life in a Destitute Shelter for the Displaced." In *Trauma, War, and Violence: Public Mental Health in Socio-cultural Context,* ed. Joop de Jong, 337-366, New York: Kluwer Academic/Plenum Publishers, 2002.

Arunatilake, N., S. Jayasuriya and S. Kelegama "The Economic Cost of the War in Sri Lanka." *World Development* 29 (2000): 1483-500.

Ascherio, Alberto, Robin Bielik, Andy Epstein, *et. al.* "Death and Injuries Caused by Landmines in Mozambique." *Lancet* 346 (1977): 721-724.

Avila, Charles. *Ownership: Early Christian Teaching.* London: Sheed & Ward, 1983.

Awad, Salwa Saad. 2002. "The Invisible Citizens Roaming the City Streets." *Educational Review* 54 (2002): 105-13.

Azam, Jean-Paul and Anke Hoeffler. "Violence Against Civilians in Civil Wars: Looting or Terror?" *Journal of Peace Research* 39 (2002): 461-485.

Baker, Rachel. "Runaway Street Children in Nepal: Social Competence Away from Home." In *Children and Social Competence: Arenas of Action,* edited by Ian Hutchby and Jo Moran-Ellis, 46-63. London: Falmer Press, 1988.

Bales, Kevin. *Understanding Global Slavery.* Berkeley: University of California Press, 2005.

Bapat, Meera and Indu Agarwal. "Our Needs, Our Priorities; Women and Men from the Slums in Mumbai and Pune Talk About Their Needs for Water and Sanitation." *Environment & Urbanization* 15 (2003): 71-86.

Barany, Z. *The East European Gypsies: Regime Change, Marginality and Ethnopolitics.* Cambridge: Cambridge University Press, 2001.

Bartholomew, Craig and Thornton Moritz. *Christ and Consumerism.* Carlisle: Paternoster Press, 2000.

Bartlett, Sheridan. "Children's experience of the physical environment in poor urban settlements and the implications for policy, planning and practice." *Environment & Urbanization* 11 (1999): 63-73.

Beah, Ishmael. *A Long Way Gone: Memoirs of a Boy Soldier.* Farrar, Straus & Giroux, 2006.

Bell-Fialkoff, Andrew. *Ethnic Cleansing.* New York: Palgrave MacMillan, 1999.

Bhalla, Surjit. *Imagine There is No Country: Poverty, Inequality, and Growth in the Era of Globalization.* Washington, D.C.: Institute for International Economics, 2002.

Biggar, Nigel. *The Good Life: Reflections on What We Value Today.* London: SPCK, 1997.

Birch, Bruce C. "Hunger, Poverty and Biblical religion," *The Christian Century* 92 (1975): 593-599.

Birch, Bruce C. and Larry L. Rasmussen. *The Predicament of the Prosperous.* Philadelphia: Westminster Press, 1978.

Birdsall, Nancy, and Michael Clemens. "From Promise to Performance: How Rich Countries Can Help Poor Countries help Themselves." CGD Brief 1 (2) Washington, D.C.: Center for Global Development, 2003.

Bloesch, Donald. *Freedom for Obedience: Evangelical Ethics in Contemporary Times.* San Francisco: Harper & Row, 1987.

Bonino, José M. *Revolutionary Theology Comes of Age.* London: SPCK 1975.

Boyden, J. *Children of the Cities.* Atlantic Highlands, NJ: Zed Books 1991.

Boyden, J. and J. de Berry, eds. *Children and Youth on the Front Line: Ethnography, Armed Conflict and Displacement.* New York: Berghahn Books, 2004.

Bradley, Christine. "Why Male Violence against Women is a Development Issue: Reflections from Papua New Guinea." In Miranda Davies, ed. *Women and Violence: Realities and Responses Worldwide* London: Zed Books, 1994.

Bringa, Tone. "Averted Gaze: Genocide in Bosnia-Herzegovina, 1992-1995," in Alexander Laban Hinton ed. *Annihilating Difference: The Anthropology of Genocide.* Berkeley: University of California Press, 2002.

Britton, Andrew and Peter Sedgwick. *Economic Theory and Christian Belief.* Bern: Peter Lang, 2003.

Brookman, W. R. *Grinding the Face of the Poor: A Reader in Biblical Justice.* Minneapolis: North Central University Press, 2006.

Brown, Malcolm. *After the Market; Economics, Moral Agreement and the Churches Mission.* Bern: Peter Lang, 2004.

Burghardt, Walter J. *Justice: A Global Adventure.* Maryknoll, NY: Orbis Books, 2004.

Caldwell, J. "Education as a Factor in Mortality Decline: An Examination of Nigerian Data," *Population Studies* 33 (1979): 395-419.

Caldwell, J. "How is Greater Maternal Education Translated into Lower Child Mortality?" *Health Transition Review* 4 (1994): 224-29.

Caldwell, J. and P. Caldwell. "Famine in Africa: A Global Perspective." In Pison de Wall Van, and Mpembele Sala Diakanda eds., *Mortality and Society in Sub-Saharan Africa.* Oxford: Clarendon Press, 1992.

Centre for Community Economics and Development Consultants Society. *Report on Social Assessment for the District Poverty Initiatives Project: Baran District.* Jaipur, India: Institute of Development Studies, 1997.

Chen, Shaohua and Martin Ravallion. "How Did the World's Poorest Faire in the 1990s?" World Bank Policy Research Working Paper Series 2409. Washington, D. C.: World Bank, 2000.

Chen, Shaohua and Martin Ravallion. "How Have the World's Poorest Fared Since the Early 1980s?" World Bank Policy Research Working Paper 3341. Washington, D. C.: World Bank, 2004.

Chen, Shaohua, and Yan Wang. "China's Growth and Poverty Reduction: Trends between 1990 and 1999." World Bank Policy Research Working Paper Series 2651. Washington, D. C.: World Bank, 2001.

Chitekwe, Beth and Diana Mitlin. "The Urban Poor Under Threat and in Struggle: Option for Urban Development in Zimbabwe, 1995-2000." *Environment & Urbanization* 13 (2001): 85-101.

Christiaensen, L., and H. Alderman. "Child Malnutrition in Ethiopia: Can Maternal knowledge Augment the Role of Income?" African Region Working paper Series No. 22.Washington, D. C.: World Bank, 2001.

Chrysostom, John in J. P. Migne ed., *Patrologiae Graeca*, vol 61, Paris: Migne, 1862.

Claiborne, Shane. *The Irresistible Revolution.* Grand Rapids, MI: Zondervan, 2006.

Collier, Jane and Rafael Esteban. *From Complicity to Encounter: The Church and the Culture of Economism.* Harrisburg: Trinity Press International, 1998.

Collier, Paul. *The Bottom Billion: Why the Poorest Countries Are Failing and What Can Be Done About It.* New York: Oxford University Press, 2007.

Cosgrove, J. "Towards a Working Definition of Street Children." *International Social Work* 33 (1990):185-192.

Coudouel, Aline, Jesko. Hentschel, and Quentin T. Wodon. "Poverty Measurement and Analysis," in Jeni Klugman ed. *A Sourcebook for Poverty Reduction Strategies. Washington, D.C.* The World Bank, 2003.

Curlin, Chen G. and S. Hussain. "Demographic Crisis: The Impact of the Bangladesh Civil War (1971) on Births and Deaths in Rural Areas of Bangladesh." *Population Studies* 30 (1976): 87-105.

Davies, Miranda, ed. *Women and Violence: Realities and Responses Worldwide.* London: Zed Books, 1994.

de Jong, Joop, ed. Trauma, War, and Violence: *Public Mental Health in Socio-cultural Context*. New York: Kluwer Academic/Plenum Publishers, 1990.

de Wall Van, Pison, Mpembele Sala-Diakanda, eds., *Mortality and Society in Sub-Saharan Africa*. Oxford: Clarendon Press, 1992.

De Onis, Mercedes, Monika Blössner, Elaine Borghi, Edward A. Frongillo, and Richard Morris. "Estimates of Global Prevalence of Children Under Weight in 1990 and 2015." *Journal of the American Medical Association* 291 (2004): 2600-06.

De Soto, Hermine G., and Nora Dudwick. "Poverty in Moldova: The Social Dimensions of Transition, June 1996-May 1997." Washington, D.C.: World Bank, 1997.

Deaton, Angus. "Counting the World's Poor: Problems and Possible Solutions." *Word Bank Research Observer* 16 (2001): 125-147.

Derluyn, Ilse, Eric Broekaert and Gilberte Schuyten. "Post-traumatic Stress in Former Ugandan Child Soldiers," *The Lancet* 363 (2004): 861-863.

Dimmelen, R. van. *Faith in the Global Economy: A Primer for Christians*. Geneva: World Council of Churches, 1998.

Dollar, David. "Globalization, Poverty, and Inequity since 1980. World Bank Policy Research Working Paper 3333. Washington, D. C.: World Bank, 2004.

Dollar, David and Paul Collier, eds., *Globalization, Growth, and Poverty: Building an Inclusive World Economy*. New York: Oxford University Press, 2002.

Dollar, David and Robert Gatti. "Gender Inequality, Income, and Growth: Are Good Times Good for Women?" *Policy Research Report on Gender and Development*, No. 1. Washington, D.C.: World Bank, 1995.

Dollar, David and Aart Kray. "Growth is Good for the Poor." World Bank Policy Research Working Paper 2587. Washington, D. C.: World Bank, 2001.

Dowdney, Luke. *Children of the Drug Trade*. Rio de Janeiero: Viveiros de Castro Editoria, 2003.

Doyle, R. "Leveling the Playing Field." *Scientific American* 32 (2005): 68-72.

Drèze. Jean and Amartya Sen. *Hunger and Public Action*. Oxford: Oxford University Press, 1989.

Drèze, Jean, Amartya Sen, and Athar Hussain (eds.). *The Political Economy of Hunger*. Oxford: Oxford University Press., 1995

Dunson, Donald H. *No Room at the Table*. Maryknoll, NY: Orbis Books, 2003.

Easterly, William. *White Man's Burden: Why the West's Efforts to Aid the Rest Have Done So Much Ill and So Little Good*. New York: Penguin Press, 2006.

Ehrman, Bart D., ed. *The Apostolic Fathers*. Cambridge, MA: Harvard University Press, 2003.

Farmer, Paul. *Pathologies of Power: Health, human Rights, and the New War on the Poor*. Berkeley: University of California Press, 2005.

Finckenauer, James O. "Russian Transnational Organized Crime and Human Trafficking," in David Kyle and Rey Koslowski, eds., *Global Human Smuggling*, Baltimore: Johns Hopkins University Press, 2001.

Finnerty, Adam Daniel. *No More Plastic Jesus: Global justice and Christian Lifestyle*. Maryknoll, NY: Orbis Books, 1977.

Forrester, Duncan B. *Beliefs, Values and Policies*. Oxford: Clarendon Press, 1989.

Forrester, Duncan B. *On Human Worth*. London: SCM Press, 2001.

Forrester, Duncan B. and Danus Skene, eds., *Just Sharing: A Christian Approach to the Distribution of Wealth, Income and Benefits*. London: Epworth Press, 1988.

Forsyth, Justin. Letter to the Editor. *The Economist*, 20 (2000): 6.

Foster, Phillips and Howard D. Leathers. *The World Food Problem*. London: Lynne Reinner Publishers, 1999.

Galeano, Eduardo. *The Book of Embraces*. New York: W. W. Norton & Company, 1992.

Gelin, Albert. *The Poor of Yahweh*. Collegeville, MN: The Liturgical Press, 1964.

Gerson, Michael. "Hyperinflation ruining Zimbabwe." *Minneapolis Star Tribune*, February 22, 2008.

Ghobarah, Hazem A., Paul Huth, and Bruce Russett. "Civil Wars Kill and maim People—Long After the Shooting Stops," *American Political Science Review* 97 (2003): 189-202.

Gibb, Richard. *Grace and Global Justice*. Paternoster Theological Monographs. Waynesboro, GA: Paternoster, 2006.

Gomart, Elizabeth. "Between Civil War and Land Reform: Among the Poorest of the poor in Tajikistan," in Nora Dudwick, Elizabeth Gomart, and Alexandre Marc, eds., *When Things Fall Apart: Qualitative Studies of poverty in the Former Soviet Union*, Washington, D.C.: World Bank, 2003.

Gragnolati, M. "Children's Growth and poverty in Rural Guatemala." Latin American and the Caribbean Region Human Development Sector Unit, World Bank Policy Research Working Paper 2193. Washington, D. C.: World Bank, 1999.

Grams, Rollin G. "From Being to Doing: The identity of God's people as the ground for building a Christian social ethic." *Transformation* 18 (2001):155-71.

Grant, Beth. "Sexual Slavery and the Gospel," in B. Brenneman, W. R. Brookman and N. Muhovich, eds., *Java & Justice: Journeys in Pentecostal Missions Education*. Minneapolis: North Central University Press, 2006.

Grant, James P. *The State of the World's Children 1995*. New York: Oxford University Press, 1995.

Graybiel, A.M. "Guide to the anatomy of the brain: the basal ganglia." in J. H. Byrne, ed. *Encyclopedia of Learning and Memory*. New York: MacMillan, 2002.

Graybiel, A.M. and S. Grillner, eds., *Microcircuits: The Interface Between Neurons and Global Brain Function*. Cambridge, MA: MIT Press, 2006.

Graybiel, A.M. and E. Saka. 2003. "The basal ganglia and the control of action." in M.S. Gazzaniga, ed. *The New Cognitive Neurosciences*. Cambridge, MA: MIT Press, 2003.

Greitens, Eric. "The Treatment of Children During Conflict." in F. Stewart, and Valpy Fitzgerald, eds., *War and Underdevelopment, Vol I: The Economic and Social Consequences of Conflict*. New York: Oxford University Press, 2001.

Gupta, S., B. Clements, R. Bhattacharya and S. Chakravarti. "Fiscal Consequences of Armed Conflict and Terrorism in Low and Middle-income Countries." *European Journal of Political Economy* 20 (2004):403-21.

Gustason, Per, Renee Norberg, Badara Samb, Anders Naucler, and Peter Aaby. "Tuberculosis Mortality during a Civil War in Guinea-Bissau." *Journal of the American Medical Association* 286 (2001): 599-603.

Gutiérrez, Gustavo. *A Theology of Liberation: History, Politics and Salvation*. London: SCM Press, 1978.

Gutiérrez, Gustavo. "The Violence of a System." in Dietmar Mieth and Jacques Pohierm eds., *Christian Ethics and Economics: The North-South Conflict*. New York: Seabury Press, 1980.

Gwatkin, Davidson, and Michel Gulliot. "The Burden of Disease among the Global Poor." Health, Nutrition, and Population Series. Washington, D.C.: World Bank, 2000.

Haidar, J., and T. Demissie. "Nutrition Situation in Ethiopia." *South African Journal of Clinical Nutrition* 89 (1999): 181-83.

Hailu, T. Wolde-Georgis, T. and Van Arsdale, P. "Resource Depletion, Famine and Refugees in Tigrai." in Adelman H. and J. Sorenson, eds., *African Refugees: Development Aid and Repatriation*. Boulder, CO: Westview Press, 1994.

Hanks, T.D. *God So Loved the Third World*. Trans. J.C. Dekker. Maryknoll, N.Y.: Orbis Books, 1994.

Hanson, N.R. *Patterns of Discovery*. London: Cambridge University Press, 1958.

Hardoy, Jorge, S. Cairncross and D. Satterthwaite, eds. *The Poor Die Young: Housing and Health in Third World Cities*. London: Earthscan, 1990.

Harries, Richard. *Is There a Gospel for the Rich?* London: Mowbray, 1992.

Harrison, A. ed. *Globalization and Poverty*. National Bureau of Economic Research Conference Report. Chicago: University of Chicago Press, 2006.

Harriss, Barbara. "The Intrafamily Distribution of Hunger in South Asia." in Jean Drèze, Amartya Sen, and Athar Hussai, eds. *The Political Economy of Hunger*. Oxford: Oxford University Press, 1997.

Hasan, Arif. *Understanding Karachi*. Karachi: City Press, 1999.

Hatzfeld, Jean. *Machete Season: The Killers in Rwanda Speak*. New York: Farrar, Straus and Giroux, 2003.

Hauerwas, Stanley. *The Peaceable Kingdom: A Primer in Christian Ethics*. London: SCM Press, 1983.

Haughey, John C., ed. *The Faith That Does Justice*. Woodstock Studies 2. New York: Paulist Press, 1977.

Haughey, John C. "Jesus as the Justice of God." In *The Faith That Does Justice*. John Haughey ed. Woodstock Studies 2. New York: Paulist Press, 1977.

Hay, Donald and Alan Kreider, eds. *Christianity and the Culture of Economics*. Cardiff: University of Wales Press, 2001.

Hays, Richard B. *The Moral Vision of the New Testament: A Contemporary Introduction to New Testament Ethics*. New York: HarperCollins, 1996.

Hecht, Tobias. *At Home in the Street: Street Children in Northeast Brazil*. Cambridge: Cambridge University Press, 1998.

Heilbroner, Robert L. *The Great Ascent: The Struggle for Economic Development in Our Time*, New York: Harper & Row, 1963.

Heinonen, Paola. *Anthropology of Street Children in Addis Ababa, Ethiopia*. Unpublished Ph.D. Dissertation. Durham, UK: University of Durham, 2000.

Hentschel, Jesko, William F. Waters, and Anna Kathryn Vandever Webb. "Rural Poverty in Ecuador—A Qualitative Assessment." Washington, D.C.: World Bank, 1996.

Hicks, Douglas A. *Inequality and Christian Ethics* Cambridge: Cambridge University Press, 2000.

Hinton, Alexander Laban ed. *Annihilating Difference: The Anthropology of Genocide*. Berkeley: University of California Press, 2002.

Hofmane, L. "Report on the Qualitative Analysis Research into the Living Standards of Inhabitants in Aluksne District." Washington, D.C.: World Bank, 1997.

Holland, J. and J. Blackburn, eds. *Whose Voice? Participatory Research and Policy Change*. London: Intermediate Technology Publications, 1998.

Holman, Bob. *et al. Faith in the Poor*. Oxford: Lion, 1998.

Hoogstraten, Hans-Dirk van. *Deep Economy: Caring for Ecology, Humanity and Religion*. Cambridge: James Clark, 2001.

Human Rights Watch/AFRICA. *Children in Sudan: Slaves, Street Children and Child Soldiers*. Washington, D.C.: Human Rights Watch, 1995.

Human Rights Watch. *The War Within the War: Sexual violence against women and girls in Eastern Congo*. New York: Human Rights Watch, 2007.

Hutchby, Ian and Jo Moran-Ellis, eds. *Children and Social Competence: Arenas of Action.* London: Falmer Press, 1988.

Iceland, John. *Poverty in America.* Berkeley: University of California Press, 2006.

Institute for Sociological and Political-Legal Research. "Qualitative Analysis of the Living Standard of the Population of the Republic of Macedonia." Skopje: Institute for Sociological and Political-Legal Research, 1998.

International Catholic Children's Bureau. *Forum on Street Children and Youth.* Grand Bassam, Ivory Coast: International Catholic Children's Bureau, 1985.

Jackson, Cecile. "Rescuing Gender from the Poverty Trap." *World Development* 23 (1996): 489-504.

Jayne, T., J. Strauss, T. Yamano, and D. Molla. "Targeting Food Aid in Rural Ethiopia: Chronic Need or Inertia." *Journal of Development Economics* 68 (2002): 247-88.

Jarl, Ann-Cathrin. *In Justice: Women and Global Economics.* Minneapolis: Fortress Press, 2003.

Johnson, Kelly S. *The Fear of Beggars: Stewardship and poverty in Christian Ethics.* Grand Rapids: Michigan: William B. Eerdmans Publishing Company, 2007.

Johnson, R.B. *World View and International Development: A Critical Study of the Idea of Progress in Development Work of World Vision Tanzania.* Ph.D. thesis. Oxford Centre for Mission Studies, Oxford, UK, 1998.

Johnstone, Patrick and Jason Mandryk. *Operation World.* Waynesboro, GA: Authentic Media, 2001.

Kabaakchieva, P., I. Illiev, and Y. Konstantinov. "Reeling from Change," in Deepa Narayan and Patti Petesch, eds., *Voices of the Poor: From Many Lands.* New York: Oxford University Press, 2002.

Kabeer, Naila. "Women, Wages and Intra-household Power Relations in Urban Bangladesh." *Development and Change* 28 (1997): 261-302.

Kassouf, A., and B. Senauer. "Direct and indirect Effects of Parental Education on Malnutrition among Children in Brazil: A Full Income Approach." *Economic Development and Cultural Change* 44 (1996): 817-38.

Keraita, Bernard, Pay Drechsel and Philip Amoah. "Influence of Urban Wastewater on Stream Water quality and Agriculture In and Around Kumasi, Ghana." *Environment & Urbanization* 15 (2003): 171-78.

Khare, R. S. *Culture and Reality: Essays on the Hindu System of Managing Foods.* Simla: Indian Institute of Advance Study, 1977.

Kierkegaard, Søren. *Works of Love.* trans. David Swenson. London: Oxford University Press, 1946.

Kim, Ik Ki. "Differentiation among the urban poor and the reproduction of poverty: the case of Nanjido." *Environment and Urbanization* 7 (1995): 183-94.

Kim, Jim Yong, Joyce V. Millen, Alec Irwin, and John Gershman eds. *Dying for Growth: Global Inequality and the Health of the Poor.* Monroe, Maine: Common Courage Press, 2000.

Kiros, Gebre-Egziabher and Dennis P. Hogan. "War, famine and excess child mortality in Africa: the role of parental education." *International Journal of Epidemiology* 30 (2001): 447-455.

Klitgaard, Robert. "Subverting Corruption." *Finance and Development* 37 (2000): 2-5.

Korey, William. "Raphael Lemkin: 'The Unofficial Man'" *Midstream*, June/July (1989): 45-48.

Kovats-Bernat, Christopher J. *Sleeping Rough in Port-Au-Prince: An Ethnography of Street Children and Violence in Haiti.* Gainsville: University Press of Florida, 2006.

Kunfaa, Ernest Y. and Tony Dogbe. "Empty Pockets," in Deepa Narayan and Patti Petesch, eds., *Voices of the Poor: From Many Lands*. New York: Oxford University Press, 2002.

Kraybill, Donald B. *The Upside-Down Kingdom*. Scottdale, PA: Herald Press, 1978.

Lemkin, Raphael. "Akte der Barbarei und des Vandalismus als *delicta juris gentium*"(Acts of Barbarism and Vandalism under the Law of Nations), *Anwaltsblatt Internationales* 19 (1933): 117-119.

———. *Axis Rule In Occupied Europe: Laws Of Occupation, Analysis Of Government, Proposals For Redress*. Washington: Carnegie Endowment for International Peace, Division of International Law, 1944.

Lopez, Humberto and Quentin Wodon. "The Economic Impact of Armed Conflict in Rwanda*." Journal of African Economies* 14 (2005): 586-602.

Lumpe, Lora and Jeff Donarski. *The Arms Trade Revealed: A Guide for Investigators and Activists*. Washington, D.C.: Federation of American Scientists, 1998.

Lusk, Mark. "Street Children of Rio De Janeiro." *International Social Work* 35 (1991): 293-305.

Lusk, Mark and Derek Mason. "Fieldwork with Rio's Street Children." In Irene Rizzini, ed. *Children in Brazil Today: A Challenge for the Third Millennium*, 157-176, Rio de Janeiro: Editora Universitaria Santa Ursula, 1994.

Lyon, James. "Yugoslavia's Hyperinflation, 1993-1994: A Social History," *East European Politics and Societies* 10 (1996): 293-327.

Mandelbrot, Benoît. *The Fractal Geometry of Nature*. New York: W.H. Freeman & Co., 1982.

Mann, Gillian. "Separated Çhildren," in Boyden, J. and J. de Berry eds. *Children and Youth on the Front Line: Ethnography, Armed Conflict and Displacement*. New York: Berghahn Books, 2004.

Martin, James. "Raphael Lemkin and the Invention of 'Genocide, '" *The Journal of Historical Review*, 2 (1981): 19-34.

Martin, Susan Forbes and Trish Hiddleston. "Burundi: A Case of Humanitarian Neglect," in N. Van Hear and C. McDowell, eds., *Catching Fire: Containing Forced Migration in Volatile World*. New York: Lexington Books, 2006.

Mawson, Andrew. "Children, Impunity and Justice: Some Dilemmas from Northern Uganda," In J. Boyden and J. de Berry, eds., *Children and Youth on the Front Line: Ethnography, Armed Conflict and Displacement*. (New York: Berghahn Books 2004.

McClan, Kimberley, and Charles Lwanga Ntale. "Desk Review of Participatory Approaches to Assess poverty in Uganda." The Ministry of Planning and Economic Development, Kampala, Uganda, 1998.

McLean, Jennifer, and Thomas Greene. "Turmoil in Tajikistan: addressing the crisis of internal displacement," in Roberta Cohen and Francis Madding Deng, eds., *The Forsaken People: Case Studies of the Internally Displaced*, Washington, D.C.: Brookings Institution Press, 1998.

Mieth, Dietmar and Jacques Pohier eds. *Christian Ethics and Economics: The North-South Conflict*. New York: Seabury Press, 1980.

Millen, Joyce V. and Timothy H. Holtz. "Transnational Corporations and the Health of the Poor." in Kim, Jim Yong, Joyce V. Millen, Alec Irwin, and John Gershman, eds., *Dying for Growth: Global Inequality and the Health of the Poor*, 177-223, Monroe, Maine: Common Courage Press, 2000.

Ministry of Economic Planning and Development of the Kingdom of Swaziland and the World Bank. "Swaziland: Poverty Assessment by the Poor." Washington, D.C.: World Bank, 1997.

Morgan, Elizabeth. *Global Poverty and Personal Responsibility*. New York: Paulist Press, 1989.

Mother Teresa. *Everything Starts from Prayer*. Ashland, Oregon: White Cloud Press, 2000.

Mother Teresa. 1997. *No Greater Love*. Novato, CA: New World Library.

Mott, Stephen and Ronald J. Sider, "Economic Justice: A Biblical Paradigm." *Transformation* 17 (2000): 50-63.

Murray, C.J.L. and A.D. Lopez. *The Global Burden of Disease*. Boston: Harvard University Press, 1996.

Murshed, S. M. *Globalization, Marginalization and Development*. London: Routeldge, 2002.

Mutebi, Frederick Golooba, Simon Stone and Neil Thin. "Rawanda," *Development Policy Review* 21 (2003): 253-70.

Myers, Bryant L. *Walking With the Poor*. Maryknoll, NY: Orbis Books, 2006.

Myers, W. "Urban Working Children: A comparison of four surveys from South Africa." *International Labor* 188 (1989): 321-335.

Nafziger, E.W., F. Stewart and R. Vayrynen, eds., *War, Hunger, and Displacement: The origins of humanitarian emergencies, Volume 2: Case Studies*. New York: Oxford University Press, 2000.

Narayan, Deepa, and David Nyamwaya. "Learning from the Poor: A participatory Poverty Assessment in Kenya." Washington, D.C.: World Bank, 1996.

Narayan, Deepa, Raj Patel, Kai Schafft, Anne Rademacher, and Sarah Koch-Schulte. *Voices of the Poor: Can Anyone Hear Us?* New York: Oxford University Press, 2000.

Narayan, Deepa, and Lant Pritchet. "Cents and Sociability: Household Income and Social Capital in Rural Tanzania." *Economic Development and Cultural Change* 47 (1999): 871-78.

Narayan, Deepa, and Patti Petesch, eds., *Voices of the Poor: From Many Lands*. New York: Oxford University Press, 2002.

Nardoni, Enrique. *Rise Up, O Judge*. trans. by Sean Charles Martin. Peabody, MA: Hendrickson Publishers, 2004.

Neuffer, Elizabeth. *The Key to My Neighbor's House: Seeking Justice in Bosnia and Rwanda*. New York: Picador, 2001.

Nicol, A. *Carrying the Can: Children and their Water Environments*. London: Save the Children UK, 1998.

Nygren, Anders. *Agape and Eros*. Translated by Philip S. Watson. Philadelphia: Westminster Press, 1953.

OECD, *Highlights of Public Sector Pay and Employment: 2002 Update*. Paris: Organization for Economic Co-operation and Development, 2002.

Ouellette, J. A. and W. Wood. "Habit and Intention in Everyday Life: The Multiple Processes by Which past Behavior Predicts Future Behavior," *Psychological Bulletin*, 124 (1998): 54-74.

Outka, Gene. *Agape: An Ethical Analysis*. New Haven: Yale University Press, 1972.

Øyen, Else, ed. *Best Practices in Poverty Reduction: An Analytical Framework*. London: Zed Books, 2002.

Patel, A. *An Overview of Street Children in India*. New York: Covenant House, 1983.

Peoples, James and Garrick Bailey. *Humanity: An Introduction to Cultural Anthropology.* Belmont, CA: Thomson Wadsworth, 2006.

Perlman, Janice E. "The Chronic Poor in Rio de Janeiro: What has Changed in 30 Years?" in Marco Keiner *et. al.*, eds. *Managing Urban Futures: Sustainability and Urban Growth in Developing Countries.* Burlington, VT: Ashgate, 2005.

Perlman, Janice E. and Molly O'Meara Sheehan. "Fighting Poverty and Environmental Injustice in Cities." in Linda Starke, ed., *State of the World 2007: Our Urban Future.* New York: W.W. Norton & Company, 2007.

Petrovic, Drazen. "Ethnic Cleansing—An Attempt at Methodology," *European Journal of International Law* 3 (1994): 1-19.

Pitman, Todd. "Africa's 'forgotten crisis.'" *Minneapolis Start Tribune.* April 30, 2007.

Pogge, Thomas W. "Human Rights and Human Responsibilities," in *Global Justice and Transnational Politics: Essays on the Moral and Political Challenges of Globalization,* Edited by Pablo de Greiff and Ciaran Cronin. Cambridge, MA: MIT Press, 2002.

———. *World Poverty and Human Rights: Cosmopolitan Responsibilities and Reforms.* Cambridge: Polity Press, 2002.

Pope, Stephen J. "Proper and Improper Partiality and the Preferential Option for the Poor." *Theological Studies* 54 (1993): 242-71.

———. "'Equal Regard' Versus 'Special Relations'? Reaffirming the Inclusiveness of Agape," *The Journal of Religion* 77 (1997): 353-79.

Power, Samantha. *A Problem from Hell: America and the Age of Genocide.* New York: Basic Books, 2002.

PRAXIS. "Partcipatory Poverty Profile Study: Bolangir District, Orissa." U.K. Department for International Development. New Delhi: World Bank, 1998.

Prunier, Gérard. *Darfur: The Ambiguous Genocide.* Ithaca: Cornell University Press, 2007.

Quironga, Jorge. "The Millennium Challenge Account: A New Model for Increased Aid Effectiveness," Institute of International Economics, Washington, DC, 2002.

Rae, Douglas. *Equalities.* Cambridge, MA: Harvard University Press, 1981.

Rahman, Atiqur and John Westley. "The Challenge of Ending Rural Poverty." *Development Policy Review* 19 (2001): 533-62.

Rahmato, D., "Neither Feast Nor Famine: Prospects for Food Security." In Zegeye A. and S. Pausewang, eds., *Ethiopia in Change.* London: British Academic Press 1994.

Rahnema, M. "Poverty." In W. Sachs ed. *The Development Dictionary: A Guide to Knowledge as Power.* London: Zed Books, 1992.

Ravallion, Martin. "China's Lagging Poor Areas." *American Economic Review, Papers and Procedures* 89 (1995): 301-5.

———. "Issues in Measuring and Modeling Poverty," *Policy Research Working Paper* no. 1615, Washington, D.C.: World Bank, 1996.

Ravallion, Martin, Shaohua Chen, and Prem Sangraula. "Dollar a Day Revisted," *World Bank Policy Research Working Paper 4620* Washington, D.C.: World Bank, 2008.

Rawls, John. *A Theory of Justice.* Cambridge, MA: Harvard University Press, 1971.

Reddy, Sanjay and Thomas Pogge. "How Not to Count the Poor." Columbia University, Department of Economics, New York, 2002.

Revenga, A., D. Ringold, and W. M. Tracy. *Poverty and Ethnicity: A Cross-Country Study of Roma Poverty in Central Europe.* World Bank Technical Paper No. 531. Washington, D.C.: The World Bank, 2002.

Rhode, David. *Endgame: The Betrayal and Fall of Srebrenica: Europe's Worst Massacre since World War II.* New York: Farrar, Strauss and Giroux, 1997.

Rice, A., L. Sacco, A. Hyder, and R. Black. "Malnutrition as an Underlying Cause of Childhood Deaths Associated with Infectious Diseases in Developing Countries," *Bulletin of the World Health Organization* 78 (2000): 1207-21.

Rizzini, Irene, ed. *Children in Brazil Today: A Challenge for the Third Millennium*. Rio de Janeiro: Editora Universitaria Santa Ursula, 1994.

Roberts, Les, Charles Hale, Fethi Belyakdoumi, Laiura Cobey, Roselida Ondeko, Michael Despines, and John Keys. *Mortality in Eastern Democratic Republic of the Congo: Results from eleven mortality surveys*. New York: Health Unit/International Rescue Committee, 2001.

Sachs, Jeffrey. *The End of Poverty: Economic Possibilities for Our Time*. New York: Penguin Press, 2005.

Sahn, David and David Stifel. "Progress toward the Millennium Development Goals in Africa." *World Development* 31 (2003): 23-52.

Salmen, Lawrence. "The People's Voice: Mexico—Participatory Poverty Assessment." Washington, D.C.: World Bank, 1995.

Sanderson, David. "Cities, disasters and livelihoods," *Environment & Urbanization* 12 (2000): 93-102.

Satterthwaite, David. "The Millennium Development Goals and urban poverty reduction: great expectations and nonsense statistics." *Environment & Urbanization* 15 (2003): 181-90.

Schnabel, Eckhard. *Early Christian Mission*. Volume 1. Downers Grove, Il: InterVarsity Press, 2004.

Schumacher, Christian. *Small is Beautiful: Economics as though People Mattered*. London: Vintage, 1993.

Sells, Michael. *The Bridge Betrayed: Religion an Genocide in Bosnia*. Berkeley: University of California Press, 1996.

Sen, Amartya. *Poverty and Famines*. Oxford: Clarendon Press, 1981.

———. *Development as Freedom*. Oxford: Oxford University Press, 1999.

Seymour, Jane ed. *Poverty in Plenty: A Human Development Report for the UK*. London: Earthscan Publications Ltd, 2000.

Shah, Anup. "Poverty Around the World," www.globalissues.org/article/4/poverty-around-the-world#WorldBanksPovertyEstimatesRevised, March 1, 2010.

Shatkin, Gavin. "Obstacles to Empowerment: Local Politics and Civil Society in Metropolitan Manila, the Philippines." *Urban Studies* 12((2000): 2357-75.

Shemyakina, Olga. "The Effect of Armed Conflict on Accumulation of Schooling: Results from Tajikistan," Unpublished Job Market Paper, 2006.

Sider, Ronald J. *Rich Christians in an Age of Hunger*. Dallas: Word Publishing, 1997.

———. *Just Generosity*. Grand Rapids: Baker Books, 1999.

Sidley, Pat. "Cholera Sweeps through South African Province," *British Medical Journal* 332 (2001): 71.

Silva, Patricia. "Environmental Factors and Children's Malnutrition in Ethiopia." World Bank Policy Research Working Paper 3489. Washington, D. C.: World Bank, 2005.

Singer, Peter. "Famine, Affluence and Morality." *Philosophy and Public Affairs* 1 (1972): 229-43.

———. *Practical Ethics*. New York: Cambridge University Press, 1979.

———. *Children at War*. Berkeley: University of California Press, 2006.

Smil, Vaclav. *Feeding the World: A Challenge for the 21st Century*. Cambridge: MIT Press, 2000.

Smolin, David M. "Overcoming Religious Objections to the Convention on the Rights of the Child," *Emory International Law Review* 20 (2006): 81-110.

Springer, M.. "Champ Chimp," *Scientific American Mind* (August/September 2006): 12-14.

Stapleford, John. *Bulls, Bears and Golden Calves: Applying Christian Ethics in Economics.* Leicester: InterVarsity Press, 2002.

Starke, Linda, ed. *State of the World 2007: Our Urban Future.* New York: W.W. Norton & Company, 2007.

Stassen, Glen H. and David P. Gushee. *Kingdom Ethics: Following Jesus in Contemporary Context.* Downers Grove: InterVarsity Press, 2003.

Steidle, Brian. 2007. *The Devil Came On Horseback: Bearing Witness to the Genocide in Dafur.* New York: Public Affairs, 2007.

Stewart, Frances and Valpy Fitzgerald, eds., *War and Underdevelopment, Vol I: The Economic and Social Consequences of Conflict.* New York: Oxford University Press, 2001.

————.*War and Underdevelopment, Vol II: Country Experiences.* New York: Oxford University Press, 2001.

Stewart, Frances and Valpy Fitzgerald. "Introduction: Assessing the Economic Costs of War." In Frances Stewart, and Valpy Fitzgerald, eds., *War and Underdevelopment, Vol I: The Economic and Social Consequences of Conflict.* New York: Oxford University Press, 2001.

Stewart, Frances, Cindy Huang, and Michael Wang. "Internal Wars in Developing Countries: an empirical overview of economic and social consequences," in In Frances Stewart, and Valpy Fitzgerald, eds., *War and Underdevelopment.* New York: Oxford University Press, 2001.

Stover, Eric, A.S. Keller, J.C. Kobey, *et al.* "The Medical and Social Consequences of Landmines in Cambodia." *Journal of the American Medial Association* 272 (1994): 331-36.

Tabutin, D. and E. Akoto. "Socio-economic and Cultural Differences in the Mortality of Sub-Saharan Africa." In de Wall Van, Pison, Mpembele Sala-Diakanda, eds., *Mortality and Society in Sub-Saharan Africa.* Oxford: Clarendon Press, 1992.

Theissen, Gerd. *A Theory of Primitive Christianity.* London: SCM Press, 1999.

Thompson, Milburn J. *Justice & Peace.* Maryknoll, NY: Orbis Books, 2003.

Thunberg, Anne-Marie. 1974. "The Egoism of the Rich." *Ecumenical Review* XXVI (1974): 459-468.

Toole, M. J. "Complex Emergencies: Refugee and Other Populations." In Barry S. Levy and Victor W. Sidel, eds., *War and Public Health.* Washington, D.C.: American Public Health Association 1997.

Toole, M. J. and J. W. Ronald. "Refugees and Displaced Persons: War, Hunger, and Public Health." *Journal of the American Medical Association* 270 (1993): 600-606.

Toole, M. J. and R. J. Waldman. "An Analysis of Mortality Trends Among Refugee Populations in Somalia, Sudan, and Thailand." *Bulletin of the World Health Organization* 66 (1988): 237-247.

————. "The Public Health Aspects of Complex Emergencies and Refugee Situations." *Annual Review of Public Health* 18 (1997): 283-312.

Transparency International. *Global Corruption Report 2004.* London: Pluto Press, 2004.

Triandis, H.C. *Interpersonal Behavior.* Monterey, CA: Brooks/Cole Publishing, 1977.

Turner, Stuart, Sahika Yuksel, and Derrick Silove. 2003. "Survivors of Mass Violence and Torture," In Bonnie L. Green. Hingham, ed. *Trauma Interventions in War and Peace: Prevention, Practice, and Policy* MA: Kluwer Academic Publishers.

Unger, Peter. *Living High & Letting Die*. New York: Oxford University Press, 1996.

UNICEF. *State of the World's Children, 1996*. New York: Oxford University Press, 1996.

———. *The Impact of Conflict on Women and Girls in West and Central Africa and the UNICEF Response*. New York: UNICEF, 2005.

———. *State of the World's Children, 2006*. New York: UNICEFF House, 2006.

———. *State of the World's Children, 2008*. New York: UNICEFF House, 2008.

United Nations Development Programme. *Human Development Report 1995*. New York: Oxford University Press, 1995.

———. *UNDP's 1996 Report on Human Development in Bangladesh: A Pro-Poor Agenda—Poor People's Perspectives*. Dhaka, Bangladesh, 1996.

———. *Human Development Report 2001*. New York: Oxford University Press, 2001.

———. *Human Development Report 2002*. New York: Oxford University Press, 2002.

———. *Human Development Report 2003*. New York: Oxford University Press, 2003.

———. *The Arab Human Development Report 2005*. New York: United Nations Publications, 2006.

United Nations Development Programme Rwanda. *Turning Vision 2020 into Reality: From Recovery to Sustainable Human Development*. New York: United Nations Development Programme Rwanda, 2007.

United Nations Human Settlements Programme. *State of the World's Cities 2006/7*. Nairobi: UN-HABITAT, 2006.

United Nations Office for the Coordination of Humanitarian Affairs (UN OCHA). *Press Release*, July 10, 2007.

Urban Resource Center. "Urban Poverty and Transport: A Case Study From Karachi." *Environment & Urbanization* 13 (2001): 223-33.

Van Hear, Nicholas and Christopher McDowell, eds., *Catching Fire: Containing Forced Migration in Volatile World*. New York: Lexington Books, 2006.

Van Til, Kent A. *Less Than Two Dollars A Day*. Grand Rapids, Michigan: Eerdmans Publishing Co, 2007.

Verplanken, Bas and Wendy Wood. "Interventions to Break and Create Consumer Habits." *Journal of Public Policy & Marketing* 25 (2006): 90-103.

Verwimp, P. "Testing the Double-genocide Thesis for Central and Southern Rwanda." *Journal of Conflict Resolution* 47 (2003): 423-42.

———. "Death and Survival During the 1994 Genocide in Rwanda." *Population Studies* 58 (1994): 233-45.

Visano, L. "The Socialization of Street Children: The Development and Transformation of Identities." *Sociological Studies of Child Development* 3 (1990): 139-161.

Visaria, Leela. "Violence against Women in India: Evidence from Rural Gujarat." in *Domestic Violence in India: A Summary Report of Three Studies*. Washington, D.C.: International Center for Research on Women, 1999.

Warah, Rasna. "Life in Kibera," in Linda Starke, ed. *State of the World 2007: Our Urban Future*. New York: W.W. Norton & Company, 2007.

Whitehead, A. "'I'm Hungry Mum': The Politics of Domestic Budgeting" in Young, Wolkowitz, and McCullogh, eds., *Of Marriage and the Market: Women's Subordination in International Perspective*. London: CSE Books, 1981.

Willard, Dallas. *The Spirit of the Disciplines*. San Francisco: HarperCollins Publishers, 1988.

Williams, Daniel Day. *The Spirit and the Forms of Love*. New York: Harper & Row, 1968.

Willoughby, Rodney E. "A Cure for Rabies?" *Scientific American* April (2007): 89-93.

Wodon, Quentin, and S. Yitzhaki. "Inequality and Social Welfare." In Jeni Klugman, ed., *A Sourcebook for Poverty Reduction Strategies,* Washington, DC: The World Bank, 2002.

Wogaman, John Philip. "Towards a Method for Dealing with Economic Problems as Ethical Problems," in Dietmar Mieth and Jacques Pohier (eds.) *Christian Ethics and Economics: The North-South Conflict* New York: Seabury Press, 1980.

Wood, Wendy. "Habits: A Repeat Performance." *Current Directions in Psychological Science* 14 (2006): 198-202.

Wood, Wendy. and J. M. Quinn. 2005. "Habits and the Structure of Motivation in Everyday Life," in *Social Motivations: Conscious and Unconscious Processes,* K.D. Williams and J.P. Forgas, eds., New York: Cambridge University Press, 2005.

Wood, W., L. Tam, and M. Guerrero Wit. "Changing Circumstances, Disrupting Habits," *Journal of Personality and Social Psychology* 88 (2005): 918-33.

World Bank. *Visual Participatory Poverty Assessment* Washington, D.C.: World Bank, 1994.

———. "Diversity, Growth, and Poverty Reduction." Washington, D.C.: World Bank, 1995.

———. "Identifying the Social Needs of the Poor: An Update." Washington, D.C.: World Bank, 1997.

———. *World Development Report 2004, Making Service Work for Poor People.* New York: Oxford University Press., 2003

———. *World Development Report 2005, A Better Investment Climate for Everyone.* New York: Oxford University Press, 2004.

———. *Global Purchasing Power Parities and Real Expenditures. 2005 International Comparison Program,* Washington DC: World Bank.

———. *World Development Report 2006, Equity and Development.* New York: Oxford University Press, 2005.

———. *World Development Indicators.* New York: Oxford University Press, 2006.

———. *World Development Report 2007, Development and the Next Generation.* New York: Oxford University Press, 2006.

World Health Organization, *Macroeconomics and Heath: Investing in Health for Economic Development,* Geneva: World Health Organization, 2001.